Consequences

CONSEQUENCES

BY

EGERTON CASTLE

AUTHOR OF

"THE PRIDE OF JENNICO," ETC.

NEW YORK
STREET & SMITH, Publishers
238 William Street

CONSEQUENCES.

PART I.

GEORGE KERR.

CHAPTER I.

HOW GEORGE KERR REPENTED AT LEISURE.

Popular proverbs—those short statements of long experience—must, from their very essence, be various and even contradictory on almost every question.

Concerning marriage especially—that most solemn, uncertain, and fatal of human engagements—do they wax numerous and conflicting, even as are the consequences of a bid at the eternal lottery.

"Happy the wooing that's not a long a-doing," is an acceptable maxim, and a wise, in the estimation at least of young and ardent love. It fits admirably with other well-known emotional prognostications anent the risky undertaking: "Happy is the bride the sun shines on," and such-like. Alas that its natural cross, "Marry in haste and repent at leisure," should ever prove equally opposite!

People who plunge headlong into very early matrimony have, as a rule, ample opportunity to test the pithiness of both proverbs.

Rapturous always their first impressions; but, in a little while, the inevitable sobering process once fairly started—with the whole of a life stretching drearily before them a lengthy series of wasted capabilities—grim their reflections on the endless consequences of one imprudent step!

The various aspects of leisurely repentance formed in the year 1857 a main theme in the mental existence of Mr. George Kerr, who was then aged twenty-three.

Arrived at the green door of his little house in Mayfair, he paused a moment in disheartened and bitter cogitation. No doubt she was lying in wait for him up-stairs, preparing a scene in punishment for their last quarrel. . . . No peace for him, night or day! Was it astonishing that he was sick—sick to death—of all this?

He turned the key in the door, and let himself in with a muttered curse on his unhappy home. Contrary to orders, when all had retired except himself, the lights were still blazing in the hall; on the other hand, the lamp had burned itself out in his smoking-room, and filled it with nauseating darkness. His savage pull at the bell brought the sleepy footman tumbling up-stairs before his eyes were well opened.

"Why are you not in bed—why is there a light in the hall?"

"Mrs. Kerr has not yet come in," said the man in injured tones.

"Not come in . . . ?"

There was a lengthy silence.

"You can go to bed," said George at last, with forced calmness. "Frst take that lamp away, and light the candles. I shall wait up for your mistress."

There had been nothing very particular about the day just elapsed. It had only differed in details from that of almost every day since chill disillusion had first entered into George Kerr's mad paradise—so few weeks after the irrevocable deed had been sealed—but it was destined to have far-reaching consequences.

From the very morning, as the youthful husband sat to a cold, ill-served, solitary breakfast—the mistress of the house as usual sleeping late in the day after the worldly exertions of the night—the sense of his injuries had been strong upon him.

Only a year ago, at that very hour, he was standing beside his bride in the solemn Cathedral of Seville, and in galling contrast to the high hopes, the proud rapture, which then had filled him, the dead failure of the present rose, specter-like, to mock him, and would not be laid again. He recalled how he had looked down with palpitating heart on the blushing, smiling face, lace-veiled, by his side; how the touch of the slim fingers, as he held them within his, thrilled him through and through; with what a tender earnestness, what faith and love —God knows!—he had vowed to cherish her till death;—recalled the tumult of joy with which he had led her down the aisle, his wife! . . .

It would be curious to look back on, in truth, if it were not almost maddening.

The quarrel had started, trivially enough, by his refusal to escort her to the ball that evening. In no humor to put himself out for her this day, he had vowed himself determined to have a quiet evening for once at any price. She pouted, protested, wept and stormed in vain, finally brushed away her tears, and, with sudden calm defiance, announced her determination to go alone.

"If you do," had retorted the husband, fairly roused, "I shall never forgive you." And thereupon he had flung himself out of the house, to seek in his club the peace and independence refused him in his home.

He had not dreamed she would have dared to disobey him openly; indeed, such an act of emancipation would have been considered so marked in those days of sterner social propriety that he had not for an instant contemplated seriously the possibility of her carrying out her threat; and his anger was deep indeed when he discovered the fact.

Gone to that infernal ball! Gone, in the very teeth of his command!

"Before heaven, she actually browbeats me!" he cried, as, once more alone, he paced the little room from end to end, gradually collecting his thoughts after the first blank confusion of his rage.

The silver clock on the mantelpiece struck twice in its chirpy way. She was enjoying herself, without doubt, not thinking of returning home for another hour or so, bathing her soul in the adulation that was as the very breath of life to her. Oh! he could see her, prodigal of smiles and those soft long looks which he had thought were for him alone, yielding herself, with all the voluptuous grace that had once enthralled him, to the delight of the dance. And her husband—dangling fool!—where was he?

He could hear the half-mocking inquiry some confidential swain would breathe into the dainty shell of her little ear, and Carmen's careless answer: "She did not know; at his club, she supposed."

And the "husband at home," viciously chewing the stump of an extinct cigar, seething, not in thoughts of jealousy—for passion had burned itself out long ago, and love had been stifled by ever-recurring disappointment—but in maddening anger at the despicable situation he had created for himself, swore a great oath that he would afford food for such laughter no longer.

Yet what to do? Ay, there was the rub!

He could not beat her, he could not break her—and she defied him.

The sense of his own impotence met him on every side.

"Yes, look at yourself!" he snarled, as he caught sight of

his morose face in the glass, and paused in his caged tramp to glare at it. "Look! think of your driveling folly, and despise yourself for one moment of weakness! You will now have to put up with the consequences, George Kerr, 'till death do you part!' . . . You are the guardian of a beautiful, brainless fool, whom you cannot control, with whom you have nothing in common but the chain which binds you together. He almost laughed aloud as he recalled the mad impatience, the tenacity, the determination with which he carried his point in the face of so many difficuties—unto this end!

And the thought of the dear old regiment he had sacrificed with so light a heart came over him with almost a passion of regret. It was the most glorious, surely, that ever glittered under the sun. Even now it was starting for another spell of doughty work in India, while he—here he was, white-faced, useless, with not even a show of happiness to set off against his waste of youth.

The weary minutes, feverishly ticked off by the little clock, had measured two leaden hours before the young man, storm-spent and heart-sick, could settle on a feasible plan of action. But at length, as the rays of dawning day were creeping through the curtain folds a glimmer of light broke over the chaos of his mind. She had promised to obey and honor him, as he to cherish her, but she was, even now, sinning against that vow. And if she refused to keep her part of the contract, why need he hold himself to his? Let her obey, as a wife is bound to obey her husband, or he would put her from him, and be surely justified before God and man in so doing.

George, under the relief of his new-found determination, flung himself on a deep arm-chair and gradually fell into a sort of drowsy, semi-conscious condition, from which a loud rattle of wheels and a sharp peal of the bell aroused him to a vivid sense of the moment's importance.

Drawing his weary limbs together, he rose with a stern composure to open the door to his wife.

CHAPTER II.

HOW HE MARRIED IN HASTE.

It is an idle exercise of the mind, and yet one which has its fascination in moments of dreamy meditation, that searching back into the far past of our own or our neighbor's life for the distant cause, the seemingly unimportant event, which may have been the starting-point in the present concatenation of things.

And yet, after all, what is often most striking in such reflections is the sometimes inconceivable smallness, even absurdity, of the incident which leads to such far-reaching results. A thought, a look, a word, is sufficient to start a new train of circumstances. Our existence has been rolling in its ordinary groove, we have been treading the road of everyday life, apparently without a prospect of ever diverging from it, when there comes a something so trivial as well-nigh to escape notice—a pebble which did but turn the wheel of fortune ever so little from its course, and, behold, what a change! What strange lands lie befo· : us!—may be, what racking experiences in the narrow circle of our joy and pain!

That the present curious relations of the last two representatives of that ancient race, the Kerrs of Gilham, would never have come about save for certain side-events, seemingly irrelevant, in the life of their grandsire, is a fact which would doubtless much vex his sturdy old ghost were it brought home to him. And yet, again, these events would never have occurred had not the course of Lord Wellington's operations in the Peninsula obliged him to attack Marmont's strong position of Los Arapiles on the 22d of July, 1812, on which day was achieved the bloody victory now heralded "Salamanca" on the colors and standards of thirty-five of our regiments. During the course of that fierce struggle it fell to the lot of Lieutenant Kerr, whose captain had already been shot, to dislodge with a company of Highlanders a party of troublesome Imperial Voltigeurs from a certain crenelated village called Santa Maria de la Peña. At a critical moment he was, through the fortune of war, opportunely re-enforced by a party of the 3d "Ligeros," gallantly led by a Spanish officer, one Don Atanasio de Ayala, anxious in his burning national pride to imitate, if possible to rival, the exploits of the Northerners.

It was a hard-fought day. By the time the Imperials had sullenly but unequivocally yielded the ground, both the Spanish and the English officer were severely wounded. Discovered side by side, scarcely breathing, but still alive, they were carted off to experience together the horrors of a Peninsular ambulance. Both were young men, almost boys. They had seen each other at work, and in the close intimacy in which they were thus thrown cemented such a friendship as is made only amid hardships doughtily shared and dangers met in common.

Now, but for that breathless meeting on the torrid crags of Arapil el Grande, certain human existences would undoubtedly, in distant days to come, when Peninsular events had long passed into the domain of general history, have moved in widely different channels—one of them, indeed, never have issued out of the store of infinite life.

In the natural course of things the friends parted, to look upon each other's face no more. Peace returned; each in his turn retired to his own home, matured, then married and settled down; the Spaniard spinning out his life in the true, lazy Andalusian way; the Englishman, when the time came, assuming the reins of government on the ancestral estate of Gilham, where, toward the end of the year 1850, an awkward fall between a double rail terminated his well-filled life at the beginning of its twelfth luster.

During the course of his allotted span this William Kerr of Gilham had reproduced his existence in three different directions. A first marriage with the daughter of an ancient house had given an heir to the proud name and wide lands of Gilham; of a second, contracted in the autumn of his life, were born two other children, who, by the way, through the irregular workings of hereditary chance, proved to be, both in look and temper, far more true Kerrs than the first-born. For the latter, although very consciously proud, as in duty bound, of the headship of his house when it devolved upon him, recalled in no particular, except perhaps an unimpeachable sense of duty, the traditional characteristics—the warm-hearted impulsiveness and easy-going spirit of his father's race.

On his accession the new squire naturally became guardian to the offspring of what, in his heart, he had always held as his sire's senile folly. Of these, the boy, George, was at that time half-way through his teens, and Susie on the threshold of womanhood—just an age when the unwelcome charge was likely to give their guardian most trouble.

He was, however, soon relieved of half his burden, for the year of mourning was scarcely out before Susie left the Court to bestow herself, and her little independent fortune, on a certain handsome, intellectual, penniless curate, Hillyard by name, and joyfully set up house in a humble Kentish parsonage on three hundred a year and her darling brother George's blessing—a commodity which this young gentleman very graciously bestowed on the couple, though personally he could not be said to think much of curates.

But George it was who all his life had been a thorn in the present squire's side, and he was not so easily got rid of—a perpetual disturbing element in the matter of Gilham's otherwise satisfactory existence, even from distant Eton. Things, bad enough in his unruly boyhood, were at their worst between them when Alma Mater opened her arms to the scapegrace. All the Kerrs who were not soldiers had been

Trinity men; and George, repairing thither as a matter of course, his career under the shadow of those time-honored walls became, in the estimation of a person of his step-brother's temperament, nothing short of scandalous. In truth, it was a succession of ridiculous scrapes and escapades which gave the pompous guardian the most exquisite irritation.

On his side, Master George, who considered himself unwarrantably hectored and curbed, and kept on an ungentlemanly short allowance, gradually fought shy of returning to his old home, despite his pretty sister-in-law's conciliating and welcoming presence. And so, there having grown no feeling except mutual dislike between the strait-laced methodical squire and his headstrong, "good-for-nothing" half-brother—who, indeed, according to the former's innermost ideas, had no business to exist at all—it was but natural that when the young man came of age, and into the unfettered possession of his own money, he should shake off his elder's control with the smallest delay possible.

This was the time when England, after forty years of peace, and at the lowest military disorganization, having settled in grim earnest to her contest with her ever-rampant Eastern rival, was sending the cream of her manhood to the Crimea.

The first use George made of his delightful new liberty was to drop academic pretensions, and to buy a commission in the Highland regiment that had known his father so well. And, curiously enough, this first independent act was the only one he ever took which met with the unmitigated approval of the head of his house, who, however strongly he might have objected to the profession in peace-time, as a snare and a pitfall for idle youth, now sincerely wished him a martinet of a colonel, and even considered without too much discomposure the possible prospect of a soldier's grave in the neighborhood of Sebastopol.

Hard and grim, however, as that experience proved, it was far from effecting the desired amendment.

On leaving Krim Tartary, the proud regiment, prouder than ever, though much thinned and battered, after its two years of relentless campaigning, was quartered at Gibraltar, and proceeded to enjoy a period of well-earned rest. George, who had escaped scot-free from the hazard of lead and steel, was changed in no way from the scatter-brain, dare-devil undergraduate, save perhaps by an increase of adventurous spirit, coupled with the fool-hardiness of one who had seen Death at close quarters, only to laugh in his face.

Andalusia in the spring of the year is, one may take it, a place where a young man of naturally warm, reckless fancy and athletic temperament easily loses his Northern deliberation, to say the least of it. Now, the subaltern, delighted to have an opportunity of gratifying his love of adventure, resolved to spend his first leave in wandering about Southern Spain, then supposed to be the home of all that was romantic, beautiful and dangerous. And refusing all offers of companionship, he flung himself headlong into the arms of that fascinating land—determined to enjoy to the uttermost all that it was capable of yielding—to fall promptly, as do all who are blessed or cursed with poetic fancy, under its most indescribable charm.

What is it gives Spain so extraordinary a spell? it would be hard to say precisely; but the sunny existence, the graceful dress, dignified old-world courtesy, old-world habits; the magnificent, sonorous tongue so sweet in love, so grave and rich in earnest discourse; the passionate yet langorous national music so stirring to young blood; all these things are components of the charm to which George abandoned himself with all the thoroughness and irreflectiveness that characterized him.

He had reached Seville—Seville, the jewel of the world as the Spaniards hold it—toward the spring of the year, the passionate, ripe spring of Spain which, like to the maidens of that sun-loved land, flowers from pale immaturity into warm development of beauty with magic quickness; and there, under the vault of burning blue, amid the contrasting light and shade, in the rambling streets of the old Moorish town, there came to George Kerr one of those episodes which are so slight, so trivial, as to pass, in many instances, all unnoted, but which nevertheless, as has been said, bring in their train consequences strange, unforeseen, and destined, perchance, to change a man's whole destiny.

In the serene enjoyment of that soundness of body and freshness of mind which belong by right to the blessed age of two-and-twenty, the young warrior, immersed in complacent appreciation of his well-merited spell of freedom and laziness, was sauntering down a narrow, silent, deserted street, toward those middle hours of the day when the Spaniard seeks his siesta, and when, according to his sententious saying, "only dogs or Englishmen walk abroad."

One of the quaint wrought-iron gateways which mark the entrance to some private house, through the fantastically interlacing bars of which the passer-by can usually descry the fresh foliage of palm, pomegranate and orange trees filling the umbrageous inner courtyard, arrested his attention. He stopped and gazed through the scroll work at the mysterious nook, while a desire, curious in its suddenness, to see something of the inner life, something more than the threshold of such a dwelling, took possession of him.

"Now, here is a place," thought he, "with a charming capacity for romance. Delicious experiences might await a man in just such a house as this—if he only had the key of the gate."

He lit his cigarette and pondered. And as he abstractedly listened to the monotonous ripple of a fountain, hidden behind the tantalizing screen of verdure, the capricious wish grew and grew in intensity, until it became almost a resolve.

All at once, with fantastic opportuneness, a delightful idea flashed across his mind. His father, from oft-quoted accounts, had had a certain Spanish comrade in the old fighting days. This gallant foreign officer, Don Something or other de Ayala, whose miniature portrait, in sky blue and silver, hung even now in the smoking-room at Gilham, hailed, if memory was not at fault, from Seville.

What if he hunted the old gentleman up? presuming him, of course, to be still in the land of the living—and why not? At all hazards, it was worth the trying.

And so well did his energy, and a fair amount of luck, serve his new purpose, that before sundown, not only had he found out that his father's old friend was alive, actually in Seville, and ascertained his address, but had likewise gathered sundry particulars concerning his family, which consisted, it seemed, but of his wife and daughter—*hermosisima,* report said of the latter, a detail which kept up the interest to its original exalted height.

The following forenoon, of course, saw George at the gate of the house indicated, which he was pleased to find wrought in still more delicious vagaries, and affording glimpses of a *patio* even greener, shadier and more tempting than that which had originally inspired him with such curiosity. He sent up his card by the old dark-visaged servant, on which to introduce himself, he had previously written, under the title of his regiment, the words, "Arapil el Grande"—the name of that place where the Spaniard had proved so true an ally to his sire, amid the blood and smoke and fury of attack.

In eager expectation, he paced up and down among the orange trees, starred with white blossoms, which filled the warm air almost to excess with odorous sweetness. A fountain rose and fell in slender columns in each corner. The courtyard was surrounded on three sides by the house, a perfect remnant of the domestic architecture peculiar to Andalusia in the sixteenth century—architecture in which Moorish fancy and luxury of detail blended with Christian simplicity. It was to the Englishman's imaginative mind as if he had stepped straight into the world of days gone by. And, behold! the heavy, nail-studded ogee door moved slowly on its scrolled hinges, and, standing framed by the darkness beyond, there appeared a peak-bearded, white-haired old cavalier, but surely just this instant stepped down from some canvas of Velasquez to welcome the stranger from the dull days of the nineteenth century into the glamourous past.

So strong for the minute was the illusion with which George was pleased to divert himself, that it was almost with amazement that he met the old man's earnest greeting, as the latter, scrutinizing his visitor with kindly eyes, came forward, holding out his hand, and saying with deep, grave voice in sonorous Spanish:

"Son of my old friend, you are welcome! Welcome to this, your house, my son!"

He was a very real personage, after all, despite his weirdly antique air; and the hand that George now grasped in true sturdy British fashion was unmistakably flesh and blood, however agedly etherealized.

Again the worn, kind eyes sought the young man's face, their scrutiny softening into benevolent pleasure as they rested on its handsome youthfulness.

"Perhaps you do not speak the Spanish tongue?" said Don Atanasio in quaint English, with a little evident and guileless pride in his own proficiency.

"I have been learning at Gibraltar," quoth George. And thus the ice being broken, the conversation progressed fluently enough.

Bending his fine old head, for he was taller than the Highlander by an inch or so, the Spaniard listened to the visitor's frank explanation of his appearance in courteous and pleased attention.

"So my old comrade—God have his soul!—did not forget to speak to his children of the Spanish friend. It is well! it is well! and a kind thought of his father's son to come and see the old man. Methinks it is as if it were the gallant William again in the flesh before me. Ah, sir! we were strong, fiery young men together, and the thought of those early days has not gone from me. You are welcome indeed! Welcome for the sake of the blood that flows in your veins, for the memory of him that is no more, and for your own sake too, most heartily."

Taking the blushing Englishman's arm, who, though touched by his host's genuine emotion, was thoroughly at a loss how to respond to these flowers of speech, he led him with dignified steps into the house.

They passed first through a dark hall, bare, vaulted, echoing to the sound of their feet, then up a flight of stone stairs into a large flagged room.

The proportions of this place were so majestic, it rose into such loftiness, spread into such spacious wideness, that, in wondering admiration, the young man halted and stared. Stately, somber visages looked down at him from their tarnished frames; tapestry rich-hued, yet faded, hung between them, out of which as he gazed there started into life the quaintest depths of fairy forests, the weirdest forms; stern suits of armor stood in stiff array along the wall, seeming to retain in their dead emptiness something of the ferocious dignity of the spirits that once animated them, and to glare upon the world with angry menace in their vacant visors. In the middle of the floor a *brasero* of glowing red copper gave the last touch of outlandish and mediæval strangeness to the scene.

A light tap on his arm recalled him to himself. Before him, as if she had sprung out of the earth, smiling, handsome, wrinkled, stood a dame with white hair, lace-veiled, of imposing proportions, clad in the picturesque national costume; a not incongruous pendant to the solemn leanness of the cavalier.

"Beloved of my soul, I present to thee the son of my brother in arms," said Don Atanasio in Spanish, as George made a low bow; "the son of that much-beloved and regretted friend Don William Kerr, of whom I have so often spoken to thee. A lieutenant of Scots, even as was his father. He speaks Spanish."

Blissfully ignorant of the chivalrous customs of the country, George proceeded to press—not knowing he should have kissed—the very small, very fat hand which, with a guttural flow of hospitable observations, was warmly extended to him.

But the whole scene assumed a new complexion when, with a patter of light, quick feet, a fourth person made her entrance into the room, and he was further introduced to "Carmen, my unique daughter."

Just at the age when in a sunny clime a woman attains the perfection of a bloom as rich and warm as the opening pomegranate flower; attired, like her mother, as were all Spanish ladies in those days, in the national dress—even in that land of exquisite maidens Carmen was a jewel.

At sight of the visitor she stopped short in an attitude of half-arch half-bashful astonishment, and George realized on the spot that he had never known before what loveliness a woman could embody. The first look he cast upon her, taking in the luster of dark eyes, the curve of red lips, the exquisitely rounded, satin-clad figure, to end respectfully on a pair of tiny slippers which just allowed a ray of tender blue stocking to peer through the cloud of black lace, was simply a revelation. It seemed to lift him into an existence hitherto unthought of.

As for the cause of his sudden exaltation, she apparently experienced some occult psychical reaction of the same kind. Such ecstasies are sympathetic. As her eyes met his they became troubled, a crimson flush flew to each olive cheek, and the modest answer to his stammered compliment died away half finished in an inarticulate murmur.

Meanwhile, all unconscious of the strange operations at work in those two young heads and hearts so near to him, Don Atanasio, with that hospitality which is part of the very spirit of his race, was explaining to his guest that there could be no question of his living at Seville anywhere but under his roof; in declaring that his house in town, his villa near Ronda, his horses, his servants, all his possessions, were at his disposal whenever and as long as the son of his old friend chose to make use of them.

And in this manner George Kerr, barely twenty-four hours after acting on a fantastic desire, the idlest freak of curiosity, found himself installed as the honored guest of Don Atanasio de Ayala y Quevedo, and already the abject slave of his daughter's bright eyes.

Under ordinary circumstances this arrangement, which did away with all true liberty of action, would very soon have palled upon him; but as it was, betwitched, spellbound, he passed day after day in a feverish dream of excitement and rapture.

He made rapid progress in the language, as well as in the favor of his simple-minded entertainers. Don Atanasio was charmed to have found a new listener for his interminable stories of the War of Independence, so modest and well-behaved a youth, who seemed content to sit for hours under his discourses, with eyes cast down, attending with such deep interest to his lessons in tactics and his account of the exploits of "El Lord" and his Spanish allies.

As for the beautiful creature, sole survivor of the many children who had once gathered round the old couple's knees, she spoke little to the stranger; but for all that, the most eloquent and passionate conversation passed daily between the two under the very nose of the watchful parents. Eye spoke to eye in question and avowal. The flush on her lovely oval cheek, the pouting of her fair red mouth, answered many a time and most satisfactorily the silent disclosure of passion which the pressure of his hand, the voiceless motion of his lips, conveyed to the object of his worship.

Long before an opportunity occurred for the open declaration of his feelings, George possessed the rapturous conviction of being beloved in return, and this state of abeyance, its delicate, exquisite joys had for him a charm and piquancy he was half loath to break through.

One day, having for a few moments eluded the surrounding vigilance, they found themselves face to face alone, and straightway the burning secret which they had shared in silence found words at last. In the somber old room, under the scowling eyes of a score of past-century warriors, just by the half-shuttered window, where a peep of green spoke of the budding orange-trees, Carmen and George talked of eternal love, and, kissing her lips, he vowed himself fit to die with happiness at her feet.

"I hear, Don Jorge, that you have seen my daughter alone to-day," said Don Atanasio very gravely that same evening. "Allow me to reproach you. Among us such conduct is thought incorrect. Were you more conversant with things of Spain, I would even call it a breach of honor."

This was a tempting opportunity for George to carry out to its obvious end the folly which filled his brain, and to avow the passion which the enthralling episode of that day had exalted to fever-heat.

"Sir," he replied warmly, "I beseech you to remember that the rules of honorable behavior differ in various countries. An English gentleman who loves a woman and would make her his wife sees no breach of honor in asking her himself. If, however, I have transgressed, I can but beg your forgiveness."

The old man's severe mood slightly softened as the youth, whose cavalier-like accomplishments he had already had occasion to appreciate, went on without flinching from his gaze:

"I bear, as you know, an ancient name, have an independent fortune, and serve in an honorable profession. I ask your daughter, whom I love and who loves me, for my wife."

This little speech, which George flattered himself was quite in Spanish style, was listened to in silence by the old Don, who considered it just pardonable in a foreigner.

"She should not have owned that she loved you," he remarked at length; "but what is done is done. We will advise."

Advise he did in consequence with his loving consort, the white-haired chaplain, and a few trusted friends—advised in much anxiety of mind, earnestness, and deliberation; and finally, in opposition to all the counsel he sought for, carried the day as his kindly old heart had prompted him from the first. His solemn approval was given to the engagement, and the young man, half bewildered with his own happiness, left the house till the time came for him to fetch his bride.

George's midsummer madness was having serious consequences. He started back on his journey to Gibraltar to beg for prolongation of leave in order to go to England and make arrangements for his new departure.

When he returned to the mess-room and announced his intention to be married, the joking which was started on the subject of the disastrous result of the sub's first leave became so ceaseless and unlicensed as to prove quite intolerable to the victim's passionate spirit. And when the Colonel, as might be expected, first pooh-poohed his request for further leave, and finally flatly refused to grant it, George, not sorry to escape the galling gibes of his comrades, and momentarily out of conceit with his regimental life and its irksome restraint, while more bent than ever from the very opposition he encountered on carrying through his determination, announced his intention of selling out.

On a certain memorable evening toward the end of May in the same year, a number of the *Times* was placed in the hands of Mr. Kerr of Gilham, destined through one minute portion of its contents to shake that worthy gentleman's soul with a very paroxysm of virtuous indignation.

He had just returned from a ride round his farms and had taken up the paper determined beforehand to disagree with most of its opinions. But he was ill prepared for such a call upon his wrath as the crisp columns contained for him that day.

"Gwendolin," said the squire in awful tones, as he stepped on to the lawn in search of his long-suffering wife, "I must beg you to favor me with your attention for a moment. Listen to this—'On the twenty-fifth of May, in the Cathedral of Seville, George Kerr, youngest son of the late William Kerr of Gilham, Esquire, late of the —th Highlanders, to Doña Carmen Maria Concepcion, only daughter of Don Atanasio Ayala y Quevedo!'—eh, what next?"

"George married!" ejaculated Lady Gwendolin in amazement. Then, seizing only the bare facts, she exclaimed with lively feminine interest: "Married to a Spanish girl; I am sure she is lovely! Oh, Willie, how unkind of him never to write! How I wish I could see them!"

"Gwendolin!" returned the squire, stiff with horror, "you do not know what you are saying? Do you not see that George"—and he shook the sheet with suppressed rage—"that this depraved man has married a Papist—a Spanish Papist? Heaven only knows what the end of it will be; perhaps he has turned Papist himself. Carmen Maria Concepcion!

Who in his senses would ever have thought of associating these idolatrous names with the name of Kerr? By a Romish priest, in the Cathedral of Seville, you understand—Seville, the headquarters of the Inquisition."

Even good-tempered, pleasant Lady Gwendolin was not above the current prejudice against other people's religion. She looked shocked and unhappy as the truth forced itself upon her, and lifted her voice in no remonstrance when her husband, dashing the paper away from him with an indecorous display of excitement very foreign to him, uttered his command that henceforth the name of George Kerr was not to be uttered in his presence, and that so long as he was master of Gilham the shadow of the shameless culprit was never to darken his doors again.

The two sturdy little boys who were being brought up so well under their father's methodical rule, who were such model little boys before his face and such incarnate pickles behind his back, now looked after his pompous retreating figure and at their mother's saddened face with round, solemn blue eyes, whispering to each other that Uncle George had done something very naughty, and wondering what it could be.

A few weeks before Susan Hillyard, in her little gabled parsonage, had received a letter from her brother, setting forth, in a few kind, careless words, the announcement of his approaching happiness.

"I know that my good little Susie," said the writer, "will love my beautiful Carmen as a sister, and rejoice that her George is the happiest man in the whole world."

Susie had wept tears of mingled dismay and tenderness, and dispatched a long, loving answer, containing the assurance of her undying affection, and her readiness to welcome with all cordiality her lovely new sister. Though somewhat inclined to fear he was risking his eternal salvation by such a step, she was immensely consoled by her husband's philosophical reception of the news; for the Rev. Robert Hillyard, notwithstanding his official position, was too liberal and open-minded to blindly condemn any creature for his creed.

CHAPTER III.

Carmen halted a moment on the threshold as her husband opened the door and silently received her; she was clad in crimson and enveloped in clouds of black lace, glorious, even against the flood of searching, morning light, in radiant youthful beauty. She looked at him; then, without a word, brushed by. Her step was alert and springy; there was not a shade of fatigue over the warm complexion, under the superb eyes, in the carriage of the lithe, rounded figure.

"That woman, my wife, is peerless—there can be no doubt of that," thought George, following her movements with a dark, abstracted look.

There was naught but æsthetic, lifeless criticism in his admiration, mingled with wonder at the uselessness of such mere bodily perfection. And, in truth, was not that very beauty of hers—she being his wife, and such as she—but part of his curse? Did not the exquisite, feather-brained creature who thus returned defiantly in broad daylight from her night's amusement bear his name and hold his honor in her hands?

His black face grew more lowering yet; with a magnificent show of indifference she was passing up-stairs, when he called to her to stop, and in so harsh a voice that it imposed immediate, if perchance involuntary, obedience. She paused, one little foot on the first step, her head thrown back, interrogating him with languid eye and raised eyebrow.

"Come into my study," he said; "I have much to say to you."

She hesitated, but, as he opened the door and imperatively motioned her into the room, look and gesture were too stern to be resisted, and, with an ill grace, a loud sigh of resignation, she obeyed. She confronted him sullenly.

"Well, my lovely Carmen," he said after a pause, "I can see by the brightness of your eyes that you have enjoyed your evening on this first anniversary of our happy union. All the more, no doubt, for the absence of your husband. But," he continued, with a sudden hard change of tone, as she ostentatiously yawned behind her fan, "I have to warn you that, while you live under my roof, it is my intention to prevent such escapades as to-night's ever happening again."

She turned upon him quickly and merely asked, with a

little toss of her head, a little tapping of the crimson slipper on the ground:

"Is that all you have to say?"

"No," answered the man. "I have much to speak to you about, and I am determined you shall hear it now. Sit down."

"I am going to bed. I am tired," she cried petulantly, but still avoiding his eye. She gathered her skirts together, and, as he would have barred her way, with a mixture of childish passion and fear, she pushed him vigorously aside with one round bare arm, and like a whirlwind dashed out of the room, slamming the door behind her.

He made a step forward. Then he flung himself into a chair, and for a long while remained motionless, absorbed in thought.

At length he rose and made his way slowly up the stairs; knocked at his wife's door and listened. There was no sound within; he tried the handle, but the door was locked.

"Carmen, you had better open; do not push this too far!" Her dress rustled as she moved about; he could hear her displace a chair, and hum a note or two of a waltz tune to herself.

His passion rose. He kicked the door beneath the keyhole with such force that, with shattered lock, it burst back quivering on its hinges.

With a scream, suddenly frozen into silence on her open mouth, she rose and stared at him, and a creeping pallor sucked the blood from her cheeks.

George closed the door as well as he could, and came up to her; he, too, was white to the lips.

"You are curiously mistaken," he said, with forced calmness, "to think you can keep me out of any room in my house. I am master here; you have forgotten it too long."

If he had not been so blinded with passion, and so hard in his new-found strength of purpose, he must have been struck by the utter childishness of the dilated eyes fixed on him.

"Listen to me," he continued, laying a cold hand on her wrist. "I have had patience; I have borne with you for a whole year. It has been as a lifetime of misery to me. I have had enough of it. I have taken my resolve—I will endure this sort of existence not an hour longer. Either you shall submit, absolutely, unquestioningly, uncomplainingly, to my will for the future; live where I please, as I please—do your duty as a wife, in humility and obedience; or, before God! I will send you back to your father!"

She wrenched her hand angrily away from him, then suddenly burst into tears. His manner frightened her. She had followed his words, comprehending their drift no more intelligently than to realize that he was very angry, as usual, because she had gone to the ball without him. But the last phrase struck home. She stepped back as if she had received a buffet.

He let her weep, without speaking. She was one of those rare women to whom tears are no disfigurement. The crystal drops welled up in her lustrous eyes, overflowed on her peach-like cheeks, without a trace of that red distortion which marks the grief of ordinary mortals.

His silence emboldened her. From tears she came to sobbing reproaches; from reproach to vituperation. Her quick blood rose as her first fear subsided, the color mantled again in her cheek, fire dried the moisture of her eye. She flung her arms about in passionate gesticulation; the extravagantly decorated draperies fell away from her bare shoulders, from the ripe perfection of her throat.

"Because," she cried, "because, forsooth, I am young and beautiful, and choose to dance and laugh and enjoy life; because I do not choose to be buried in your dull, your stupid country, I am to be cast off in disgrace! And you dare tell this to me, George—to me who have given up all, all for you —my land, my people, my parents? Oh, my God, is it possible? Have you no shame, no heart?"

She paused, panting, and plunged a long look into his fixed, expressionless eyes. Never had she looked more beautiful than in her present self-abandonment.

Now, Carmen, dense though she might be in most matters requiring nice discrimination, or even the use of common sense, had a keen enough perception of anything that touched her personal vanity. She suddenly read that in the young man's eyes which was, as she thought, a revelation of her victory. And on the spot all her misgivings vanished as if by magic. A self-satisfied smile hovered for an instant over the red lips; then, with the insolence of her newly-found security, she resumed her seat before the glass.

"God knows I have had cause enough to regret the day when you came to me with your false promises and lured me from my beautiful home. How have you kept them? You have neglected me, abused me, but I refuse the position you so kindly offer me of a separated woman. I will not have this undeserved shame cast on me; I will not lose my proper place in society—what you cannot do, shall not do, is cast me away before the world like a mistress you are tired of."

She looked over her shoulder and shot a conquering glance at him. She saw that he was shaking with a nervous tremor, that his eyes were averted as if in fear. She read defeat, she thought, in every sign, and her foolish heart bounded for pride.

She compared the rapture with which her slightest favors had been received by humble adorers but a few hours ago with the scowling, downcast countenance of him who, in his own right, now stood in her sanctum. And he, above all men, blessed in the possession of such a pearl—he it was who this night had in his anger threatened to cast it from him.

She set her little teeth at her own glowing image; dearly, dearly should he smart for this, for she could punish him, and would, till he groveled at her feet. Not till she had half maddened him by her disdain and the glacial barrier that would be raised against him would she permit herself to relax in her severity.

She loosened her long tresses, and, passing her jeweled fingers through the heavy black masses, turned them like a mantilla round her bare shoulders; then, suddenly pretending to recollect herself in the midst of another proud look in the glass, she rose, and, with an insufferably dramatic air, "Have the goodness to leave my room!" she said, loftily, extending her arm and pointing to the door. "You wished for separation: you shall have this much of it. Go!"

The compression of George's hands on the chair grew so violent that the muscles of his arms started into view beneath the sleeves. He looked at his wife with a bloodshot, threatening stare.

"Ah, you wish to rid yourself of me! You shall have your wish. It is not you who cast me away; it is I who renounce you!" And, with the gesture of a stage queen, she drew her wedding-ring from her finger.

"For the outside world I shall still wear a ring, but not the one over which you made at the altar your perjured oath of eternal love. Take it—I have done with it and you!"

She flung it at him and then confronted him, maddening enough in her insolent beauty to drive a calmer man to frenzy.

And the frenzy came, and bringing with it visions of the insane joy of destruction; the overmastering impulse to seize in his arms the woman who thus taunted him, and crush the very life out of her beautiful, proud body, to force forth her last agonized breath in one long delirious embrace—not of love, for love is tenderness, but of triumph and rage.

He felt himself grow pale as the tiny amulet struck him on the mouth. Nothing was heard in the room but the constant matutinal chirrup of the birds outside the light window and the rattling of the discarded ring. Then, suddenly, with an inarticulate imprecation, he sprang forward.

She gave a stifled shriek of terror and pain as she found herself helplessly bound in his arms, her supple frame vainly writhing in his mad grasp, while a harsh, unknown voice panted in her ear:

"Our last day! so be it, Carmen! I will see you tamed—or kill you!"

At first she fought like a tigress; but what could her woman's strength, even in terror, do against his fury? In his cruel grip she soon ceased to struggle. Resistless at length, she lay across his arm, crushed, well-nigh annihilated.

With her submission, his triumph gave way. Blank and dazed, he released her, and she fell prostrate before him. He stood, glaring at the lovely form at his feet, seemingly lifeless, save for an occasional convulsive sigh.

After a while that, too, ceased, and for one agonized ghastly moment he thought her life was gone. But presently, when, covering her face with the mantle of her hair, she took to crying, gently and piteously, like a child, his senses came back; the horror of the disgrace he had brought upon his manhood overpowered him, and he fled from the room.

CHAPTER IV.

THE DEMON WHISPERS.

The one sense which now encompassed George's whole being was of shame. Out into the deserted street he dashed, driven by a mad desire to fly from his own disgrace. Bareheaded, frenzied, rushing purposeless this way and that, he might have been stopped for a madman indeed, had not the early hour presented but a lifeless town to his first precipitate flight. But presently, as the furious intensity of emotion subsided to a duller misery, he slackened his pace, and monotonously followed any street that led ahead, dimly finding some relief in the persistent motion.

Eastward his course lay—far to the east. If his disheveled attire and the desperate look on his face had excited ere now suspicious curiosity on the part of the rare policeman, milkman and early stall-keeper of deserted Mayfair, they naturally attracted more rudely obtrusive attention among the busy toilers of Tower Hill and Hackney.

George began to realize that his evening dress, under the bright sun of six in the morning, in the Whitechapel Road, was a warrantable cause for the loudly expressed derision which followed him on every side; and he bethought himself to purchase an overcoat and a hat, fit for daylight wear, at the first Jew clothier's he could find. Freed from further popular persecution, he fell back more doggedly than ever on his melancholy tramp, whither he knew not. On and on till the sun was already on its downward course, and the turmoil of the great town had reached its climax. Then he found that his aimless wayfaring had brought him back to the land of clubs.

In an utterly prostrate condition he had just sufficient strength and wits left to crawl into his club and order some food. But when it came, the very sight of it sickened him, and the servants looked askance as he drearily ordered brandy and ice, and drank immoderate quantities of the insidious mixture.

Staggering to the smoking-room, he fell into the lap of the first armchair, and sank back overpowered, his giddy brain slowly revolving under the pulse of the only two thoughts left in it—that he was a miserable, degraded, futureless man, and that sleep was the only blessed thing in life—until suddenly all sensation ceased and he was plunged in profound torpor.

The Middle Ages accepted as an adequate explanation of many obscure mental phenomena the theory of unseen evil spirits haunting the path of each human life, ever on the alert to pounce upon their victim at the first sign of weakness, and, when once it was fairly in their eager clutches, devoting their demoniacal ingenuity to its utter perdition, until a hitherto happy or blameless being was plunged in black despair or reckless vice.

To such a familiar demon had George fallen a victim.

The voices of members broke his sleep, and instantly the worry was upon him stronger than ever, clutching into his heart, filling him with still more despairing inability to settle a definite line of conduct.

He tried to sleep again; a painful activity seized upon his brain. He took up a paper and tried to read; his mind was paralyzed.

Presently, as if from an immense distance, his attention was drawn to a paragraph he had been mechanically scanning for some time. It concerned the suicide of an officer, and gradually George's wandering faculties became fixed upon its meaning. A young captain of Hussars, popular, well-to-do, a favorite with men and comrades, believed by all to be in the best of health, the best of circumstances, who seemed, and with reason, up to the day of his unaccountable action, perfectly satisfied with his lot, had been discovered shot through the head, under circumstances conclusively proving that he had fallen by his own hand.

"Was he married?" wondered George, and read the paragraph again. There was no mention of a wife, and he put down the paper with a sort of vague surprise. "What a fool he was to kill himself!"

He took up a fashionable journal, and sighed impatiently as he skimmed over strings of titles and lists of entertainments; then the sensational heading, "Suicide of an Officer," leaped out of the page to his brooding eye once more. He perused the second account with greater interest and deliberation. It was more detailed, and dwelt with gusto on the horror of the spectacle, the grief of relatives and friends, the strangeness of the deed.

"He may have been married in secret—a low marriage, perhaps!" thought George, working round again to his fixed idea.

Well, if he were to leave this world, he must do it in an orderly gentlemanly fashion; the affairs of his household must be arranged; his accounts paid; his last directions written down to the minutest item. It was an interesting, even amusing, exercise for the irritated mind to think out the proper manner of accomplishing this, and to picture the unimpeachable, systematic state in which George Kerr's affairs would be found after that gentleman's sudden demise.

Ballasted with a definite object for action he quitted the club in a mood very different from that of an hour ago; curiously placid, gently sad, rather superior and benevolent toward mankind, as befits one who now has it in his indisputable power to place himself beyond the reach of all earthly disappointments.

CHAPTER V.

THE LAST PIPE OF TOBACCO.

With great deliberation he had himself shaved. Then he hailed a cabriolet and drove off to his solicitor, from whom, after a somewhat lengthy interview, he extracted a promise to have forwarded to his house early next morning some fifteen hundred pounds, drawn upon capital, and an exact statement of his financial affairs. The man of law was filled with the gloomy conviction that so large a sum could be required in such a hurry for no other purpose than the defraying of some gambling debts.

"I hope you mean to turn over a new leaf, Mr. George," he said, somewhat severely, as his client rose to go. "Yours is a tidy little property, but it will not stand many years of this work."

The young man turned round from the threshold with a

pale and meaning smile. Oh, yes, he was going to turn over a new leaf—that very day! And still grimly smiling at the thought, he jumped again into his cabriolet and gave the driver the address of his own house.

His wife's little victoria was waiting at the door, and the footman stood on the steps with a rug over his arm, gaping at his master as the latter drew up.

A chill struck over George as once more he entered his home, and was greeted by the ring of his wife's voice on the stairs, raised in angry rebuke to her maid. Those angry, overbearing tones which Carmen's voice—the music of which had once been so sweet to him—could assume at times, had been one of his first disenchantments.

In the midst of his self-centered cogitations he stood amazed, aghast! Was it really possible? he asked himself in utter bewilderment. Going out! She was actually going out, intent as ever on finery, admiration, amusement, a few hours after what had happened, while he——

The thought of what he was about to do rose before him, vivid, specterlike. And he halted on the threshold of his room, paralyzed in awful realization.

Another woman, with higher ideals, more refined organization, would have been filled with contempt for the man who could use such violence to a woman, were she not depressed with shame and remorse for having brought so low the one whose name she bore. But it was not so with George's wife. When she had regained some calm, the thought of her husband's passionate outbreak, ending in her own complete defeat and subjugation, was recalled as a stirring, novel experience—fearful, in a way, to look back upon, but not without some wild savor.

In her self-conceit, she never doubted but that, for all his threats, he loved her still; never doubted but that, although she had angered him out of bounds, the moving spirit of that anger had been his mad passion for her. She would win him back, now, by every fascination and art she could devise. Oh, the triumph of bringing once more to her feet the man who had meant to kill her in his rage! And again the joy to own herself vanquished, and him the master, after all!

But as the hours wore on there was no sign of his return, and Carmen found herself standing by the window watching every passing conveyance, starting at every bell with her heart in her mouth, now angry, now frightened, now on the point of tears. There arrived opportunely a new gown from the dressmaker. She must try it on, and then she would drive. She would be back in time to see George before dinner. In a renewed access of good spirits she was proceeding down the stairs to her carriage even as her husband entered the house.

His hand was on the door of the study when he heard the rustle of her dress approaching. The sound conjured up a swift bright vision of the past.

Down came Carmen, triumphant in the newest Paris fashion. Perceiving her husband, she stopped short and gave a faint cry. Then, with an effort, she descended slowly to the foot of the stairs and paused again. She was pale, and, as he saw, was trembling. Then, with a very forced smile:

"Well, George?" she said, almost meekly.

Her whole behavior and appearance were as a terrible revelation to his guilty conscience. She was afraid of him, poor silly butterfly thing, fluttering along in the enjoyment of her beauty and bright attire, to see her shrink from him like that, and then pitiably try to conciliate him while she trembled at the bare feeling of his proximity! It brought home to him more than ever what he had done—laid his strong hand in violence on a woman. With a sort of inward groan, too bitter to find voice, he turned and rushed into his study, leaving Carmen blankly staring at the closed door.

"He is still angry," she thought.

Then she boldly opened the door of his study and popped her head in. His back was turned to her; he was staring out of the window. Something in the commonplace attitude gave her courage.

"George!"

He turned round sharply and faced her—pale, silent, forbidding—looking at her with distant gaze. She stammered, retreated, and finally, in desperation, assuming an airy tone, which sounded hideously incongruous to his ears:

"Remember, we have people to dinner to-night, and afterward the opera. I'm going out now; good-by."

He heard her hasty steps across the hall, the banging of the house-door, and presently the sound of carriage-wheels rolling away. Then he laughed aloud in bitter mockery of himself and her. Poor Carmen!—unlucky woman!

"A pistol and one moment of firmness," he muttered. "Yes; that is the only way out of it."

He took down from a trophy a pair of richly-worked Spanish pistols, that of the old Don's wedding gifts which had best pleased him, and tried the works one after another. But as he considered their graceful shape and exquisite ornamentation before loading, a sneer came upon his lips.

"Bah! they are too beautiful to be good for anything."

He replaced the weapons and unlocked a case of dueling

pistols, hair-triggered, of the latest pattern; selected one, loaded it carefully, and laid it on his writing table.

In this grim company he spent the next two hours, putting order among his papers. Since, shortly after his marriage, Carmen's incompetence had forced him to take upon himself the management of the household, all bills and accounts, whether for himself or his wife, were left in his room., Everything was at hand, therefore, and, after some determined work, in unimpeacheable order.

Then, after a long muse, he took out a copy of his will and satisfied himself that matters lay even as he still wished. The tenor of that document was of the simplest. All his assets went to his wife, subject to some trifling legacies and a bequest of a few thousands to his sister.

With the money that he expected the next morning, to be employed according to his written instructions, he considered that all debts could be settled, and the establishment broken up without any of the lamentable confusion which generally follows such a catastrophe as was going to happen in his household.

And as to Carmen, did he not know her well enough to foresee how she would take it all? After the first shock, the first scenes of hysterics and lamentations, she would not be long before discovering some solace in her lot. She would be free, the sole mistress of a pretty fortune, probably return to Spain, marry again, and spend very happily the remainder of this brief human existence.

"And so my last instant has come," he thought, dreamily taking up the pistol, and slowly pushing the hair-trigger back.

The sharp click struck disagreeably upon his jaded nerves, and with a sort of revulsion he paused, but only for a moment.

His heart ceased beating, and he closed his eyes and gently pulled the trigger.

In the silence of his awful expectation there fell the sound of another sharp click—that was all.

George opened his eyes, dropped his hand and looked round, faint and dazed.

So here he was, alive.

Heaving a deep sigh, and intensely irritated at the thought of having experienced all this emotion uselessly, he rose, and walked over to the window to examine his weapon. The hammer had fallen to half-cock.

Very much oppressed, and again with a sickening sensation of faintness, he dashed up the casement and leaned out for a breath of air. His groom was passing down the path toward the stables, puffing vigorously at a strong clay pipe. A whiff of blue smoke floated across George's nostrils.

The smell of the tobacco brought a dimly soothing sensation to his overstrained nerves. The grateful herb was an old and trusty friend to him, and now the scent evoked a sudden craving. He, too, would smoke a last pipe before leaving this world.

A short clay was selected from the rack. This he filled slowly and with an earnest countenance lighted it and sank back in his favorite arm-chair, inhaling the sedative fragrance and stretching his weary limbs.

He unconsciously enjoyed the luxury of complete relaxation of mind. He had ceased to suffer, almost ceased to think; his eyes listlessly followed the curls of blue vapor in their fantastic rising through the air, while he mechanically puffed what, to one in his condition, was the most beneficent of essences. And thus by degrees he fell into that restful state of day-dreaming when ideas meet each other and float vaguely through the mind.

"If death be rest like this, then death is sweet indeed— And so George Kerr is dead, poor fellow! Life is a dream, changing, inconsistent, incomplete—of which the whole meaning vanishes on waking. If the dream is pleasant, then sleep on as long as possible; if it is painful, shake yourself, make one effort and wake."

And he turned his eyes lazily toward the pistol, and sagely thought, "No hair-trigger this time!"

But he was so tired that he had not the heart to move, and so remained passive, while again his thoughts wandered away in the blue.

"And yet there are good things on earth, otherwise no man could bear to live; there are dreams within dreams; how few indeed the seeds that fall on congenial ground; how rarely those souls meet who might live harmoniously together! Make one mistake, take one wrong turning, and a whole life is spoiled. What use in experience, save to show you, too late, what might have been avoided and the trammels that never can be shaken off."

He puffed again; the pipe was out. Regretfully he looked at it, wondering whether he might indulge himself in another; but the tobacco was beyond reach on the mantel-shelf; the pistol was still farther away. He fell again to musing, contemplating and weighing in his hand the tobacco-dyed clay.

"I should have liked to go to India with the brave fellows when they deal with those murderous devils."

Here he made an effort and got up; not to fetch the pistol,

however, but—almost mechanically—to fill his pipe again. "Pity I did not think of it a little sooner; perhaps I might have worked it, and been even now with the old corps; they would have welcomed me back, no doubt." The new train of thought, leading, as it did, away from present unpleasant combinations, was a welcome one; it was, therefore, with proportionate irritation that he found himself recalled to the actual ugly state of things by a discreet tap at the door, accompanied by a confidential cough, unmistakably proceeding from the footman.

"Come in!" he cried savagely. "What the devil do you want now?"

A fumbling at the handle reminded him that he had locked himself in, and he strode across the room to remove the obstacle.

"Beg pardon, sir," stammered the man, who entered with visible embarrassment, which the sight of the open pistol-case and its scattered contents considerably increased. "Mrs. Kerr has come in, sir, and she sent me to remind you that there is company to dinner to-night; and will you please to give me the key of the cellar for to get out the champagne and burgundy?"

The message was a second and equally feeble attempt on the part of Carmen to provoke an interview, if possible a reconciliation; but to George, full of his preconceived ideas, it was but another gross impertinence.

His first movement was one of anger, but the next moment a very different mood was upon him.

He burst out laughing. What a farce it all was! He had been going to shoot himself while she was thinking of the champagne!

He turned to his desk for the keys, while his shoulders still shook with vainly-suppressed laughter.

"Here you are," he cried good-naturedly, tossing the bunch toward the man; "and tell Mrs. Kerr I beg to be excused from dinner."

That laugh did George good, and the soothing, grateful fumes of his old friend had begun. What! was his melancholy madness really dissipating? He yawned and stretched himself, and looked around the room.

He discovered that there must have been a thunderstorm somewhere; for the brooding heat of the day was replaced by invigorating freshness, the trees in the little garden dripped with glistening rain drops, and there rose up a delicious scent of damp verdure mingled with the vague fragrance of early summer flowers.

For a few seconds the would-be suicide remained lost in

mute enjoyment of the sunset hour, seconds during which the mere fact of existence was sufficient for content. Then his mind awoke to reflection.

Here a clatter of plates and glasses, as the footman passed the door to lay the table in the adjoining room, recalled his consideration to more sublunary matters—that he was hungry—prosaically, ravenously, absurdly hungry.

Calling out to the servant, he ordered some meat and bread to be immediately brought up to his study, together with a bottle of "that burgundy."

The man, delighted to see his master reverting to more human instincts, and flattered by the unwonted familiarity, hastened to lay the cloth on a card-table, which he covered with a substantial spread.

George sat down with a serious but much less meditative countenance, and opened immediate relations with the ancient bottle.

He was half-way through his repast when the sound of people moving into the dining-room brought him back to the sense of his incongruous position.

On the other side of that wall his wife was entertaining guests whose names he did not even know, while he, the master of the house—unnoticed, unmissed—partook of his improvised meal in the solitude of the back chamber.

"Well," he communed with himself, "I have not shot myself, after all, and it is perhaps a good thing; I am not going to, either, that seems pretty certain." This, filling his third glass. "Now what am I going to do? The state of affairs that has so nearly made a corpse of me cannot be risked again. No; from this moment the sort of life I have led here is over. I drink to a better one, whatever it is to be."

He rose from the table and again sought his arm-chair; not to muse this time, but to reflect with all the earnestness and intelligence of his eager mind on the possibility of starting on a fresh journey in life, free and unhampered by a single tie of the old existence—alone in the world again.

George Kerr was dead. The chance thought was taking root, and rapidly growing into shape. Why not let it be so? It was no fault of his if George Kerr's death was not an accomplished fact; but for the most unforeseen of hazards, George would now be of this life no more.

Life in the future must be out of England; nay, across the ocean. The old world was no place for his new career; he must have fresh fields, fresh motives, a new birth, as it were. Above all, he must be unknown.

"No one will miss me much. As to poor Susie, she is so wrapped up in her parson and her chicks that, however she may fret at first, the hundred a year she will gain by my death will be more useful to her than her good-for-nothing brother."

He must choose some perfectly definite mode of death, and so act as to appear to the most critical to have perished thereby. Death by drowning, then, alone, could answer his purpose and excite no suspicion. An accident, a boat on the river—better still, at sea; body lost, but boat recovered.

It was best, too, that for the world at large his demise should have the appearance of being accidental.

He would be poor, of course; but, with the money to arrive next morning from the solicitors, rich enough for his energy. What a happy thing had been that quixotic notion of his to leave his widow so large a sum in hand!

Satisfied with the arrangement of matters so far, he emptied his bottle with much relish, and went out to develop, under the silent trees of Berkeley Square, in so far as was now possible, the most minute details of his scheme. Later in the evening he returned with every particular clearly settled in his head.

Tired out by all the harassing emotions and fatigue of the last twenty-four hours, he flung himself on a camp-bed in his dressing-room, and slept heavily and dreamlessly till morning.

It was nearly midnight when Carmen returned from the theatre. The maid, who waited in her room, longing for the hour of her release to bed, heard footsteps coming up the stairs—so heavy, wearied, lagging, she could scarcely believe that they were those of her mistress, who was wont to trip in so lightly.

Still more surprised was she to mark the depression of manner, the strange gentleness, unprecedented in the usually irascible Spaniard. In all the time she had been in Mrs. Kerr's service she had never known that mood.

When the duties for the night were accomplished, and she was about to retire, Carmen called her back.

"Mr. Kerr," she said, with a slight hesitation, "is he out?"

"Oh no, madam!" retorted the maid cheerfully. "Mr. Kerr has gone to bed in his dressing-room, and has not stirred since eleven."

Carmen tossed her head and flushed.

"There, that will do," she said sharply. "Leave me."

Alone, she stamped her foot with the petulance of a thwarted child; then she knocked a chair down, coughed, rustled her dress—all in vain.

She bent her pretty ear to listen at the door; nothing but the sound of the regular breathing within broke the stillness.

The daylong effort of acting indifference had tired her.
She had no wish to thwart him more; she would be humble.
She only wanted to be forgiven, but a strange diffidence kept
her from him. He had dined by himself in his room, he
had retired without seeing her, and was now sleeping—sleeping while she cried.

Now and then she would hold her breath and again listen.
Surely George would hear her, would feel she was miserable,
ay, that she was repentant, and he would hasten to her, overcome with remorse; with the old tenderness, the old caresses,
she now yearned for so passionately.

At last, in an agony of sobs, burying her face in the pillow
to shut out the darkness of her solitude, she cried herself to
sleep.

On what trivial events does the course of a whole life depend.

CHAPTER VI.

THE SEAFOAM BIRTH OF DAVID FARGUS.

Early in the afternoon of the next day George entered the
Old Quebec Hotel, Portsmouth. That old-fashioned and dingy
hostelry was associated in his mind with the brightest epoch
of his life. Here, new to the delights of his new-found independence, to the soul-stirring prospect of active service,
he had spent the night previous to his embarkation for the
Crimea in the company of a brace of ensigns recently joined
like himself.

But it was from no sentimental attachment to the past
that, at so critical a moment, he chose to return to that well-
remembered haunt, but because its position at the entrance of
the harbor was best suited to his plans.

After depositing his luggage and ordering a good dinner to
be ready in an hour's time, he sauntered along the quay of
the Camber toward the Logs to look for and engage a likely
craft for his strange purpose.

An ancient mariner instantly woke up to the prospect of
business.

"Nice evening for a sail, sir. Tidy little boat there of
mine; take you round the harbor in no time."

"Which is your boat?" asked George, pausing; then,
thoughtfully surveying the one indicated, which in truth
seemed as good as any he would be likely to find: "Do you
think it could take me across to the island to-night and bring
me back to-morrow morning?"

"Couldn't find a better sailing boat in the harbor. I'll bring her round in a jiffy."

"Stop a minute, my man!" cried George; "I can't start for a couple of hours at least; but if you will take her round to the harbor about six o'clock you may come and fetch me at the Quebec."

"Right, sir, shall I bring my son to look after the boat?"

"I want no one. I shall sail her myself."

"Well, you see, sir——"

"Well, my good man, I fear your boat will not suit me if you object to trusting it to me. I want particularly to be alone; and if I can manage a boat myself, I can pay for it, too!"

"All right, sir, all right! No offense; I only want to oblige; some gents like to have a man to mind the boat. I shall have her round at six. Good-day, sir."

George returned to his hotel and ate his dinner with the consciousness of one who knows that his physical energies will soon be severely taxed; drank his pint of port, then repaired to his own room and seated himself on the sill of the bow-window to ruminate.

And so this was the last day—indeed, the last few hours—that remained to him to spend under the old personality. That night George Kerr would sink to the bottom of the sea and disappear forever from the list of English subjects, while in the room of that unlucky being would rise one David Fargus. David Fargus, for the nonce passenger to the New World; where to in particular the future to decide.

That morning, in London, he had risen early and ordered the astonished James to pack up, noiselessly so as not to wake Mrs. Kerr, the few necessaries sufficient for a couple of days' outing. Before leaving the house he had withdrawn a hundred pounds from the money that Perkins, faithful to his promise, had already sent by a confidential messenger, and placed that sum in an envelope, together with his written directions that all his personal debts, as per list inclosed, should be paid therewith. To this he had further attached his solicitor's statement, addressed the whole to his wife, and left it in the drawer of his writing-table.

The remainder of the notes, with all the loose cash he had in the house, he had taken with him. Having thus finally settled everything to his satisfaction, he had driven to the station, stopping, however on his way, at a suitable shop to purchase a certain bag of water-tight material, which was to play an important part in his scheme of supposed accidental death.

This bag he now took out of his portmanteau and carefully packed with a complete suit of clothes and change of linen, towels, etc., not forgetting a flask of old brandy. All these articles together barely half filled it, but he nevertheless tied the mouth with minute precautions.

"There! it is water-tight, I hope. Rather heavy, but it will float easily enough; it might even play the part of a life-buoy on emergency," thought he, as he mentally compared its weight with its bulk. Then, spreading out a quantity of banknotes, gold, and silver, on the table, he proceeded to count:

"One thousand three hundred and ninety pounds notes; seven pound ten gold; eleven and seven pence small cash—the capital of David Fargus, Esquire; about equal to one year of George Kerr's income. Not much, perhaps; but more than enough for that valiant soldier of fortune!"

The notes were carefully wrapped in oiled silk, and, together with the cash and his watch, placed in a money-belt which he wore next to the skin.

These preparations finished, he took out some note-paper with his crest and address, sat down to the writing table, and, after a few minutes' reflection, indited his last letter to his wife:

"THE QUEBEC HOTEL, PORTSMOUTH.

"CARMEN: After what happened two nights ago," so ran the document, "you will hardly be astonished at, nor, I suppose, regret, the step which I have taken. Life with you has become impossible. Your behavior is such as no man could ever forgive. But I am too sick at heart even to wish to punish you, and since, as you said yourself on that eventful night when I was able fully to understand your true character, you would lose your position in the eyes of the world—that was all you thought of—if I sent you away from me, I have taken all my measures to prevent reproach falling on you.

"Every one will believe in the 'accident' you will hear of.

"I leave you to seek your happiness in the path you have chosen; you are now mistress of your own life, but you may thank your fate that we have no children, or I could not thus give you your liberty and the untrammeled possession of my fortune. Fare you well, Carmen; I make you no reproaches; at the moment of parting forever they would be idle. I hope sincerely that you may still find happiness on earth, though you could not find it with me.   GEORGE KERR."

"P. S.—I left my last directions with a sum of money in the drawer of my writing table."

The old resentment had burned within him hotly as he wrote, and as he read the letter over it did not strike him as too harsh. Directing it to Charles street, he sealed it carefully with his signet-ring and went out to post it himself.

As he returned he found his boatman waiting for him, this time in a very conciliating mood.

The sack, carefully concealed in the folds of a great-coat so as to look like a bundle of rugs, George carried himself to the boat, then shoved off, set his sail, and, under the breath of a fresh northeast breeze, nimbly slid away on his curious expedition, while the boat proprietor gazed after him with a critical air and condescending approval of the manner in which the Londoner steered and tacked, until the boat rounded Block House Point and disappeared.

The solitary sail at the sunset hour on that superb roadstead, so typical of England's greatness, was impressive and melancholy. And George felt the sadness of it all steal round his young heart.

"What! qualms already, David Fargus? This will hardly do when the hour for action is so near, and we have to kill the body of George Kerr and to effect the transmigration of his soul into your personality."

His scheme was tolerably complete already, and during the long hours he had to cruise about Spithead, waiting for darkness to set in, there was ample opportunity to settle all details and adapt them to the topographical requirements of the case.

"Yes," thought George, as he turned the boat toward the glowing west," that patch, for instance, where the gorse creeps down almost to the water's edge, would not be bad. Nearly equidistant between the two coast-guards' huts, too. Ah, yes; hereabout must be the watery grave of George Kerr.

Yet another hour to wait and the tide would turn outward—so said the calendar—while the moon would not rise before ten. At the turn of the tide, therefore, should the plunge be taken.

The tide which he waited for would take the boat, when left to herself, sufficiently far out to sea to afford no indication of the place of the supposed accident.

At length the nine strokes of the hour floated away on the wings of the night air from some old church-steeple, and George nerved himself for his critical task.

His boots and clothes, strapped into a tight parcel and weighted, were dropped overboard. When he had ascertained that they had duly sunk, he threw the buoyant bag on the water, felt if his money-belt was secure, placed his foot on the gunwale, and noiselessly capsized his craft.

The icy mantle had hardly closed round his shoulders when he began to wish he had sailed in closer to the shore before making the plunge.

He breasted the dark waves with methodical vigor, all his energy, mental and physical, fixed upon the task. Yet the twenty minutes he had allowed himself as its outside duration elapsed, and he did not seem to have advanced much closer to the somber line that represented the coast.

In the old times George had excelled in swimming, as in most forms of athleticism, but the lazy life led since his marriage, and especially the worry and fatigue of the last days, had lowered his powers more than he could suspect. After another immense effort to increase his pace, he felt, with horror, that his strength was giving way. At length, but some twenty yards from the shore, he ceased to make any headway, at all, and floated helplessly at the mercy of the current.

The time he had allotted for the ordeal had already merged into twice its length, the periods of deadly oblivion were growing more frequent, more prolonged; had it not been for this buoyant bag, to which, all unconsciously, he clung with unrelaxing grasp, it is more than probable that David Fargus' career would have proved a short one indeed. But all at once a sharp pain in the knees recalled his wandering senses. The conflicting tides, which at that part run parallel to the shore, had brought him far away from his intended landing-point; but friendly they had been, and had thrown him on the strand at last.

The joy of feeling the solid earth again, and the violent pain in his limbs, restored his waning energy; he gathered together all his strength for one last exertion and struggled up on the beach.

Shivering, almost palsied; for, colder even than the water, every pulse of the breeze cut into his benumbed nakedness like a knife; he staggered along the shingle in search of some sheltering nook, fearful of awakening the attention of chance watchers—coastguards or sentries—for, towering on his right, rose, black against the starry sky, the walls of old Fort Monckton.

As he expected, he came upon a suitable nook at the head of the Kaponier, offering all imaginable advantages under the circumstances; a screen from the blast, and especially from the inquisitiveness of any flying sentry who might take it into his head to cast a glance over the parapet; and, what was not to be despised by a man numbed almost to rigidity, steps to sit upon.

Painfully opening the faithful bag with stiffened fingers, he first brought out the flask and took a long draught of its contents, which coursed through his system like fire, and gave a welcome fillip to the exhausted heart; then, wonderfully invigorated, found his towels and fell to rubbing himself with increasing energy, and so gradually brought some warmer movement into his circulation.

"And now the transmigration is effected!" His spirits mounted to a sense of triumph in the glow of reaction—and felt as though it were indeed a new life pulsing through his veins. "Here is David Fargus, risen, like a son of Neptune, from the foam of the sea, drying his dripping hair in the darkest corner of an antiquated piece of fortification—a quaint birthplace, truly!"

By this time he was dressed in the rough blue suit he had provided for himself, with light shoes on his feet and a yachting cap on his head. He folded his life-saving bag, pocketed his flask, and clambered gayly again on to the glacis.

Making straight for the lights of the little village of Alverstoke, through the gorse, he soon came upon a hedged lane, which, upon inquiry of a passer-by, he learned led to the highroad. This he tramped vigorously along, avoiding the town for fear of some remote possibility of recognition.

Three days later the brave steamship *Columbia* was cleaving through the waters of Southampton Harbor, outward bound.

Smoking his pipe on the fore-deck and perusing with much interest the graphic account given by some local paper of the melancholy death by drowning of one Mr. G. Kerr, of London, sat Mr. David Fargus, second-class passenger to Vera Cruz.

CHAPTER VII.

THE REV. ROBERT HILLYARD GARNERS DOCUMENTS.

The Rev. Robert Hillyard sat in his study apparently reading, in reality brooding over the difficulties of adapting a small income to the requirements of a large family, when Susie came into the room, her pretty worn face full of trouble, the last baby on her arm, and an open letter in her hand.

"Please read it, Robert," she said in a trembling voice. "I am afraid something is wrong."

Then she put the baby on the floor to creep, cast herself down on a chair, stretched out her arms over her husband's desk, and broke into tears and sobs.

Her George! her darling George!

The curate kindly laid his thin hand on her sunny hair, and kept it there while he read the letter, characteristically, without stopping to ask her for an explanation.

It was written in a wild, irregular hand, and worded so confusedly that he had to peruse it twice over before he could gather any definite meaning therefrom.

"I write to you," it began abruptly, "because I do not know who else to turn to, or what to do. Your brother George has left me, and he says he means to kill himself. I am the most miserable and guilty of women. Come at once and I will show you the dreadful letter. You will perhaps know what to do. If George is dead, you will say it is my fault. I know I have done wrong, but God is my witness how I now repent.

"Your distracted and unhappy sister,
"CARMEN."

The curate put the letter carefully in his pocket, and turned to his wife with a few words of comfort.

Pitying her suspense, he formed the prompt decision of taking the next train to town and ascertaining himself the state of affairs. This, and the hope that matters were really not so bad as they might seem, did a little to stop the flow of Susie's tears.

Then she had to pack a bag for the curate and get him something to eat before he started, and collect all their available funds to give him—very little it was; such a journey was to them a terrible outlay. As soon as this was accomplished, and she stood by her husband's chair, watching him hastily swallow his poor meal, she had recovered her usual calm exterior.

"Robert," she said hesitatingly, "what does she mean by guilty?"

"We cannot tell, my dear," said the curate gently; then he kissed her and walked off to the station.

When some three hours later he stopped before the little green door of 3A Charles street, and glanced at the bright boxes of geranium in the windows, the red blinds, the fresh paint on the walls, he could not help contrasting in his own mind the gay outward appearance of the house with the tragedy he expected to hear of within its walls.

His first act was to walk to the window and pull up the blinds, regardless of the figure reclining on the sofa, which at his entrance had immediately raised a handkerchief to its eyes and given vent to a faint sob. He was determined to fulfill the unpleasant task he had taken upon himself to the best of his power.

He took a chair and sat down beside her. The vision of almost startling beauty she presented to his gaze, heightened rather than obscured by the sweeping folds of black lace with which she was enveloped, failed to strike him otherwise than again unfavorably. Nevertheless, his tone was kind as he addressed her, although the sense of the terrible importance of the hour filled it with a solemnity which alarmed her.

"Mrs. Kerr," he said, "I have come to see how I can help you; but, if you wish me to be able to be of any real use, you must tell me everything without reserve. Have you heard nothing of George since the letter you wrote about, and which contained such a terrible threat?" -

Carmen shook her head without speaking.

"Then I must see this letter first of all; where is it?"

She pointed to an envelope on her dressing-table.

Mr. Hillyard took it and went to the window, where he perused its contents with a face which grew sterner every moment, while Carmen watched him apprehensively and felt her fears increasing to positive terror.

After a pause Mr. Hillyard turned slowly round and looked at her with a searching condemning gaze.

"There can be no doubt, Mrs. Kerr, that your husband accuses you of conduct which has driven him to contemplate suicide. Let us hope, in God's mercy, that he has stopped on the brink of such a crime, though he seems to be terribly in earnest. When did you receive this letter?"

"The day before yesterday."

"And you have done nothing—sent no one after him? This letter is dated Portsmouth; why did you not go there yourself? a timely effort on your part might have averted the calamity; he even gave you his address; how do you know that he may not have been almost hoping for some explanation —an act of repentance from you? At least you might have written instantly to his elder brother or to us."

"I don't know; I did not know what to do. I thought George would be sure to come back; that he wanted to frighten me. But I have heard nothing since; oh! what shall I do?"

The curate leaned against the chimney-piece, wondering indeed what could be done now. He contrasted in his mind the unfortunate young husband, flying, as he thought, a dishonored home, with the resolve of not surviving his shame, and the guilty wife, lounging on her cushions by the fire in comparative apathy.

It was, therefore, in a hard tone that, after a lengthy pause, he requested her to narrate exactly the events which had led to this climax, and with a great deal of impatient incredulity that he listened to Carmen's limited view of the whole affair. That any young man should threaten to destroy himself merely because he did not like living in London was too preposterous an idea to be entertained for a minute; such, however, was the gist of her narrative, for the simple reason that she herself was incapable of seeing any deeper motive in their periodical altercations. And as she recapitulated them her natural combativeness gradually assumed the mastery. The very querulousness of her tone more than ever convinced him that this woman must indeed be guilty of some unavowed misbehavior.

With great indignation he at length got up, and, holding out the letter and angrily tapping it with his finger:

"In my opinion, Mrs. Kerr," he cried, "your conduct is inexpressibly shocking. With this letter before you—the last, probably, that the man to whom you have joined your life before God will ever have written, and in which, indeed, his principal thought seems to be that of sparing you merited sorrow and shame—you can still give way to these recriminations, hedge yourself in this useless reserve. All that you told me is perfectly inadequate to explain the despair of my poor Susie's brother, once the gayest, the most open-hearted fellow that ever lived! At your own call I have come to help you, and to help him, if it be God's will; but this I insist on—it is indispensable to success—you must tell me the offense your husband distinctly accuses you of. My character as a gentlemen and a clergyman ought to satisfy you that any confidence will be sacred, and that I shall comply with George's generous wish that you should be spared all exposure."

At these words, at what she thought was wilful and insulting misapprehension, the anger which had been gathering in Carmen's heart during the last minutes burst forth.

She glared at him fiercely, and, getting up in her turn, "Mr. Hillyard," she cried, "I did beg for help from a friend, but you would come here as a priest. You are no priest in my eyes. I have nothing to tell you. Under the hypocritical pretense of helping me in my dreadful trouble, you would merely try to worm out secrets that have no existence. Why did not Susie come? She would not be so cruel; she would have advised me and consoled me. But since you will do nothing but insult me, you may leave me!"

She sank back on her sofa, sulking, while the curate, bewildered, stood wondering whether he was indeed making a grievous mistake, or if the woman before him was really the commonplace sinner he had imagined.

Be it as it might, he resolved to waste no further time in fruitless endeavors to obtain reason and assistance from her, but to devote all his energies to the task of finding out for himself what could be done in this desperate case.

A knock at the door stopped him as he was about to take his leave. The maid entered with a letter, which Carmen seized, opened and read with dilated eyes. All color fled from her cheeks; she fell on her knees with a wild scream.

"It is true!" she sobbed. "He is dead! And he said it was I who forced him to do it. . . . What does it mean? Oh, my beautiful George! can you prefer death to me?"

With worst forebodings, Mr. Hillyard picked up and read the letter, which ran thus:

"THE QUEBEC HOTEL, PORTSMOUTH.

"SIR OR MADAM: A gentleman, who gave his name as G. Kerr, and whose portmanteau bore the address we now send this letter to, came to this hotel on Wednesday afternoon last. After dinner he went out alone, in a sailing boat, announcing his intention to sail over to Ryde and return the next morning. The next day, however, the boat in which he had gone out was discovered some distance out at sea capsized. It is greatly feared—indeed, it is only too probable—that the unfortunate young gentleman has met with a fatal accident, as nothing has been heard of him since.

"His luggage is still in our possession, and we should be much obliged by receiving instructions as to what we are to do with it. The proprietor of the boat also has a claim for damage and salvage money.

"We are, Sir or Madam,

"Your obedient servants,

"LAMBKIN BROTHERS.

"To the Occupier of No. 3a Charles street,
    "Berkeley Square, London."

This communication removed any hope or doubt; an accident which has been announced by the victim in one letter, and related by witnesses in another, is but too palpably an accomplished suicide. The curate looked at Carmen; she was rocking herself backward and forward in an agony of tears. To him this passionate sorrow, following on her anger and previous apathy, was almost incomprehensible; yet he was touched with pity.

"Mrs. Kerr," he said more gently, as he placed George's letter and that of the landlord in his pocket-book, "I shall immediately go down to Portsmouth myself and see what can be done. I regret that any reproof of mine should have added to your misery at such a moment. The best, the only thing I think of to help you now, is to take on myself the responsibility of investigating matters and carrying out George's last wishes. Therefore, as he mentioned in his letter to you a packet containing directions and money to be found in his study, I ask your permission to take it. I shall render you later an account of the trust."

But seeing that he spoke to deaf ears, that the poor creature was incapable of comprehending, even of listening to him, Mr. Hillyard, thinking it cruel to abandon her in such a condition to the mercy of servants, resolved to pen a hurried letter to Susie before leaving the house.

"DARLING WIFE (he wrote): I fear the bad news is but too true; I am just off to Portsmouth, where the dreadful affair has taken place. Useless to bid you hope. Your sister seems in a terrible plight. I cannot make her out; but the one thing is certain, that she wants help and consolation. Might you not come up and see her through it? I leave all this to you."

He rang the bell, and gave the letter to be posted at once. Then, opening George's desk, he took possession of the papers indicated and hurried away to the station.

It was very late that night when he arrived at Portsmouth; he was received with much satisfaction at the Quebec, where, no better tidings awaited him. "The gentleman was surely drowned, though his body might never be found in such a tideway."

The next day he had an interview with the boatman, and was still further confirmed in the theory of premeditation by the old man's account of the manner in which George had insisted on starting alone on his ill-fated expedition. As a witness at the subsequent official inquiry, Mr. Hillyard easily reconciled it with his conscience to keep in the background all he knew of the real nature of the accident, and the verdict found was, in consequence, of "Death by misadventure."

Having satisfied all claims at Portsmouth, Mr. Hillyard returned to London and went to the solicitor, with whom he had a consultation.

He found Susie at Charles street, unremitting in her attentions to her sister-in-law, whose violent grief was no doubt sincere, and whose miserable condition removed all harsh feelings from Mrs. Hillyard's heart.

George's will was read, all debts were paid, and the announcement of his death by accident inserted in the *Times*.

The next thing to be setted was Carmen's future. One of Mr. Hillyard's first acts on arriving at Portsmouth had been to write to Mr. William Kerr, informing him of all he knew, and asking for his advice. He was too well acquainted with the family pride of the Kerrs not to feel sure that the squire would be more anxious even than himself to keep secret the true cause of his brother's death. But although he did not anticipate much help from that quarter, he was nevertheless surprised at the utter want of feeling displayed in the answer which was delivered to him next evening at Charles street:

"MY DEAR ROBERT: I have just received your letter of the 17th inst., informing me of my step-brother's miserable end. Inexpressibly shocking as such news must be to me, I can hardly say that I am surprised. Neither am I willing to undertake any responsibility whatsoever in the matter.

"When my step-brother contracted his undesirable alliance I forbid all intercourse between him and us. I owe it to myself to persist in this course. As to his widow, I have never recognized her, and I do not wish even to inquire into the details of her conduct. I regret for your own sake that you should have allowed your good-nature to draw you into this disgraceful business.   "Yous sincerely,

"WILLIAM KERR (of Gilham)."

All Mr. Hillyard's manly and benevolent feelings were roused by this narrow-minded brutality, and he immediately offered the shelter of his own house to Carmen, who, however, declined to avail herself of it, announcing her intention to return to her father as soon as she possibly could, and pressing the moment of departure with feverish haste.

In a couple of days more the Hillyards returned to their quiet home. After dinner, as they sat together in their little dining-room, Susie observed to her husband, with a certain diffidence, "Do you know, dear, I don't think that poor woman is so much to blame as you seem to. She is but a child in mind. I believe her worst sin has been her utter inability to enter into an Englishman's life, especially poor George's."

Robert Hillyard answered nothing; he looked very grave, and put down untasted the glass he was raising to his lips. For nothing in the world would he have dispelled Susie's charitable innocence. As she looked at him wistfully, waiting for his verdict, he merely kissed her tenderly, and said, "I wish there were more women like you, darling."

CHAPTER VIII.

UNLOOKED-FOR LEGACY OF GEORGE KERR.

May again; a bright fresh morning, with dappled blue sky —just such a day as that which had seen the transmigration of George Kerr's soul into the person of David Fargus, three years ago.

Gazing from the other side of the pavement at a certain deserted-looking little house, in Charles street, Mayfair, by number 3A, apparently absorbed in the contemplation of an agent's advertisement, which adorned the ground-floor windows, stood a man whose still young face, hardened and weather-beaten, gave token of other than home experiences.

At length, rousing himself from deep abstraction, with the air of one who takes a sudden resolve, he crossed the street and rang the bell. A melancholy looking woman of the genus caretaker opened the door, after a somewhat lengthy delay, and requested him to state his business.

"I see this house is to be let furnished, I should like to go over it." The refined voice was in curious contrast with the unfashionable attire; the woman hesitated, and measured him slowly with her eye. Had he an agent's card?

No; the stranger had been merely struck with the house as he passed by. It did not matter.

"Well, I suppose it won't make much odds for once. 'Ouse is a nice 'ouse; I'll bring you through it."

She led the way, and he followed across a small tiled hall into a room on the right.

"This is the smoking-room," she said, and fell into an attitude of patient waiting.

The visitor gazed about him with a sort of dreamy wonder. With the dust and grime of town upon everything, changed though they were for the worse, every item of the surroundings was painfully familiar. He laid his hand on the oaken writing-table with a lingering touch. The caretaker looked at him with unintelligent wonder, and he awoke from his dream of bygone days.

"Who does this house belong to—now?"

"It belongs now to Sir Reginald Vere, sir; he bought it, furniture and all, from the former howner," she answered glibly enough. "That is to say on that gentleman's death; it was a regular tragedy, I've heard tell—for he committed suicide! Oh, it wasn't here, sir! But the 'ouse is a nice 'ouse, and I can't say as I have found it haunted."

She stopped and dragged a dirty forefinger through the dust of the table beside her.

"Sir Reginald Vere, he didn't seem to care for it, somehow," she continued, after a slight pause, encouraged by her visitor's silent look of inquiry, "and the tradespeople say as how Mrs. Kerr, that's the widow of the gentleman as made away with himself, couldn't get out of it soon enough—though that's not surprising, considering she had his death on her conscience. She went to Spain, she did. I've heard them say she was a queer one. Anyhow, she took on awful—cried herself ill, she did. They say she used to scream o' nights that his ghost had come back. But I can only say I haven't seen him, and I've slept here alone these twelve months now."

But here the stranger interrupted the slow, monotonous trickle of words.

"I do not think I need trouble you to go up-stairs; I have seen enough, thank you."

The woman watched him as he strode away with dull satisfaction.

"I would never say anything against the place, though I think the 'ouse is a nice 'ouse, and ten shillings a week is ten shillings a week. But who would have thought a big strong man like that would be frightened away by the fear of ghosts!"

So Carmen had grieved; the theory of his death had been sown broadcast, and she had borne the odium of it and the sorrow.

Were it even only for ever so short a time, were she perhaps now happy, consoled, as glad of George Kerr's death as was David Fargus, he could never atone for the wrong he had done her.

Conscience smote him keenly; failure seemed to breathe upon his brilliant scheme. Ah, how harsh had been that last letter of his! He had not thought of her enough. What a memory for the solitary woman in the watches of the night, when she had screamed at her own sick fancy! He could not regret his liberty, but it would forever be embittered by the thought of this.

And, as he wound toward his hotel, the whole future and past seemed now to assume a different aspect, and new plans began to agitate his mind.

Everything had prospered with David Fargus up to this. The three years spent in Mexico, Central America, and the Southern States had been full of daring enterprises, as congenial to his high energy as they had proved profitable to his material welfare. He had not known during their lapse one single moment of regret or an instant of the old distaste of life.

But on his arrival at Liverpool, something in the very air of the country—in cloudy sky and narrow horizons, as the express flew Londonward with him through the green bosom of the land—had dashed the exuberance of his spirits. The sight of the little house, and a sullen depth of anger against his wife, a feeling he had believed dead with the old self, had stirred within him strangely. On hearing of her grief for him the revulsion of feeling had been all the stronger for the hardness of these thoughts.

It seemed to him, with that hot impulsiveness of his—of which David Fargus had to the full as large a share as George Kerr—as if he could never again taste peace till he had seen with his own eyes what had become of the woman he had abandoned in gayety of heart and misjudged in all sincerity. She had gone to Seville. Well, Seville was as easy a place for David Fargus to reach as London had been; and with his usual decisiveness the original plan of an English tour was abandoned in favor of instant departure for Spain.

A fortnight later the diligence from Cadiz deposited, for the third time in his life, George Kerr, or, rather, his alias, within the gates of the eighth marvel of the world.

Thirty years ago it was still considered advisable for travelers, whose knowledge of "things of Spain" was sufficient to bear out the disguise, to conform to the dress of the country; David Fargus's life in Spanish America had sufficiently familiarized him with that swaggering indolence, that careless, amiable self-confidence, supposed to be specially characteristic of the *majo*.

Therefore it was a very creditable Andaluz that emerged from the Cadiz diligence, clad in brown velvet, silver-buttoned jacket and embroidered leather gaiters, with silken sash binding his lithe waist, clean-shaven, but for a small bunch of scientifically darkened whiskers on each cheek-bone, and the indispensable black cape, brilliantly lined inside, carelessly thrown over his shoulder, many a well-favored cigar-maid—good judge in such matters—cast, as she hurried by from the tobacco factory, a provoking look at him from the bold languor of her eyes.

His first care was to reconnoiter the familiar neighborhood of Don Atanasio's house. In those days private houses of the middle class were generally ready to supplement their income by the reception of "guests;" and the same evening he had found and engaged a ground-floor room, the window of which commanded a view of that very gateway which was such a historic landmark in his life. A pure Havana to the host, a pretty compliment to the wife and daughter, and he was at home in his new quarters. His Spanish was sufficiently fluent to support the volunteered information that he was an American from the Southern States, who had lived much in Spanish lands.

Spaniards are, as a rule, reticent on the subject of their private affairs. It concerned nobody that the guest should spend his mornings with unvarying regularity in watching some opposite house from his grated window; that of an afternoon he should take post on the shadow side of the street, "embossed" in his cape, puffing at the eternal cigarette, waiting patiently for a glimpse of a well-known figure. There is always a sufficiency of neat ankles and roguish eyes in Seville to justify such an occupation.

Yet the days dawned and closed without bringing any result. True, Don Atanasio and his wife passed daily under his eyes, walking devoutly to mass of a morning, or setting forth on the sunset drive—but they were always alone; and it smote the watcher with an odd feeling of guiltiness to mark how aged they had become. Few people came to the old house, and after a few days he knew them all by sight. But of the beautiful form he had loved and hated, he saw not.

At the end of a week he began to despair of success and was meditating some method of carrying on his search in a less guarded manner, when the problem was solved in a way he had never contemplated.

It was early in the day; bringing in one hand the matutinal cup of chocolate, surmounted with a roll of whitest bread, and in the other a basket of dazzling linen—for your true Spaniard prides himself especially on matters of cuff and shirt-front—his host had just entered the room. Depositing the basket on the bed and the breakfast on the sill of the window, he paused for a few minutes' social chat with his guest, who, at the moment, stood leisurely lathering his chin with his fingers preparatory to a clean shave.

"It will be a hot day, señor, for the bull-fight. Chiclana will do it from the chair to-day."

"Indeed," said the presumed American.

The host refolded a Government cigarette.

"Yes, señor. I have never been in your country, and I should say you would hardly ever have seen the like of him. We, in Seville, never have since Montes, and never shall again." This was conclusive.

But somehow or other his listener did not seem so interested as he should have been in this momentous topic; he was all absorbed in looking at a woman who now emerged from the gated portal of the house opposite, leading with tenderest care a tottering little child. Half-way across the street she looked up and he recognized Doña Concepcion's face, transfigured by an anxious, tender smile.

Following his visitor's intent gaze, the landlord came close behind him to look out over his shoulder with good-humored curiosity, puffing at the same time a rich fragrance of garlic upon him.

"Aha!" he cried; "so the little one is better to-day, and going out for a walk. Jesu! Maria! how doting the grandmother is!"

The grandmother! Carmen was an only child. She had married again, then! Well, he was glad her grief had not proved so overpowering, after all.

"It is a pretty child," he said, after a pause, resuming his

shaving operation with elaborate indifference. "Whose is it?
You say the old lady is the grandmother."

"Yes, señor, and the little chap is the light of her old age.
He lives with the old couple in that great house yonder. Ah,
it is a sad story!"

David Fargus passed the razor over his soapy cheek, while
his ear was bent to listen in keen suspense. Leaning against
the wall and unrolling another cigarette to make it afresh, the
Spaniard proceeded:

"Well, señor, Don Atanasio de Ayala's daughter, who lived
in that house, as pretty a girl she was as any in Seville—and
you must know Seville has the prettiest in the world—married, some years ago, an Englishman. Many wondered at
Don Atanasio for permitting it. In this case, at all events, it
did not prosper. A year later the poor young lady returned
here, a widow. The townsfolk talked much about it here in
Seville; she was well known for her beauty. Some said the
Engishman was killed; some that there was an accident.
Anyhow, he had gone where heretics go, and she, in widow's
black, with a face white as a sheet, the image of dolor, and
yet still so lovely that people stopped in the streets to see her
pass. But it is said she could not get her spirits up again.
You should have heard her sing; many a time we listened
from here; it would have made a paving-stone glad. She
was always ailing and fretting, and not even the thought of
the little one to come could draw a smile from her, and so she
had no strength left. A month before the Easter following
she died—of that pretty little boy you saw there. It was
thought the old ones would have died, too—never was seen
such grief; but they had to live for the *pobrecito*. No wonder the grandmother dotes upon him. I am glad he is better.
I must not chatter so while you shave."

The American had dropped his razor, and was gazing, open-
mouthed, at space—a deep red streak lengthening down his
chin.

He started to a remembrance of his position, and seizing
a towel, buried his face in it under pretense of stanching the
blood, but in reality to hide the pallor he felt upon him. And
then some one within impatiently summoned his host away,
to his great relief.

He fell into a chair in an agony of thought. Carmen
dead!—the child-wife he remembered to the last as the very
incarnation of youthful strength. She had returned to her
old home, mourning for the man who had so selfishly deserted
her; returned, believing herself a widow, to die herself—to
die in giving life to his son!
He hid his face. The clever scheme, what was it but cow-

ardly, despicable, hideously selfish? And then the child!
O God, what a miserable chaos it all was! That last terrible
scene between himself and the willful creature he had meant
to subjugate came back to mind now with glaring vividness!

And he who had abandoned his wife must now abandon
their child—ay, must. So skillfully had he encompassed the
death of his old self that any other course would be impossible.
For the boy's own interest it was best so, perhaps. The
child's fortune was well assured—it would accumulate during
his minority. He would be brought up a Spaniard—that was
possibly again an advantage for him; it is easy to enjoy life
in that sunny land, away from the constant battling for distinction, which is the bane of an Englishman's existence. He
must remain forever dead to his child as he was to the whole
world.

After a long battle with himself, he rose and rapidly finished dressing. As soon as he had seen the entry of his
son's birth in the town registers, satisfied himself of the truth
of the piteous story, that chapter of his life would indeed be
closed forever. And afterward, his one desire was to fly as
soon as possible from the place.

At the Casa di Ayuntamiento he found that the simplest
plan was to ask for an attested copy of the birth of the child,
giving himself out as a distant relation of the family anxious
to verify the fact. With the help of a graciously-offered
gratuity and a well-turned apology he obtained, without too
much delay, the desired document, which bore witness to the
entrance into this world on March 22, 1858, of one Luis Jorge
Kerr y Ayala, son of D. Jorge Kerr, of London, England, de-
ceased, and of Doña Carmen Maria Concepcion de Ayala y
Quevedo, of Seville, his wife.

*   *   *   *   *   *   *   *   *

The many friends David Fargus had made during his three
years' life in the New World remarked a change in him when
he again returned among them. It was in no very marked
way, perhaps, that he was altered; the pleasant manner, the
indomitable energy were still the same; but an infectious
careless light-heartedness, a certain boyish spring that had
made him such a favorite with them, seemed to have gone
from him, to give way to a premature sedateness of manner.
There was no moroseness about him, he was still a genial companion; but his laugh was more tardy, and the ring of his
song and jest was heard no more round the camp-fire.

PART II.

DAVID FARGUS.

CHAPTER I.

ON THE OTHER SIDE OF THE HILL.

Twenty-five years had elapsed since the imperfect play of a
hair-trigger, while it marked the decaying hour of the frivo-
lous, brilliant existence of Carmen Kerr, became the starting
event of a new and vigorous career for one David Fargus.
His had been on the whole a fine life since then—a life of
active independence which had stamped its character of decision and self-reliance upon him.

In his hale middle age, while his body was scarcely past
its prime, his mind had but reached its full power. His was a
mind destined of its innate excellence to profit peculiarly by
the improving influence of years and experience—all quali-
ties which render a man easy and pleasant of access and increasingly fascinating in intercourse.

His personality, too, had, under his new name, become
famous in his adopted country.

On his first return to the New World, at the time when the
Seceder's resistance to the ideas of the North was waxing ever
fiercer, he was just in the mood to throw himself heart and
soul into any great national movement, in the hope of losing
the haunting entity of his former self.

The interest, moreover, of that many-sided question was
deep enough in itself to engross a young man of romantic and
chivalric tendency, and he naturally ended by attaching himself unreservedly to the Seceders' cause.

It could not be long before his special value as a leader of
men made itself felt among the Confederates, and it was at
the head of a corps of those unparalleled Southern Horsemen
that he finally acquired the renown which students of military
history have learned to associate with the name of Colonel
Fargus, Stuart's lieutenant and *alter ego*.

A shoulder lacerated by a splinter of shell during the masterly retreat of the last day of Gettysburg, and the great scar on the right cheek—the work of a half-warded Federal bayonet in that fatal encounter—were the sole mementos of his own personal dangers.

But at this period of his vigorous maturity David Fargus, seemingly the most successful of men, with nearly every desire of his hot youth realized, and, according to the common idea, without a care in the world, came suddenly, as it were, to a standstill in his prosperous career, and confessed to himself that it was not enough.

In the journey of life the beginning of the third score in a man's years is to him as the crest of the mountain's range to the explorer. The ascent may have been arduous, but the traveler was fresh and eager; the day increased in brightness as he went on, the horizon expanded—ahead was the goal. Once reached, however, there comes a change; the wayfarer has lost his keenness; there are, it may be, scenes more beautiful than he has yet beheld, but at every step the prospect grows restricted, the world is darkening, the lonely wanderer feels his energy slowly but surely give way to a yearning for home and rest.

Years and their memories had gathered on his head—not so many, nor yet so heavily, as to bring any foretaste of old age with them, but enough to make him think more of the past and look less to the future. The change which always comes over a man's views and desires when it strikes home to him that he is done with the ascending portion of his life, had begun to show itself to him in an indefinite but haunting regret for the land of his youth.

On an expedition—connected, it is true, with some important speculation, but undertaken principally with a view to seeking in physical fatigue and mental labor the recovery of his wonted placidity—he was suddenly laid low somewhere out of the civilized beats by a severe fever. His vigorous frame repelled the onslaught with little loss of power, but five nights of bodily anguish left their mark upon him.

The first time he found himself again in "a city," where he could confront a looking-glass, he was startled to notice sundry flashes of silver about his temples and mustache. This was the first obtrusive sign of the advancing age he had been given to speculating about of late—the reality, beginning of the end.

Before so very long, then, he must resign himself to being "an old man."

Abstractedly gazing at the keen-featured image before him, he fell into a painful meditation. At the worst of his recent fever a rough comrade, who had tended him in that shanty where he lay, with faithful devotion, had one sultry, tempest-threatened night entertained grave doubts of his patient's recovery. It was in the darkest watch of those hours as the fever-stricken man lay trembling between consciousness and delirium—his pulse at its highest, burning with dry, scorching heat; had it not been for the rain at dawn—who knows?—he might now be lying under the red clay in that dreary waste, with a ruggedly-hewed stone, or, perhaps, not even that, to mark the grave of David Fargus. Staring at the twitching fingers, the ceaselessly tossing head, his sick-nurse had removed his pipe and delivered himself of the following remark:

"I reckon, Colonel, if you wish to add a codicil or two to your last will and testament, you had better jot them down at once. Pity your folks ain't here!"

The brutal phrase had remained in his mind, and now it came back with a revealing sense of his own absolute loneliness.

Friends he had in plenty; but a relative, his own flesh and blood—David Fargus, the lonely bachelor, owned none such on earth. Ah! but George Kerr? He had had kindred. The sturdy young generation, springing from the old tree, would have been something to be proud of now. George Kerr had had a brave little sister; they had loved each other with the tenderness born of childish associations, of the best and purest part of life. Poor Susie!

And then there rose a vision of another child-face, a baby-face with great dark eyes and an aureole of yellow hair, and though resolutely forced in the background of his mind, never forgotten, and he had never so much as touched him!

At the end of so many years it was strange how the thought of the child disturbed him. He must now be a grown man, if he still lived. After all, what did it matter were he alive or dead? It was but another fortunate creature spared the evil of existence. What reason had he to expect the boy to have escaped the taint of the life he had himself condemned him to?

The boy came from a good stock on both sides—who could tell? He might have developed into the sort of man fathers are proud to own.

But man, who can rule an empire, has little power to control the small realm of his own brain; he may lead an army of thousands, but he is impotent to quell absolutely a single persistent idea.

By degrees, the determination taking root, he discovered himself, almost with surprise, making actual preparations for departure, and devising various schemes for tracing his relatives, and perchance, playing the part of beneficent genie in their lives.

This resolve once come to, a definite object again before him, his trouble of mind disappeared.

And thus, on a certain June morning in 1881, he found himself once more on the way to the old country, and in that state of freedom from ties and trammels which had remained for David Fargus one of the necessities of existence.

Now, as he stood on the quarter-deck of the Cunarder bound for home, and watched the shores of his adopted country slowly recede and fade into the horizon, the anithetical nature of his present errand, compared with his first crossing of the ocean, gave a kind of solemnity to the occasion. How different the spirit in which he was now setting out in mature age—on a venture as uncertain, as myseriously attractive, as that which had started his second self!

But as the days rolled by and the proud ship plowed her way through the salt furrows—every minute, every throb bringing him nearer to his desire—though his interest in the enterprise became more absorbing, the first sanguine glow of expectation gradually faded.

Men who have seen and done much in life remain seldom long sanguine, and David Fargus, while determining his course of action, kept rigidly before his mind the possibility of the unknown son being after all, dead, or, if alive, unworthy.

But he had not been in London more than a few days—a delay inevitable for the arrangement of his monetary affairs, and actively spent in settling the same—when one of those strokes of luck which are, after all, more frequent in life than pessimists would have us believe, saved him a long and useless journey.

CHAPTER II.

THE FIRST LINK—A GOLDEN ONE.

It was on the very evening before his intended departure.

Waiting in the drawing-room of the Naval and Military—most comfortable of London clubs—for the appearance of the friend whose guest at dinner he was to be; Fargus was absently perusing some Service weekly paper, when, under the rubric "Furloughs to England," he came across a name which instantly arrested his wandering attention.

Fargus found his gaze riveted on the small-type paragraph: "L. G. Kerr, —th Dragoon Guards." And when his host

entered and introduced the fellow-guests collected to do honor
to the American celebrity, Fargus had to make an effort to
shake off a spell of deep abstraction.

So the young generation kept up the old traditions of
devoting their life's energy to the country's service. This
unknown Dragoon Guard, L. G. Kerr, seemed to loom in the
background of every subject of conversation, and engrossed
much of the attention which should have been bestowed on the
exceptional cookery and select vintages provided for the guest
of the evening by a true connoisseur.

Was he nephew or cousin, or a more distant scion of the
dear old family? G. stood for George, of course. It was a
favorite name among the Kerrs. But L.? What did L.
stand for? Where could he have seen those two letters in
conjunction that they should seem so strangely familiar?
L. G.—Lionel George, Lawrence, or Lewis? Lewis . . .
Luis!

"Colonel Fargus, you are eating nothing. Waiter, give
Colonel Fargus some more wine."

With a hand that shook in very unwonted fashion, David
Fargus straightway drained the refilled beaker. Lewis
George! why, those were the names that had formed the
refrain to his thoughts for the last month! Lewis George,
or, rather, as the Spanish had it, Luis Jorge, the name of that
white-faced babe, Carmen's child.

"Yes, as you say, Major Fraser, nowhere in the world does
one drink a better glass of champagne than in England—the
mother country as we call her—and I have traveled a good
deal . . .". And so the dinner wore its dreary length till
its close.

Colonel Fargus' host was reaping the usual bitter reward
of inviting a lion to partake of his hospitality, with the hidden purpose of making it roar for the entertainment of his
friends. The best effort of the *chef,* the Perier-Jouet '74, the
most delicate turning of the conversation to well-remembered
subjects, were all in vain. The Colonel was abstracted, spoke
with an effort, and in that most convivial of hours, after a
good dinner, left the '47 port untasted merely to toy with the
olives on his plate.

Nor in the smoking-room did matters improve. Puffing
mechanically at the superb Larañaga, chosen for his especial
delectation with such minute care, Colonel Fargus sat cross-
legged in his deep arm-chair, and let his eyes roam dreamily
round the room. All at once he rose, and, addressing his host
with the well-remembered and peculiarly charming smile that
would have been sufficient to remove impressions even more
unsatisfactory, "Excuse me," he said; "I see an Army List

yonder. I have a reason for wishing to consult one—the fate of an old friend I am anxious about. May I look at it for a moment?"

The disappointed entertainer gave the required permission with all the good grace he could muster, and watched his guest's proceedings with a certain curiosity.

Fargus withdrew to some little distance from the group, and holding the book under the light of the lamp on the chimney-piece with one hand, rapidly turned over the pages with the other. Presently he started violently, and then became absorbed in the contemplation of one page for such a lengthy period that Major Fraser lost patience, turned his back upon him and gave him up as hopeless, to devote himself to his other guests.

But the celebrated Southern was, for the moment, Colonel David Fargus, the American, no more. He was George Kerr, English, of England's best blood, and he had a son who was a soldier of the old country. "Lewis George Ayala Kerr. Born March, 1858." Ay, that was the date, not the shadow of a doubt—there he was, even if the Spanish name beside the English ones had not been proof sufficient. "Gazetted from the R. M. C. in July, 1878, to the —th Dragoon Guards." In three years the young man had seen service enough to warrant the pride that swelled the father's heart as, when sufficiently recovered from the first bewilderment of his discovery, he noticed the crossed swords before the names and turned to the War Service references. "Attached to Sir H. Gough's Cavalry Brigade in Afghanistan; present at the march from Kabul to Kandahar." And again: "Attached to the —th Regiment in the Transvaal." Truly a goodly record for so short a time!

Fargus closed the book, and with a curious smile on his face, a bright, far-off look in his eyes, returned to the smoking circle and joined in the conversation. And now he talked enough to satisfy all the expectations of host and guests.

But over and above the exchange of words, the interlacing of ideas and sound wisdom, born of his own warlike experience, with which he delivered himself anent the mismanaged, disastrous, and bloody business of the Boer campaign, were surging private brain-pictures of the little dark-eyed boy he had seen but once; the child who was now an English soldier—and a dashing one, since he had been twice allowed to see service away from his regiment—an English horse soldier in that glorious old corps that for two centuries upheld the prestige of English valor in Spain, in Flanders, in France, the Crimea, India. With the remembrance of its noble motto there came before his mind the gallant sight of heavy horse as they had dashed past the Highland Brigade to scatter the distant swarming mass of Russians on the morning of Balaklava. With what envy, what enthusiasm he, the beardless ensign, had watched them as they rushed to the front! And his deserted boy was one of those! It was a novel and delicate emotion to think, all of a sudden, with a sense of pride, of the son he had abandond.

In accordance with his new schemes, the very next day found the American alighting among the yellow sands, the heather, the fragrant pines of Sandhurst, and wending his way through that picturesque corner of Hampshire, which meets Surrey and Berkshire.

Skirting the placid lake, hemmed in by greenwood and timber, on one side of which the mature students of the Staff College master the more recondite mysteries of warfare, while, on the other, downy-lipped cadets wrestle with its rudiments, he walked up the broad gravel road leading to the Grecian portico of the Military College, and quietly enjoyed his thoughts and his cigar.

And he paused for a few moments, drawing pleasure from the fancied vision of his son among those eager polo-players that were just now careering in wild confusion on the football plot. The father's curiosity was not devoid of anxiety as he made his way over to a much be-medaled staff-sergeant, who was standing under the portico, and realized with a strange mixture of feelings that, for the very first time, he was about to speak to some one who must have known his son.

Accosting the veteran, he went straight to the point, with a simplicity that robbed the errand of half its strangeness.

A young gentleman, by name Lewis G. Kerr, whom he had reason to be interested in, had been through the College three years back. He was most desirous for some information concerning him.

The sergeant-major glanced sharply at the speaker; then, after a second's hesitation, touched his cap and professed himself both able and willing to assist him.

"There was a Mr. Kerr here, sir, some years ago. I remember him well. He was gazetted to the —th Dragoon Guards, I believe. Out in India now. He was a fine young gentleman, liked by most. If you will come with me, I can find out a bit more about him for you, from the back registers."

And acquiescing, Fargus was piloted through long, echoing passages to the adjutant's office, where the register in question was soon produced.

"Here you are, sir, Kerr, L. G., Gentleman Cadet, University Candidate, B. A., Edin. Born in Seville, Spain, 12 March, 1858—he had a bit of a foreign way with him, too,

now I think of it, though he did not like to have it said of
him—son of George Kerr, Esq., late —th Highlanders, de-
ceased. Educated Edinburgh University; Trinity College,
Cambridge. London address: Staples Inn, Holborn. Gazetted—and so on. Is that the young gentleman you wanted
to hear about?"

Fargus nodded silently, drew out his note-book, and carefully jotted down the memoranda. "A scholar, too! How
well the lad has got on!"

"You say you remember him well, sergeant-major?" he
went on aloud, in his quiet voice, as, the business completed,
they turned away and strolled again toward the parade-
ground.

"Yes, sir, very well. A smart young gentleman; good drill;
good at gymnastics and games. I remember him throwing
the hammer, Highland fashion—not running, as they do here
—no one could come near him at that. I am a Scotchman
myself, sir, and I have never seen it better done—so was the
instructor, too, for the matter of that, but Mr. Kerr beat
him."

The visitor had lit another cigar, and now stood on the
steps of the portico, slowly puffing blue smoke and abstractedly gazing into space. The old sergeant, who, finding that the
more good he narrated of the quondam cadet the more the
stranger's face brightened, now warmed perceptibly to the
work of airing his reminiscences, and, after a pause for approval, took a fresh start.

"Good at book work, too, I believe; but that had not much
to say to things in that year, for they bundled out all the
young gentlemen at the end of their first term; we thought
we were going to fight the Russians once more, as you
know, sir."

Fargus looked down at his informant's breast, and noticed
on the broad expanse of the staff tunic the green-edged pink
ribbon and the curly Crimean clasps—honorable badges he
had himself been entitled to of old.

"It was cold work in those trenches there, was it not?" he
said, indicating the decoration with a significant gesture;
"I—that is, I have some old friends who went through it all.
What regiment were you in?"

"It is curious, sir, but I was in the —th, the very regiment
this Mr. Kerr's father belonged to. I think that was what
made the young gentleman take to me first. On parade it
is not a question of choice. Many and many is the talk we
have had about the old times. Not that I could tell him
much about his father, for I was not in his company, and
I scarcely recollect him, save that he was a finely set-up

young officer and wild like. But Mr. Kerr that was here, he would come and get me to talk of him and of our doings; he seemed never to tire of hearing me speak about his father, little as it was I could say, though he never even saw him himself, as he told me. Yes, sir, he was a nice young gentleman, and steady—as young gentlemen go."

Here was a link in the lengthening chain—a golden one. The boy had not been brought up in ignorance of or indifference to the father who died to him before he saw the light. Discoveries such as these, made with facility now that he had the proper clew, seemed to bridge over the dark abyss of time.

"Well, I am really much obliged to you."

"Don't mention it, sir. Thank you, sir"—dexterously slipping into his pocket the sovereign which the visitor pressed into his white-gloved palm. You are a relative of the young gentleman, I suppose, if I may make so bold?"

"No," answered Fargus dreamily, after a pause; "his father—I knew his father well in my young days. I am only a friend—a well-wisher to the son."

The veteran eyed him investigatingly.

"Perhaps you would like to see his likeness. Each batch of young gentlemen have themselves taken regularly in York Town. They are so pleased when they first get into their uniforms, you know. It is just over the road, sir. I can show you the way."

It was evidently a happy thought, for the stranger accepted the proposal with alacrity.

Sergeant-Major Short would have been more than human if his curiosity had not been thoroughly aroused. Having conducted his interlocutor to the photographer's door, he retired into the shade of a neighboring public-house to watch his further proceedings.

After a while the stranger emerged from the studio, and walked very slowly along the road leading to the station. He held a small card in his hand which he seemed to contemplate from every point of view with absorbing interest.

With such notes as Fargus now carried his further course was one of very plain sailing. The same afternoon he pushed as far as Cambridge, and the next morning, beneath the July sunshine, saw him strolling down the majestic, but at this vacation time deserted, King's Parade toward the well-remembered Gothic archway of that noble college which had known so many generations of Kerrs.

The head porter was soon forthcoming, and at his courteous request condescended to show the stranger over the venerable institution, little wotting how familiar every stone rose before his gaze.

Cambridge was a more likely place for Lewis Kerr to re-visit on his return home than Sandhurst, and David Fargus deemed it prudent to adopt more devious methods of inquiry than in his previous voyage of investigation. He therefore suffered himself to be conducted tourist fashion through dining-hall, library and chapel; he admired, criticised, and wondered, and finally succeeded in producing in his decorous guide the desired loquacity. It was easy to get him on the subject of generations of students, and a not unnatural transition to mention, as an instance, a certain family—the Kerrs of Gilham—whom the tourist had known in days gone by.

Yes, there had been some at Trinity to his own knowledge. But there were none now. No; there had not been any since a Mr. L. G. Kerr; and that was four or five years ago. He (with some disgust) had left before his degree—had gone, it seemed, into the army. He could not say if he was of the family the gentleman had known—they came from Yorkshire. This Mr. Kerr used to go there, now he remembered, by the way, with his cousin, Mr. Hillyard, a lecturer at one of the colleges, very highly thought of in the University. Perhaps the inquirer knew him? No; well, he was away now, any-how; Gilham, he believed, the name of the place was.

David Fargus seized with avidity upon this first piece of news. So, despite the squire's enmity, the posthumous son had after all been made welcome, and acknowledged in the old home. The great man waived the trivial personality of the youthful undergraduate—B. A. though he was of some Scotch University or other, he had left before his degree—an act of obvious folly, for he might have made a career at the University.

It was with a feeling almost of tenderness that he stepped into the small green-paneled room, with mullioned ogee win-dows looking over the old court—the rooms where his boy had passed so important a part of his life, and which, by a pleasing coincidence, were situate on the same stairs as those where George Kerr had spent his short and profitless spell of University life. Then the caressing thought came that per-haps there was more than mere coincidence, that the boy had probably found out where his unknown father lived, and had taken a sentimental interest in establishing himself near the place.

After a short conversation on general topics, undertaken with a view to draw the other's attention from the subject of his inquiries, Fargus thanked him and took his leave.

But he failed not to stop at the first bookseller's and purchase the reference books of the required date. Here he found information which amply compensated him for his lack of success with the lofty head-porter.

That evening Fargus ate his solitary dinner to the accompaniment of many pleasant thoughts.

Before leaving the table he drew the photograph from his pocketbook, and gazed at it long and with keen scrutiny; then he filled his glass to the brim and drank, with a mental toast, to the original.

CHAPTER III.

MORE LINKS IN THE GOLDEN CHAIN.

"Pending the boy's arrival in England," had thought Fargus, while maturing his plans at Cambridge, "I may as well carry on my investigations at Gilham."

To do so without betraying himself or his purpose only required a little management. The most direct way was, if possible, to settle within convenient distance of the Court for a few months; this accomplished, he would be, in some respects, even more fortunately situated than the best supported detective, having the advantage of really belonging to the society he intended to mix with.

Glancing through a list of suitable residences in that part of the Riding which is associated with Gilham, the familiar name of Widley Grange arrested his attention. Widley Grange—the "Lone Grange," as it was popularly called—the very place!

This was the very place for him, and he soon closed an engagement with the agents.

The house was, in its old-fashioned way, in solid repair, and furnished comfortably enough. The local agent had, at his request, engaged two reliable female servants, sufficiently past their prime for a bachelor establishment; and he had secured for himself in London a competent factotum, destined to act as coachman and valet, and with recommendations high enough to warrant the corresponding altitude of salary. To this discreet and capable person he intrusted the installment of his luggage, the choice of the few rooms to be inhabited out of the numerous and rambling suites, and the general preparation of house and stables. He himself remained a few days longer in town to settle private points of business—among these one which had cost him many hours of anxious deliberation.

He was too much alive to the risk of missing his son, despite the elaborate and plausible scheme by means of which he meant to come across him naturally, to leave such a contingency unprovided against, and there seemed to be but one safe way out of the difficulty. Finally, though not at first without repugnance, he entered into negotiations with one of the more respectable private inquiry offices, where he obtained the services of a trustworthy agent, who was to watch for the arrival in England of a certain subaltern of dragoons, and to furnish a daily report of his subsequent movements.

Satisfied on this important point, Fargus took the road again to enter upon the possession of his little estate and commence the operations which were to bring him once more into contact with his next of kin.

He was much attracted by the aspect of the ancient dwelling-place and the wild beauty of its surroundings when he now beheld them after so many years. And the familiar coat of arms, weather-beaten and defaced by time, on the crumbling key-stone over the hall door, made him feel, for the first time after his long wanderings, as if he had come home at last.

His newly discovered attendant received him with the respectful confidential greeting of an old retainer.

"I hope you will approve of my arrangements, sir. You see, the bedroom for yourself next to the visitor's room, as you ordered; the dining-room and the study according to your directions. The kitchens and the female servants' rooms are quite at the other end of the house. I myself occupy a room over the stables."

Fargus looked round the large beam-ceiled, wainscoted hall allotted to him as study with decided approval. With a smile of commendation he noted the odds and ends of the best furniture sagaciously collected from different parts of the house, and the trophies of heterogeneous weapons he had accumulated during many wanderings arranged on one side of the mantelpiece, not without a show of experience, to balance the rack containing guns, rifles and rods, on the other. Opening out of this "study" were the two curious, irregularly shaped bedrooms, with climbing roses peeping in at the windows, and full of the sweetness of the old-fashioned flowers in the neglected garden beyond.

On the threshold of that destined for "the guest" Fargus again paused. If things prospered him, here he might one day hope to harbor his son.

"Yes, Turner, everything is as I wish; you could not have done better."

The new habitat was, moreover, thoroughly congenial to

his tastes; it was singularly in harmony with his present pursuit; he could remain as long as necessary, look about him without exciting comments, and on occasion dispense hospitality.

Two days after his arrival, on returning from a ride to the local town, he found that his first visitor had called: Major-General Woldham, Woldham Hall, as testified the card.

Well, it was even better, perhaps to make his first appearance in county society elsewhere than at the Court itself; and there could be no more favorable opening than this. After a due lapse of time, he rode forth to return the call.

There are no spots in the kingdom where the special beauty of prosperous English scenery combines more harmoniously with undisturbed associations of the past than in Gilham and its neighborhood. Woldham Hall itself, albeit a building of no pretentious dimensions, is one of the most perfect specimens of fifteenth-century half-timber—so-called black and white—houses now extant. With its gables and bay windows, latticed casements, its oaken panels and ceilings, stairs and galleries, and the wondrous fancy of the black timbering on its white plaster-work, this ideal mansion rests with quiet but conscious pride between a tenderly nursed terrace lawn on one side—the velvet-nap bowling-green of former days, bounded now by a flower-grown baluster where, in less secure times, the moat ran its sluggish course—and on the other a luxuriant demesne of orchards, rose and kitchen gardens, hothouses and shrubberies, which encompasses and screens with pleasant motley growth such marring adjuncts as offices and stable yards.

David Fargus, turning from the white dust and glare of the highroad into the cool green shadiness of the grounds, promptly fell a victim to the temptation, and started across the short tuft at a hard canter. But arrived at the clump of fir-trees which he had thought must mark the part of the avenue he aimed at, he found he had lost his bearing, and was about to retrace his way, when a deep-mouthed, interrogatory, menacious bark made him rein in his horse and look in the direction whence the challenge seemed to proceed.

Here a graceful picture met his eyes; a tall girl, whose bright brown head was bared to the summer breeze, whose shapely figure, clad in white, detached itself vividly from the somber background, stood leaning against the trunk of a giant fir. Her clear large eyes looked with quiet inquiry at the intruder; one slender, buff-gauntleted hand was twined restrainingly round the neck of a large retriever, who, sable-coated, quivering with defiance, stood ready to spring forward in his mistress' defense.

For a moment, bathed in the full splendor of the sun, Fargus, curbing his impatient mount with firm hand, paused to enjoy this unexpected vision. Then, uncovering himself, and bowing, with the ceremonious courtesy habitual to him, he advanced a little closer on his dancing bay, and addressed her:

"I fear I am a tresspasser," he said, looking down at her with the grave eyes that lent a touch of melancholy to his smile; "I must beg your forgiveness for this intrusion; the thick turf was so tempting, and I was rash enough to try a short-cut to the house. General Woldham kindly called on me, at Widley-Grange," he added, as a sort of self-introduction. "I hope I may find him at home?"

The girl, returning his gaze with an easy directness charming in its modest absence of self-consciousness, answered, smiling back:

"I am Maude Woldham—my father is out driving; but he cannot be long now." Her voice was singularly harmonious, and it fell pleasantly on the exile's ear. Then she added, releasing the retriever, who, satisfied that his interference was no longer needed, bounded up to make friendly acquaintance with the horse:

"But will you not come up to the house? Mr. Fargus, is it not?"

Bowing acquiescence, he accepted the offer.

"I must show you the way," said she, laying one hand on the satin-smooth neck of the horse. "No; pray do not dismount. I like walking fast, and I am sure your horse hates being led—I know mine does."

The frankness of her manner, the maidenly freedom of her wide-set gray eyes, the delightful ease of movement with which she stepped over the uneven ground and bravely kept up with the steed's impatient gait—all this compelled Fargus' interest and admiration.

His fair conductress brought him round by the stables, modern in their irreproachable neatness, while delightful in their carefully restored antiquity; here, at her call, clear and true as a silver bell, appeared a white-haired groom to take the visitor's horse; then they proceeded together into the great, cool hall—in summer-time the usual sitting-room—the wide doors of which were open all day to the flower-scented air and to all comers.

A smiling butler, ancient like the groom, promptly appeared with a silver tray laden with tea and other good things; Fargus sat down and looked around with increasing content—

everything was homelike, hospitable, simple with the simplicity which only the most perfect refinement can produce. The old hall, all oak from floor to ceiling; the bowls of roses on the carved tables, darkened and polished by age alone; the girl in her young, warm-blooded beauty, and the old house, fitting in with the time-honored surroundings while gracefully contrasting with them—it all formed an attractive picture of English home-life at its best.

On her side, Maude Woldham, as she poured the yellow cream into his cup and cut the home-made cake, observed her new acquaintance with a little wonder and a good deal of approval.

"Yours is a wonderful mansion!" said Fargus, taking his cup from her slender hand, sunburnt over its whiteness with delicate amber. "Apart from its actual beauty, there is that ideal charm of old associations and memories which fail us so completely in our surroundings. We Americans who are unpractical enough to hanker after such things have to seek them in the mother-country—and lovely she is to us."

"I am glad you like our country," answered the girl, with kindling cheek and eye; "and still more that you like my home. I love it—every stick and stone of the old place is dear to me. You cannot think what a relief it was to come back to it after three months in London." Then, glancing at him curiously and a little shyly, "I did not know, however, that Americans were ever unpractical," she added with a mischievous smile.

"I can hardly lay claim to being the typical Jonathan," retorted Fargus, smiling too; "and America is a large place, you know. I come from the South, where practicality is scarcely the predominant national virtue."

"How do you like the Grange?"

"Better and better every day. I congratulate myself on having been fortunate enough to secure it."

"And have you made out your relatives?"

"I have made them out right enough," said Fargus slowly. "I could claim kinship, I believe, with no less a person than the squire. By the way, I like the homely fashion in which every one hereabouts talks of Mr. Kerr as 'the squire,' just as your father, I hear, is 'the general.' But I am certainly not going to do so. I prefer standing alone too well."

"So you are kin to the squire," Maude said musingly. "Well, I think you are quite right in not caring to claim the connection. Have you seen your landlord yet? horrid old man!"

"Then I may infer the Kerr family does not find favor in your eyes?"

"The Kerr family? I did not say the family. Oh, Lady Gwendolin was charming, and Susie—dear Susie Hillyard, I loved her.

"She was the squire's half-sister," continued Maude. "Mr. Hillyard was the Rector of Gilham for five years; that was how I knew them. Susie was like a mother to me. Her death was the first sorrow I ever knew."

"So she is dead?" said Fargus, after a long pause.

"She died last year, only six months after her husband. Her daughters live in the village; they are dear good girls," with an expressive movement of shapely shoulders. "Yet so unlike their mother. Then there is Charlie, the brother—a great man, they say, at the University. And there is another Kerr I like. Dear old Lewis!" She indicated with a smiling gesture a framed photograph, half hidden behind the roses on the table.

"May I see?" asked the visitor quietly.

"Mr. Fargus, how foolish you must think me! As if all this could possibly interest you."

"I assure you," said the other, still extending his hand, "it interests me exceedingly to hear about these people. Now this other Kerr, whose portrait—thank you."

He took the portrait to the light. The same face as in the Sandhurst one, which even now, in a hidden recess of his pocketbook, lay on his breast; but older, manlier, more vigorous.

"You seem quite absorbed in your soldier cousin," said the girl.

Fargus put down the portrait.

"Your English uniforms, with their perpetual changes, are a puzzle to me," he said with an effort. "I dare say I, too, should have liked that—extremely distant relative of mine. Now, where does he come in?"

"Oh, he has a strange history. His father, poor Susie's brother, was, it seems, a very wild young man. He married a lovely Spanish woman, and a year had not gone by when he was drowned. She died, in Spain, when Lewis was a baby, and Lewis was brought up by his grandfather, and only came to England on his death. Susie loved him so, and it was when he was staying with her that I saw him first. Mr. Hillyard brought him over to the Court, and you cannot conceive his uncle's rudeness to him—at his own table, too. We were there—papa and I—and it made us so angry that we had the boy to Woldham on the spot. Dad and I always think alike.

"That finished the squire with me forever, you know. So I do not think Lewis had much loss there. He went to papa for advice in everything, and now my dear old dad, having done such a lot for him, is as proud as Punch of his *protege,* follows all the *Gazettes,* and thinks him on the highroad to glory. It seems he has done wonderfully well for the short time he has been in the service."

The father listened in silence. Susie dead! He had feared to meet his sister—partly for the perspicacity of her loving eyes; partly, on the other hand, from a repugnance to be greeted as a stranger by her who had been the one pure affection of his youth.

And now she was beyond his discovery! . . . Well, the slender pink-cheeked little sister of his young days would still live for him. But he would yet devise some good for her children. She had not deserted his as he—the father—had done; ay, and like the highly virtuous Squire of Gilham, who had seen fit to visit the father's sins upon the innocent son! Fargus' cheek glowed at the indignity he would have smiled at had it been offered to himself.

All that was bitter. Yet sweetness was there, too, coming from this fair-faced, starry-eyed girl, who spoke so bravely of his boy, and touched his portrait with such tender fingers.

Fargus aroused himself from his fit of abstraction in time to see Maude turn joyfully to a white-haired, erect old man, who had appeared at the open door, and proudly lead him forward to introduce him as her father.

"Glad to see you, sir; glad to see you!" said the general, who had little bright-blue eyes under immense bushes of white eyebrows, and an air of extreme military severity which ill concealed a kindness almost amounting, as all said who were fortunate enough to know him well, to weak-mindedness. "This puss would not let you go, she tells me; I am glad of it."

"I did not need much pressing," said Fargus, returning the cordial handshake.

The old man subjected him to a scrutinizing, twinkling survey, and marched him off to the smoking-room in a most friendly manner. His comfortable opinion was enhanced on the production of a deep-colored pipe from the stranger's case, and when, after half an hour's genial conversation, Fargus rose to take his leave, the general seized the pretext of a passing shower to press him to remain and dine there in so homely and hospitable a manner that refusal would have seemed ungracious.

It was a pleasant meal.

Fargus heard nothing more that evening on what lay nearest to his heart. On the contrary, the turn of conversation obliged him to talk much himself and often about himself.

The general's innocent curiosity about the New World and his own experiences were such that he could not, without affectation, have avoided doing so.

Presently the general made a discovery which brought his delight to a culminating point.

The conversation turned upon military questions—the old soldier, as Maude said, was never thoroughly happy unless he talked shop. After delivering himself of divers very sage remarks on the War of Secession, in which he displayed the most guileless state of fog on the complicated history of that movement, and after being tactfully set right by Fargus, he suddenly exclaimed, good-humoredly:

"You must have been something more than a looker-on, I'll warrant."

"I raised and commanded a regiment of horse under Lee," answered Fargus in his quiet manner.

Maude looked up quickly at the long scar which started from the iron-gray wave of hair at the temple and disappeared in the close-trimmed peaked beard; her father was silent for a moment. But as the visitor attempted, unobtrusively, to launch another topic, the general exploded.

"Why, damme!" he exclaimed, in his excitement, "you do not mean to say you are *the* Colonel Fargus? How stupid of me! I should have recognized the name at once. But why have you dropped your rank? Why hide a glorious title, sir?"

"Oh," rejoined Fargus, "remember we were rebels. Moreover, among the Yankees, colonels, even generals, are rather common."

But the general was started. He would have no evasions; the Potomac, Gettysburg, all the terrible and gallant episodes of that obstinate struggle, had to be descanted on, until Maude saw, perhaps with some relief, the quartet of small Wold-hams trooping in for dessert.

This created a diversion. It was pretty to see them run to Maude, to see her bright girl-face soften with a maternal tenderness, to watch the liberality, tempered by prudence, with which she distributed good things among the little folks. The children, chubby-faced, clean-skinned, satisfactory speci-mens of the young generation, hung round the elder sister, and peered at the stranger's commanding face with round blue eyes. But his smile and gentle voice soon won them from their fears, and before long the two youngest hopes found themselves seated, one on each knee, absorbed in the contemplation of his repeating watch.

Presently Maude rose, observing that Billy Winky was coming, and marshaled the little battalion bedward.

There was the presiding genie of that house that had, it seemed, always held out its hospitality to the fatherless boy, where he had found friendship and support, where Susie was talked of in loving words.

She heard the champing of Colonel Fargus' horse and the beat of a restless hoof on the gravel beneath the window; then her father's cheery "Good-night," then the retreating sound of the horse's feet along the winding road until it faded into the night's stillness.

CHAPTER IV.

THE DANCE OF DEATH.

Before a week had elapsed the tenant of the "Lone Grange" had glided into close and friendly relations with his neighbors of the half-timber house. The general had stopped once or twice, on his way to or from the county town, to smoke half a pipe and have another interesting chat with his new acquaintance, each time conveying him back in triumph to lunch or dinner at the Hall, where Maude always gave him the welcome. The Hall party, children and all, had come to tea at the Grange, where Maude had taken possession of the tea-table, under the spreading chestnut, and ministered to her host's comfort, while he looked on in æsthetic enjoyment of the situation.

Round the central figure of the group, that image of radiant girlhood and womanly sweetness, he had already begun, half unconsciously, to weave a series of rosy schemes, in which a certain unknown son of his played a prominent part. For Maude spoke of Lewis frequently, and always with affectionate interest. It was Lewis who had given her the black retriever, her faithful guardian; it was Lewis who had set up the basket swing for the children—they were then toddling babies; Lewis who had first ridden her bay pony, etc., etc.

Fargus, with much private satisfaction, had drawn his own surmises. Indeed, he ended by settling quite comfortably in his own mind that the young mistress of Woldham was an attraction which must inevitably draw the boy there as soon as might be on his arrival.

It was therefore a grievous blow to all his plans when, after some three weeks of this pleasant intercourse, Maude's immediate departure for a month's stay at Homburg with an invalid aunt was announced. The girl herself evinced a vexation which corroborated his own private ideas. There was a cloud on her face, usually so bright.

"Oh, how I do wish I could stop here! But Aunt Annie is so delicate, and as I half promised her in London, and now she counts upon me, I cannot leave her in the lurch. As for dad, though he has the boys, he is always miserable when I am away. Happily, he has got you; you will go and see him now and again, will you not?"

She gently drew her fingers from the friendly grasp which had grown warm and close round them. Looking up to him with swimming eyes, she met his kindly, searching glance. But he could not put his sympathy in words. It would be sad indeed, when the young soldier came home in the first flush of his joy, to find his mistress, the light of the old place, gone!

The next morning came a letter to the Grange.

Not an interesting missive to look at; a long envelope, indited in a clerk-like hand, dated from the "Private Inquiry Office," set forth that the troop-ship on board which, as had been ascertained, Lieutenant L. G. Kerr was a passenger, had been spoken off Gibraltar on the previous Saturday, and was expected to-morrow at Portsmouth, whither an agent was about to proceed, to report daily the movements of the gentleman.

Fargus turned from the window with a sigh and a smile. Was he building on sand, after all? He knew that his son was a scholar, a keen soldier—also a favorite in a certain guileless, warm-hearted family; but that was all. There might yet be bitter disappointment for these hopes which had waxed so strong of late. Well, well, these first movements of the boy—which, poor fellow! he little suspected were to be noted and reported on—would no doubt reveal the young man's real character.

This plan of spying on his son had been prompted by a desire so free from all vulgar curiosity, so pure and unselfish in its ends, that it had now lost all its odious significance to the father. He waited for the morrow's letter with deep anxiety.

As he stood thus absorbed in thought, again feeding upon the future, despite all wiser determinations, the door was opened by Turner's noiseless hand, and the latter announced, with his usual soft impressiveness, "Mr. Hillyard."

Fargus laid down his pipe. With some emotion rose before him the image of the toddling infant boy at Susie's knee. And he turned round with a cordial smile to greet his sister's only son. But the first glance was a disappointment.

There was naught in the visitor's features or countenance which recalled the dear memory.

The keen face, with its pallid beauty; the gray eyes, observant and secretive; the powerful forehead and the firm mouth, the cool, self-possessed bearing of the stranger for whom he had that instant felt a movement of spontaneous affection, although eliciting his admiration at once, made a chilling impression. There was naught of Susie there. It was only a presentment of the father, a man whom Fargus knew to have been both good and true, but for whom George Kerr had never had other sympathy than that produced by the knowledge of his little sister's happiness.

"While I am happy, Colonel Fargus," the visitor said, as they shook hands, speaking in a clear, precise, rather high-toned voice, "to profit by this opportunity on my own account, I must first of all inform you that I come here as the representative of my uncle, Mr. Kerr, with whom I am stopping a few days. He has asked me to call upon you, and to express his regret that his present weak state of health should debar him from coming himself."

"I am very glad to see you," returned David Fargus, motioning his guest to an armchair, and pushing the box of cigars toward him. "As for Mr. Kerr, I shall myself visit him at the Court."

"That is just what I was going to ask you to do, colonel," said Charles Hillyard. "The squire wants to know if you will waive ceremony and come to lunch to-morrow. In the country, you know, people do not stand hard and fast on etiquette, so you will excuse formalities. I believe, however, that is not what you suffer from most on the other side of the ocean."

"Pray tell your uncle I shall have great pleasure in coming," answered Fargus, with that grave simplicity that always proved a barrier against undue familiarity.

Here the conversation languished again. Charles Hillyard looked curiously round the room, then, in a puzzled way, at the stranger, who sat in a dignified silence waiting for him to speak. He made a fresh start.

"We have heard a great deal about you from General Woldham," he said, with well-assumed cordiality, which had not, however, the genuine ring to his listener's ear. "He rode over to see the squire yesterday, and spoke mainly about you and your prowess. You have quite won his heart, colonel."

Under the grave gaze fixed on him Charles Hillyard faltered a little, and the cheeriness of the last remark was slightly overdone in consequence.

"Pardon me," interrupted Fargus, smiling, "did not the

general also tell you that when I had done with my military life I bade good-by likewise to military rank? I do not call myself colonel."

The gentle rebuke brought a quick flush of surprise and a light glow of annoyance to the visitor's face.

"Pray forgive me," he said, with instinctive good breeding, "though my mistake was a natural one. To those who have read something of your national conflict, it is hard to dissociate the name of Fargus from the prefix under which it has become so well known."

The elder man acknowledged, in his own mind, the cleverness with which his nephew had disengaged himself; he appreciated, too, the tact the young man now showed in not resting on the complimentary amendment, but changing the subject naturally by a question about the Lone Grange.

"We lived here after my father's death—until my poor mother followed him, in fact." The sadness that deepened in Fargus' eyes was absent from Charles' unsoftened face. "I know every nook and corner of the old place," he went on. "Do you not find it rather large and rambling?"

"I have made a nest for myself in these four ground-floor rooms; the rest is condemned, save, of course, servants' offices, which are sufficiently remote to be ignored altogether. I am perfectly content."

"It is a curious choice," commented Charles.

Charles looked at his cigar meditatively for a while, then, after another rather hard stare at his host, rose to take his leave.

"Well, then, to-morrow at one o'clock," said Charles, with his spasmodic friendliness.

The other accompanied him to the door, where he remained a few seconds after his guest's departure, lost in thought.

As the young man's slight, well-balanced figure rounded the grass-plot and passed by the overgrown garden, a shrill, childish voice cleaved the air.

"Well, Charlie, have you measured him? How long is he?"

"Playing truant again, I see!" he said sharply, then shook his finger and passed on.

"Who is it, Turner?" asked Fargus, in some surprise, turning to the servant, who was hovering near the door after letting the visitor out.

"The young masters from Woldham Hall, if you please, sir," replied that discreet person. "They said they preferred to wait till Mr. Hillyard had gone, and they would stroll in the garden. The cook, sir, wanted to interfere, as they was eating the peaches, but I said that I thought you would be displeased if they were disturbed."

"Quite right, Turner. Tell the cook all the peaches are to be reserved for the young gentlemen. And ask them to come in."

But at that moment there put in an appearance on the greensward two sturdy little figures, which made up for shortness of limb and chubbiness of cheek by a prodigous amount of mouse-colored cord gaiters, an easy carriage of the hands in trouser pockets, and an independent manner of walking.

"Good-afternoon, sir," said the elder of these persons, who had three more buttons to his gaiters than the younger and weaker copy of himself, lifting his cap.

"How do you do, my man?" said Fargus, in far too complete sympathy with the spirit of his small visitor to think of kissing the fruit-stained face.

"We just rode over to see you," continued the sportsman, "'cause it's so dull at home without Muddie. Yes, thanks, I'd like tea, and so would Tom. We've had fruit in the garden. Cook came out with a rolling-pin, but Turner said we might go on. We like Turner. We didn't come in at once, you know, 'cause of Charlie. We thought we'd wait, 'cause we don't like Charlie."

The pair sat down side by side on the sofa, with the gaitered legs a long way off the ground, and smiled confidently at their host, who looked back at them with pleasure and tenderness.

Lewis, too, had no doubt been just as sturdy, brave-hearted a little lad. What pleasures, of the purest in existence, had not his father deliberately denied himself, when he had left to others the task of leading the little spirit from childhood to boyhood.

"Did Charlie measure you?" burst forth the elder boy again. "I shouldn't have let him measure me; I'd have hit him in the eye, I would. Did you hit him in the eye?"

"Not exactly," said the man gravely; "but I did not let him measure me."

The boy swung his legs ecstatically.

"He came last night to dinner, you know. Father talked of you; father likes you, so do we; we think you are the nicest man we ever saw. Charlie said he thought you would turn out a fr—, a fr—, it wasn't a frog, but it was something like it. And he said he'd soon take your measure. Father said you were a great man, and father got quite red and rapped the table, and we laughed, and Muddie told us to keep quiet. Muddie and Charlie walked up and down on the terrace afterward, and when Muddie came to put us to bed her face was quite red, too. And she wouldn't talk a bit. And when she kissed us, I said, 'I hate Charlie, Muddie; I love Mr. Fargus.' And now I'll have tea, and so will Tom."

"And so my clever nephew thinks I am a fraud!" said Fargus to himself, as the little pair, escorted by the respectfully protective Turner, at length departed full of cake and bliss, and proud joint-possessors of an Indian arrow.

Next morning the bay horse carried his master across the purple heather, on to the well-known Gilham road, through the great gates, under the limes and chestnuts; finally before that picturesque massive pile that had seen the dawn of George Kerr's strange life.

"All comes in time to him who can wait," thought Fargus, as he dismounted before the porch he had not seen for some thirty years. "Ah! good-morning." This aloud to his nephew, who appeared on the steps and gracefully came forward to receive him.

He ushered the visitor into the dining-hall with an apology. "If you do not mind waiting a second or two—this is the most ancient part of the Court, contains the best pictures, and is generally supposed to be the show-room—I will go and announce your arrival."

And thus did David Fargus find himself once more under the converging gaze of his ancestors.

"Back at last, after thirty years!" he muttered in answer to their mute greeting. "And only home, after all, under a false character. What do you think of him?" And slowly he went round the room, stopping to interpellate each vigorous old Kerr face with half-smliing, half-sad recognition.

The stern blue eyes of William Kerr looked down reproachfully at his son. "How could you give up our name, deny our country and our forefathers!" And yet the kindly mouth whispered to the mind's ear another greeting: "It is well you have come back at last—do not go again."

It was a noble portrait.

Full of unwonted emotion under the memories of that long-forgotten affection of his childhood, Fargus turned to seek, in the feminine gallery, for the delicate outline of the young mother who had died in giving him birth.

But although female ascendants figured in goodly array and almost unbroken sequence, from the languorous-eyed, curly locked, very bare-bosomed beauties of Restoration days, to the smiling, good-natured image of her who had been his step-brother's faithful wife, the sweet young face which in former days had hung in the place of honor over the high mantel-board had disappeared.

"William all over!" said he to himself, with a sudden uprising of the fiery spirit he had believed dead this many a year. "And it tallies well with his treatment of my boy. But may be he has not done with that branch of his family yet."

The opening door and the slow advance of a gaunt and tottering figure broke in upon this train of thought, and David Fargus, turning, saw the present head of his race. He had been prepared for a change, but this wreck of a strong man he had not looked for. The squire was, after all, but sixteen years or so older than he; but while he felt, in mind and body, all the vigor of maturity, his brother was indeed an old man—his face bore that drawn, distressed look which so painfully betrays the loss of vital power.

He received Fargus with a feeble reflex of the pomposity which had once been so irritating to the latter. For one instant, as they took their seats at the table, Fargus felt his self-possession fail him beneath a curiously intent look which appeared suddenly, like the up-leaping of a dying flame, in the squire's eyes. But the danger was over almost as soon as perceived.

"I thought I had seen you somewhere before this," the old man muttered, "but it was a mistake."

Then he drew himself together and addressed his visitor on the broad subject of America, after the interested manner of an English county gentleman who has a proper appreciation of the superiority of his own status.

"My son, sir, has just been there," he explained with complacent civility. "He is a great traveler, and is making the Grand Tour—in our days a Grand Tour must needs be round the world."

"Lucky fellow!" put in Charles in his dry way.

"He has been two years away. He is my only son now, and we English landowners think our heirs should remain as much as possible on the estate, that they may learn the duties of their position in life."

Fargus admired, as the meal proceeded, the tact and patience with which Charles humored his uncle. For his part, he strove to maintain the conversation at a tolerable degree of interest. But the elaborately served and lengthy repast was so like those which used, in days gone by, to try his boyish patience so terribly, that it produced an almost dream-like effect upon him.

Fargus found it hard to combat the melancholy that was taking possession of his soul, though the fare was of the best, though Charles spoke brilliantly and interestingly—as though with the desire of effacing the disagreeable impression of the previous day—though the squire himself, when they adjourned to the terrace for coffee and cigars, had wonderfully unbent to his guest and seemed a little brightened and invigorated.

Suddenly a tall figure appeared on the sward and hurried toward them. At sight of him Fargus started to his feet with a presentment of evil. It was only the rector, but his was a pallid, disturbed face, and he held an orange-colored envelope in his hand. The squire, undisturbed by such forebodings, called out, for him, quite cheerily:

"Halloa, Mr. Mivart! You are just in time for a cup of coffee."

The unwilling messenger of evil gave a piteous look at Charles.

"What is it?" whispered the latter hastily.

"Bad news."

The old man caught the words. He rose at once, straightening his feeble form to rigid attention.

"My son?" he cried in a loud voice.

After a terrible attempt to break gradually the whole misfortune to the unhappy father, the truth had to be told. His son, the last remaining child, was dead.

For a moment the squire stood with outstretched arms; then his face grew purple, his eyes started from their orbits; before they could receive him in their arms, so swiftly came the stroke, he had fallen forward on the walk.

As they raised him, and beheld the distorted countenance streaming with blood, the swollen discolored neck and upturned eyes, Fargus alone retained enough self-command to give him immediate help.

"I have seen this before—cerebral hemorrhage," he said, quickly loosening the old man's collar and raising his head. "I should bleed him if I dared. Charlie, send some one for the doctor. You and I must at once bring him into the house."

Charlie appreciated the calmness and authority of the stranger at this crisis, and begged him to remain till the doctor should have made his appearance. The clergyman soon made an excuse to withdraw. Thus Fargus and his nephew found themselves silently watching in the darkened room by the stricken father's bedside, listening to the stentorous breathing which alone betokened life, and busily renewing the ice bandages they had laid on his forehead.

When the doctor arrived, the visitor from the Lone Grange, in his turn, was glad to leave. The doctor's look as he had bent over his patient had been ominous, and confirmed his own opinion of the case; within a very short time the last but one, ostensibly, of the direct line in that ancient house would have joined the majority.

At the moment when all life-energy would have finally radiated away from that prostrate body, the rightful ownership of those noble lands, the headship of "name, arms and estates," would devolve, *de jure,* on the stranger of the Lone Grange, but *de facto,* unless the latter chose to prove his identity, on a certain young soldier who, surely, was far from dreaming of such an accession of fortune.

The letter which awaited him on his hall table—in the envelope of the "Argus Office"—was, at such a juncture, invested with a new solemnity of interest. It ran, however, thus:

"DEAR SIR: In accordance with your request, one of our agents yesterday attended at Portsmouth on the arrival of the Crocodile troop-ship, and thus reports on the movements of the officer whom you wish us to watch.

"The gentleman in question did not seem to have any duty to see to. Soon after disembarking, about 11 A. M., having arranged about his personal luggage, went to the Naval Club in company with a friend. About an hour later he came out alone, took a long walk by himself along Southsea Beach, returning in time to catch the afternoon train to London.

"From Waterloo Station he drove straight to Staples Inn, Chancery Lane (where he has rooms inscribed with his name). He came out, three hours later, in evening dress, drove to the Army and Navy Club, Pall Mall, and, after an interval, apparently for dinner, walked over to the St. James' Theatre, where he engaged a stall. He had no intercourse with any one, and after the performance walked leisurely back to his rooms in Staples Inn.

"We will continue to acquaint you daily with the results of our observations.   We are, etc., etc."

With a sigh of relief Fargus laid down the letter. Simple enough, these "movements," yet pleasing in their very simplicity, and, coupled with what he already knew concerning the young man's energy and courage, completing the favorable portrait he had so laboriously collated. He would be worthy of the new and weighty position he would so soon be called upon to fill.

The next morning early he rode over to the Court. Charles Hillyard was standing in the porch.

The squire was dead, and Fargus, tactfully shortening the interview, rode away in a very reflective mood.

Once more in his own room, he sat down to write a short note to the "Argus Office."

"DEAR SIR: Be pleased to look at the obituary notices in

the morning papers during the next few days, and, as soon as you notice announcement of the death of Mr. William Kerr, of Gilham, Yorkshire, to forward at once a copy of the paper, with the entry very conspicuously marked, to Mr. L. G. Kerr, at his chambers in Staples Inn.

"You will understand that this must be done in a strictly anonymous manner."

"This, I fancy, will bring the boy down—for the funeral, at least," he said to himself, as he closed the letter.

But, three days later, when that ceremonial took place, and Fargus attended at the Court, among the numerous guests assembled to render the last honors to the host, there was no one to be seen who could in any way be taken for the person he so longed to meet.

After that solemn rite, with its painful, unnecessary, attendant pomp and, show, much disappointed and perplexed, the father walked back with General Woldham until they reached the point where their homeward roads diverged.

"By the way, general," he asked, as if casually. "who comes in for the place now?"

The general puffed.

"Why, I suppose it will be Lewis Kerr, now in the —th D. G. Curiously enough, I was just this instant talking about him to Charles Hillyard, who says he ran up against him in town yesterday. I knew he must be coming back, though I did not expect him so soon. But he apparently declined to come down for the funeral."

"That is curious," said Fargus.

"Very. It is the last thing I should have expected of him. It is not like Lewis. An event like this should bury all feuds. Decency, sir, should have brought him down."

Fargus returned to his house in a discontented mood. The evening post brought a partial explanation of the puzzle, and decided his own course of action. The agent's daily letter ended by the statement that, on the evening of the previous day, Mr. Kerr had driven, with luggage, to Charing Cross Station, booked for Homburg, Germany, and started for the Continent by the mail. The agent had parted company with him at Dover, "not having received instructions to follow the gentleman out of England."

CHAPTER V.

Although Society has been crowded out of the mansions of its past glories by the swarming influx of the toilers who supply its ever-increasing demands, we can yet count one class of men who, of necessity, live much of their life in the original dwelling-place of their order—the students and adepts of the law, who still people those ancient colleges, the Inns of Court and their dependencies.

There stood in days gone by a goodly number of such hostels or inns, forming the individual colleges of what our old annalists termed the "Third Universitie of England," but few have retained to the present time their collegiate character.

Yet among those institutions which have passed from their high estates as houses of learning and dignity to the degradation of depending for existence on lay patronage, there still remains one whilom Inn of Chancery, very much as it was beheld of Shakespeare and inhabited of Johnson. Its aspect on the Holborn front presents its seven gables, its bulging corbeled stories of stout beam and hard petrel, untouched by the ravages of time, practically unchanged since the last Tudor; and clinging to its flanks, as moss to a mighty tree, may be seen just such a parasitic growth of booth and open shoplet as it, no doubt, always shielded from the days of its first erection. There are the winding, crazy stairs that creaked beneath the great lexicographer's ponderous tread, the paneled rooms filled with the memories of four centuries, the quiet courtyards, oak-ceiled hall, capacious ghostly kitchens and cellars; altered now in their resigned decay from the time when Stow wrote of the "Fayrest Hall in this great law University," when ruffling mootmen and utter barristers filled chambers and gardens with as much rollicking life as does the modern under-graduate his more prosperous college on the banks of Cam or Isis!

This is old Staple Inn, a too rare relic of "Old London" architecture, built on the original site of that Hall of the Wool Staple Merchants where Chaucer dealt with Custom receipts, the obsolete cognizance of which—a staple of wood—is even now borne on its escutcheon.

Staple Inn has become rather shabby in itself and in its inhabitants. Fallen from the honorable intention of its founders, it has had to seek support from such as choose to give it, and few men who can afford the comforts of modern chambers seem to care for the thought of settling in that aged haunt, and any one capable of appreciating the charm of seclusion in the very heart of London—the charm of living amid scenes sacred to the doings and thinkings of so many bygone generations—could with but little expenditure of trouble and money make for himself such a nest in the old rookery as he would be loath to exchange for all the nineteenth century Queen Anne glories of sky-threatening mansions in more favored quarters.

This is precisely what had been done with a set of attic-rooms overlooking Holborn on the one side, and the sleepy courtyard on the other. They had been cleaned and painted for the first time, perhaps, in this century; their dingy, shivering casements replaced by new frames and light-stained diamond panes; the dilapidated outer-door had made way for a solid "oak" of college-pattern, over the lintel of which the name of the enterprising tenant was plain to see, in white letters on a black ground. The old chambers had first assumed this unprecedentedly rejuvenated aspect on becoming the town residence of Mr. Lewis G. Kerr, B. A., Edin., during his under-graduate days at Cambridge. And so dear to the heart of their occupier did they finally grow, that when, in the course of events, he exchanged the gown for the sword, and went over the seas on his country's service, he could not make up his mind to part with his quaint *pied-a-terre,* but kept it on as the shrine of his household gods, with the comfortable feeling that here he would, at least, always have a home to return to.

And now, on a hot July day, the young dragoon, back again at last, bronzed out of all recognition by the Indian sun, thinned, hardened, something battered by long months of Central Asian campaigning and a spell of South African experience, withal more vigorous than ever, stood in the middle of his attic abode, between portmanteaus and bullock-trunks—gazing with dreamy pleasure on the dusty surroundings which brought him back in imagination to so many chapters of his life now closed forever.

Here, after his regiment, was his home; in a corner, the half-suit of armor worn by some Castilian ancestor, about which there still hung the quaint old-world atmosphere of the proud though tumble-down home of his boyish days; on three of the four walls the black-oak bookcases, crammed with the most motley collection of volumes, some in the gorgeous armorial bindings of college prizes.

Mr. Kerr traversed his domain with a restless step, now lightly fingering some dust-covered chattel associated with a thousand unimportant memories, now pausing by the door to open the solemn "Grandfather's clock" and restore its suspended animation, and through a glamourous illumination of shafts of dancing motes there came back upon him, one after another, each different phase of his past life, inextricably associated with the memorials surrounding him.

There, before him, hung the water-color sketch of his father, in Highland uniform, and the miniature frame containing his Crimean medal and clasps; the exquisite head, also in water-colors, of the young mother who had died in giving him life; they had hung in his nursery in far Seville, where he had been taught to kiss them night and morning and babble a prayer for the dead Padrecito and Madrecita; round them were woven almost his first memories.

And in a corner of the bookcase, affectionately preserved in all their shabbiness in a row to themselves, there were the queer old school-books in which he had first begun to learn under the good old English monk, chosen for the high post of tutor to the orphan boy as much by reason of his nationality as of his attainments.

What delightful hours those were in the shady court!

How he had longed for the unknown, far-off England! Don Atanasio had promised to bring him here himself when he was old enough for an English school. The dear old grandfather! It was for his conscientious self-abnegation in bringing up this, the last scion of his own race, as belonging by greater right to the dead father's country, that surely he, Lewis Kerr, owed his memory the keenest gratitude. And yet when the time came for him to go, and that by himself, all in his new mourning—for but a fortnight before they had laid the great hidalgo in his grave—how bitter had been the parting! How terrible it was to feel so alone on the threshold of a new life, with no one but a new guardian, Reverend Mr. Hillyard, unknown but as the writer of two stiff, cold letters, between him and absolute isolation!

He saw himself again on the deck of the mighty steamer as she throbbed away in the blue and yellow dawn from the coast of Spain; a small, shivering boy, for all his thirteen years, trying hard to combat the tears that would rise to his eyes, to struggle against the heavy pain at his heart, which, nevertheless, beat high with the thought of seeing England, his country, at last. And then the arrival. How well he remembered it all—the cold welcome, the sickening disappointment, until "Aunt Susie" first dawned upon his life, and her warm arms opened to the desolate little foreigner, never to close to him again until they grew cold in death.

He had been determined to assert his claim as an Englishman, in spite of his disadvantages; and he had succeeded. Even before the happy spell of student life at Edinburgh, he had forced himself to the front, made himself respected in class-room and playground. But, oh! that glorious feeling of freedom when at sixteen he found himself practically his own master in the severe old Northern city, where the rough but genuine cordiality of his older fellow-students made him, for the first time since his arrival from the distant land of his birth, feel at home. That was a happy era, for it was during his first session there that Robert Hillyard was presented with the rectorship of Gilham, and that thus was brought about the meeting with Maude.

Eight years ago! It was quite a journey down the stream of life to look back upon, and strange to think that the love of a little lass of fifteen should have outlived all the experiences, the long absences, the many changes.

She had come upon him at a very bitter moment, but the warm partisanship of the gray-blue eyes, blazing from under a cloud of tumbled brown hair, the thrill of the girl's voice, as he had first heard it, calling to him in pretty, eager conciliation, had more than made up for the offense.

He turned half round in his chair to look for the shield of arms, displayed over the chimney-piece, between the escutcheon of Alma Mater and that of his particular college. There the "sable bend, engrailed, on the field," of Kerr of Gilham, quartered the foreign and more canting arms of Ayala, a "caravel on a stormy sea, in the heavens a solitary star."

And now the contemplation brought him back to that memorable forenoon, the only occasion on which he had set foot in Gilham Court, when Aunt Susie and the rector had marched him forth to introduce him to the head of his family. As they paced through the prosperous country scenery, he had been amazed to hear that so many of the broad acres of rich pasture land, stretches of plowed fields, of green woods and fern-grown covers, belonged to Mr. Kerr, of Gilham, that relation of his who had never bestowed so much as one sign of interest on him. And then a winding in the high-hedged road brought them in front of a towering gateway, a curious emotion crept round his heart as he recognized in the escutcheon over the keeper's lodge those very arms of Kerr by which he had been taught in the distant land of his birth to set such store. There was the home of his English forefathers; his heart had swelled with so many feelings that he could not trust himself to speak. In silence he had threaded his way up to the noble, time-mellowed manorhouse that had been his father's home. Would he ever forget his reception? How the squire had all but disowned him, almost shown him the door!

As, crimson with indignation, he had risen to take his leave, and shake off his feet the dust of that inhospitable house, there sprang up in the far end of the great room a little figure with gold-brown hair. Too confused then to notice all that passed, he had retained but disjointed memories of the sweetest face ever seen; of the pressure of a little bare, brown hand; of a tall, white-haired man who likewise loomed upon him in some unexpected way, and to whom Aunt Susie, pale and with a troubled countenance, introduced "my brother's son;" of pleasant words and warm proffers of hospitality. This was the beginning of the intimacy at Woldham Hall, when life had assumed such a new meaning under the light of Maude's eyes.

The dreamer laid down his burned-out pipe and glanced once more at the coat-of-arms. His star! before him always, in fair weather or foul, in the days when he had fancied by academic distinctions to win his fastidious little lady's favor, before he had discovered her paramount weakness for "buff and burnished steel," and battlefield honors. His eyes wandered to the Trinity escutcheon with its golden book, closed, on the chief of gules. Those were good days, too. He did not regret his present choice, for all it had cost him the loss of that high degree he had once aimed at, but he would always be glad of his years in the great quadrangle.

"I wonder who would have enjoyed this superb Villar had chance decreed that my bones now should be blanching on Afghan gravel, as those of so many better fellows. Ah, I suppose you would, old chap."

This mental apostrophe was addressed to one of the portraits he had just installed on the writing-table; that of his cousin, quondam coach, and bosom friend.

Charles Hillyard, Fellow of his College, lecturer in Moral Sciences, a writer, already of some note, was one of those men who never can pass unnoticed anywhere. The head Lewis was gazing at through the smoke of his cigar was such as a Vandyck would love to paint; with aquiline features, high forehead, and deep-set gray eyes; a thin but powerful face, surmounted by a wavy growth of light hair, and accentuated by a light mustache, curling upward in a way that gave a curious permanent look of sarcasm to the grave, compressed lips. It was a face that might have seemed equally typical of cavalier, artist, or thinker.

"Not one of the least pleasant events of my return will be the first evening we spend again together, dear old chap, and have another of those long jaws which used to follow our coaching in the tutor and pupil days. And, by Jove! I must write to you this very evening. I dare say you will not be sorry, either, to see my bullet head again."

CHAPTER VI.

MIDNIGHT CONFIDENCES.

Late in the evening of the next day Lewis was leisurely wending his way back from his club, his thoughts for the moment much and pleasantly occupied with anticipations of proximate meetings with his old chum and his friends in the North.

As he came through a certain dark short cut for foot-passengers from Lincoln's Inn Fields—which opens into Holborn just by the glaring portal of that choice place of entertainment yclept "The Royal," there appeared, across the torrent of light which makes its entrance so obtrusively resplendent, a certain tall, familiar figure, a well-known, keen, pallid face.

"The very man himself, by Heaven!"

He was rushing forward, hand outstretched in all glee, when a second look brought him to an abrupt standstill. Charles was not alone; he was doing escort duty to a tall young woman, whose face was concealed behind a thick veil, and who held him with close familiarity by the arm. She was quietly and neatly dressed, but as ladies do not generally perambulate such quarters in company with bachelor friends at eleven of the night, Lewis discreetly drew back into the doorway of a small tobacco shop behind him, not to put his grave and reverend tutor of yore out of countenance.

The couple took a step or two into the comparative darkness of the alley, where the young woman lifted her veil and raised her cheek for what was evidently a farewell kiss. When they again emerged into the light, her companion hailed a hansom, in which he proceeded to install her, closed the doors without getting in, and called out to the driver some address which had no meaning in Lewis' ear. But as the hansom swung round, and its occupant, bending forward, sent another kiss from the tips of her fingers to the stationary figure of his friend, the young man caught a fair view of her unveiled face for the first time. He started violently. It was not imagination—features, smile, look, the wave of the hand itself, the little toss of her head, ay, the very voice, now crying out, "Good-night, good-by"—it was Maude! And yet not Maude—another glance at the handsome creature, whom, during a short pause, occasioned by the block of vehicles, he had time to examine more critically under the crude electric light, was sufficient to prove the folly of his first impulse, although the marvelous resemblance increased rather than diminished on scrutiny.

As he gazed after the retreating hansom conflicting thoughts rushed wildly through his brain. What was the meaning of this? Maude, the refined maiden, isolated in her romantic home, and this very independent young woman, so indescribably not a lady, who composedly drove away alone in a hansom at midnight?

"If it were not for the likeness, of course, I should not bother my head about it," he thought, looking toward his cousin, who still stood in the same place. "I don't want to pry into his private life; I dare say he is no better or no worse than other men. If it were not that he knew Maude so well, I should be tempted to think it was a mere coincidence; there must be something beneath it," and through the confusion of his ideas there suddenly broke the memory of a certain night, years ago now, when his friend had spoken strange words to him, conveying nothing to his loyal mind; unheeded, then, but which now, in the light of this meeting, returned upon him pregnant with baleful meaning.

Could it be that Charles, too, had fallen in love with Maude? could it be that, loving her hopelessly, he consoled himself thus—his friend, whom he had set on so high a pedestal!

"I will not judge till I hear his story," and, resolutely emerging from his concealment, he sprang up to the object of his thoughts.

"Why, Charlie! what can a man of your serious turn be doing at such a time in the neighborhood of these haunts? Anyhow, I am glad to meet you, old man!"

"Hallo, Lewis!" exclaimed Mr. Hillyard, drawing back a pace, with a perceptible start. But the discomposure was too transient to attract his companion's notice; in another instant their hands were warmly clasped, and, surveying his quondam pupil from head to foot:

"So you are still in the land of the living!" cried the "coach." "The last I heard you were skirmishing with Afghans."

"I am, as you see, glad to be of this world still, especially at a meeting like this. You did not get my letter, then? I sent it to Cambridge. How is the world behaving to you?"

"Much as before; you need not have expressed so much suprise at meeting me here. I came up for some tiresome business connected with the 'Philosophical,' and afterward felt the want of something nice and idiotic to vary the entertainment and sweep the cobwebs from my brain."

Lewis evinced no sort of consciousness under his friend's scrutiny, and the latter proceeded more easily:

"And so here you are again. I think I can guess what has brought you back."

"What do you mean? What should have brought me back but my first long leave?"

"Indeed! nothing else?" then, after a moment's reflection, in a careless tone, "In that case I think I may have news for you. It is not really pressing, I assure you. Where are you staying? I am meditating supper before catching my train at Euston—will you come with me?"

"I am at my old rooms at Staple's, of course. They are close by; why shouldn't you come to me? And, I say, now I have found you, I am not inclined to let you go in such a hurry; if you don't disdain an improvised couch, I can accommodate you with lodgings as well as board."

"That sounds plausible," said Charles; "done."

At a pleasant pace, in keeping with the warmth of the July night, they soon exchanged the bustle and glare of Holborn for the quiet courts of the old Inn.

Ascending the rickety corkscrew stairs they entered the attic room.

After feeling for matches and lighting his lamp, the host relieved his guest of hat and stick, and, perceiving sundry letters and papers strewing the floor beneath his open letter-box, picked them up and turned them over in some surprise.

"Hullo! who the dickens has sent me a *Morning Post,* I'm sure I never ordered one; some way of advertising, I suppose. What are these? Circulars, circulars, price-lists—rubbish!"

And, tossing the collection on to a side table, he turned gayly to his friend:

"Now, Sir Cavalier, make yourself at home while I get supper ready."

"So you have kept up this den of yours. What on earth could induce any one in your circumstances to fix upon a ramshackle Inn like this, when there are chambers to be had in St. James' and other civilized parts, I cannot conceive."

"Without noticing your disparagement of my residence," said Lewis good-humoredly, "I may point out that under present circumstances it would be absurd for me to keep up an expensive establishment I should only live in for very few days at a time. Furthermore, were I ten times a millionaire, I would not give up this haunt of mine for anything, 'leather and iron dragoon' though I be. And lastly," he went on, as he selected some special wine-glasses from a cupboard, "the ownership of these rooms at the time when I threw in my lot with 'Tommy Atkins' bridged over the difficulty of storing away all my books, old oak, old arms—all the 'kickshaws' you used to scoff at, in fact, you Philistine!"

"I should have thought club chambers for yourself when you came up, more rational, but you were always a little cracked, you know; and I see that you have not changed."

"I'm glad I have not," returned Lewis simply.

"It's very pretty," continued the other, looking about him critically, "but it must be extremely uncomfortable."

"Geometry doesn't infest my life," said Lewis, dragging forward to the table a three-legged stool for himself, and a four-legged one for his guest; "and as for solidity, the Chestnut battery itself galloping past in Holborn would not so much as shake my old panels. . . . But come, you don't seem to be in a sympathetic mood; sit down. But never fear, I will pour no inferior stuff in your cup to-night. Now, let us see. Turn about and look into my cellar. Choose your tap; I have still some of those choice friends you made acquaintance with up at Trinity—like us both, a few years older; and the better for it, I hope, old man."

Carefully fitting a ponderous black key into the lock of the seventeenth-century coffer under his window, he lifted the lid, and, with a twinkle in his merry brown eyes, beckoned to his friend.

"Here you see, on the right, some of the richest juice the sun distils from Burgundian hillsides. Now choose your particular 'wanity,'" Lewis concluded with a laugh, suddenly changing his style. .

"Pour me out some of your 'aurum potabile,' since caviare is to be the first thing," said Charles, with his slightly contemptuous smile, sitting down, notwithstanding, readily enough, and helping himself to the toothsome conserve.

Charles, on his side, took up his glass and closed his eyes with mock solemnity as he swallowed the contents.

"Ah! what a fine thing it must be to be able to gratify one's epicurean tastes! I never was over-wealthy, as you know, but since my poor governor's death, which you heard of when you were out in India, I have had to rely entirely on my own exertions."

Lewis was the last person who could resist him under such circumstances; with a warm revulsion of feeling he rejoiced to find himself falling once more under the old spell.

When at length they had done full justice to the improvised meal, the dragoon sprang to his feet, and, for the sake of greater stretching room, pushed the little dining-table away into the pantry, ensconced his friend in the arm-chair, chose his best cigar for him, and filled a favorite pipe for himself with a lightening heart.

"Now, Charlie," he remarked cheerily, dropping on the stool in front of him, and stretching his hands on his knees, "this is indeed like old times, isn't it? What a piece of luck to meet you to-night! Do you remember how you used to lecture me, *extra horas,* on the necessity of seeing the world and giving up my silly habit of day-dreaming?"

"I do; and now that you have knocked about a little more, you have no doubt learned to look at life from a more practical point of view."

"Perhaps I have, in certain things. But let us hear more about yourself."

"About myself I have little to say; my life is quite as monotonous as it was."

"Indeed!" said Lewis, hesitating for a moment to go on with what he had on the tip of his tongue, for fear, by entering on delicate ground, of bringing about an unpleasant tension. But until he had cleared up what was on his mind, he felt he could not remain at ease with his friend, and he was longing to have things straight between them again; to sweep away the barriers that seemed to have risen in his absence to mar their sympathy. "Do you remember," he began slowly, as if choosing his words, "a certain sultry evening, a little before the final, up at Trinity? I had that day announced my intention to enter the service, and came to your room just as one of your new pups was about to leave you—Wagner-like—in Dr. Faustus' den, full of awe for your severe wisdom. I, however, who knew your private self intimately, found you in an unwontedly soft and melancholy mood. Do you remember that evening?"

Charles turned his head rather suddenly, and looked keenly at the speaker.

"Yes—I think I do; well?"

"We drifted into poetry, music, romance, not to say sentiment. I believe you actually quoted Heine."

"Quite a graphic picture! Well?"

"You who never spoke of your own inner thoughts, so that I believed you really were blessed with an adamantine indifference to sentiment, for once you unbosomed yourself and told me that you were in love."

An indefinable smile curled Charlie's thin lips; he turned half round on his chair and looked straight at his friend.

"Your story interests me much. Proceed," he said mockingly.

There was a moment's pause. Lewis, doggedly bent upon satisfying himself, resumed with an effort:

"Well, we found out that the music told us the same thing; I wondered who was the lady of your hopeless dreams —for you spoke of them as hopeless—don't blush; who could resist you?"

"I think I see now what you are aiming at; but still, go on."

"You spoke again out of your dark corner where your piano was stowed away—your words were so unlike what I was accustomed to hear from you. 'I sometimes wish,' you said, 'I had never had music instilled in my soul. When I hear melodies like this, with all their yearnings, it sets me mad for the unattainable; in fact, old fellow, it plays the devil with my common-sense.' Unfortunately, just as I was worked up to an intense state of sympathy for you, in came your gyp with your lamps, and the whole scene underwent a complete transformation. 'Pray don't imagine, my boy,' you then said, 'that I am a soft idealist, a gentle lunatic like you. I have been hard hit, I grant you that; but as the soothing dock grows near the stinging nettle, I trust I have found my antidote to hand.' And you suggested the case of a man who should come across a woman the very image, the 'double,' of her who had ensnared him. 'Now, your idealist,' said you, 'would go moping about forever for the want of his particular bunch of grapes, but your sensible man takes the one that is within his reach, and is thankful.' I never dreamed you were really speaking of your own experience—never dreamed that so extraordinary a coincidence had come your way, nor that you and I, sympathetic though we were, had the misfortune to fall in love with the same girl—until to-night!"

Charlie remained silent for a moment, knocking the long ash off his cigar with his little finger.

"Ah! so you did see her, then. Well, I confess that you are about the last person I could have wished to meet me with that girl. London is large enough to justify me in hoping that none of my acquaintances, let alone my intimates, would run across me under the circumstances. However, a total absence of coincidences in this haphazard world would, after all, be stranger than the least likely of accidents."

It was indeed typical of the man how soon the erstwhile coach managed to resume the tone of ascendancy.

"The little I told you," he went on, "the shadowy suggestion I then threw out, encompassed the broad facts. It was simply an astonishingly complete instance of personal likeness; but you were able to-night to judge for yourself of what my feelings must have been, my mind being filled with one particular image, when I first came across the girl you saw me with an hour ago."

Charles mused a while, to resume reflection:

"When I saw Maude Woldham, after a long interval, she had grown from a little girl into the handsome woman who has turned many heads since she bewitched you. I must say that, for the first time, I understood the general infatuation, and felt alarmed to 'find myself falling in the same way. I realized one day that as long as I remained within the reach of her influence I should do no good. I went away; but somehow or other I could not shake off the impression after all, even in the midst of the hardest work. And, with that decision, which you are, I believe, pleased to admire in me, I resolved never to return to Gilham more. That summer, therefore, I spent my vacation on a boating trip from Oxford to Maidenhead. Well, here is the story: One hot afternoon I was silently sailing past those meadows below Cookham. On the bank, within four yards of me, I suddenly saw her, as I thought—there she was, fast asleep among the buttercups, in the shelter of the hedge. At the moment I thought it was an hallucination. I let my craft run aground, and the grating of the keel awoke the vision, who started up and looked at me, blushing like a poppy. Then my sail entangled itself in some overhanging bough of the hedge, and the stream turned my boat round, so that I had to land. She was lovely—you have seen her, and know the original—and I must suppose my midsummer madness was contagious. The accident sufficed for an introduction, and that meeting by the water's edge was the turning point of two lives."

"By all that is absurd, you have not gone and married her?" cried Lewis.

"No; but it is nearly as bad," returned Charles, with a kind of sneer; "instead of letting that curious experience remain an idyl, I allowed it to form the first canto of a long history, yet to be concluded. Yes, the day is evidently past when I could lecture you on the subject of foolishness. I willfully entangle myself in the new meshes. The long and the short of it all is that I never could make up my mind to give up that easy prize. Haunted as I was by what I thought an impossible phantasy, I hankered for its commonplace, but palpable, image whose love had not cost me even an effort to win."

"A pretty kettle of fish!" ejaculated Lewis. "And who is she?"

"The daughter of a comfortable hotel-keeper somewhere up the river, and who, by the way, is apparently not at all reconciled to the present state of affairs. Pretty for a college Don!"

"And how on earth can you ever get rid of this poor girl now?"

"I hold it a wise axiom that says, 'As you make your bed, so you lie.' As it is, well, it is not so bad. She is the handsomest creature I know, one excepted, and devoted to me. When I come down every week, tired out, I find a cheerful companion, with no too exalted ideas to fret herself or me. There are undeniable advantages in such a state of things. She is perfectly satisfied with matters as they are. Since I have chosen the path, I make the most of my journey."

Lewis did not answer. He was certainly no precision in matters of morality, but there was unmistakable disenchantment in finding the friend he had been in the habit of looking up to as the archtype of intellectual refinement so cynical in acknowledging a commonplace intrigue.

For a long time the pair remained in reflective silence.

Had Asmodeus, the Bottle Imp, been liberated in London by some modern Don Cleofas, and alighted with him during his discreet explorations on the roof of old Staples Inn that night, he might have thought it curious to bid his companion look into the attic room, while, for his benefit, he read the inner thoughts of the two men who alone were still awake at that late hour.

"That slim, graceful figure you see there, lying his lazy length in the armchair, the pale, romantic beauty of whose face would seem lit as by an intense inner life, is at this moment brooding over some secret temptation. I can not tell you, Don Cleofas, what his plans are, for they are only half formed, and I can read but what is; but his thoughts are full of doubt and desire.

"As for the other, with the close-cropped brown head and the unromantic breadth of shoulder, who is squatting on his three-legged stool, with a short pipe hanging under his thick, bristly mustache, and with his round eyes staring abstractedly at his lamp, he is back again to memories, and far away from here. A winter scene in a Yorkshire glen, under a dark gray sky; a small lake, imprisoned below smooth, black ice, surrounded by silent pines, asleep and solemn under masses of hoar-frost. A slender girl, freshly blossomed into maidenhood, whose black velvet skirts, heavily furred, are swaying rhythmically to and fro, revealing the daintiest foot as she skates in long, entrancing sweeps beside him, her little hands imprisoned in his, while some rebellious locks of brown hair, escaping from her fur cap, flutter ever and anon across his face. Now she stops, panting and tired, and the breath from her parted lips condenses in iridescent beads on her long eyelashes. How he loves her—loves her very shadow! Can she hear the sweet accompaniment playing in his heart to his occasional impersonal remarks? 'How grand that slaty sky! and that mysterious, silent, wood, under the dazzling hoar! Do you not like to hear those crows calling to each other the news from distant parts?' Witch as she is, fairy-like, surely she hears his meaning rightly. 'How beautiful is the place where you are, for I love you! Were you away, how desolate, despairing this snow-laden sky, what a dirge of misery those calls!' Would you hear more, Don Cleofas, of the youth's love-sick fancies, or shall we flit further?"

"Why don't you tell me something about Maude herself?" suddenly asked Lewis, starting from his abstraction.

"About Maude Woldham? What can I tell you about her? That she is still Maude Woldham, you know yourself, I suppose?"

"Yes, I know that. But where is she? What has she been about all these years? Or are you ashamed to talk of her?" cried his companion, rather petulantly.

"Not at all, my dear fellow. She is now, I think, at Homburg, combining fashionable amusement with a cure for her aunt's nerves. As to her doings in general, what can I tell you but that she has gone through the usual mill of girls after they are brought to town to be presented? Half a dozen proposals, it appears. The legend is, that she does not want to marry, on account of her old father. My opinion, however, is that the right man has not yet come forward."

Charles noted with a smile the effect of his last remark.

"I am sorry to see that you have not been cured. Is it possible you are still reckoning on a similar state of mind in her?"

"What do you mean?"

"I believe it is openly admitted that the girl was fond of .you, as the saying goes. But even if she were still the same——"

"Oh, I know your cynical talk about the folly of marriage."

"Well, perhaps I ought not to preach wisdom now, after the confession which accident has forced from me. To cure this monomania of sentiment, since more radical remedies are not available, I should prescribe a little everyday, dragoon-like dissipation. I think it would prove invaluable in your case."

"Oh, master!" interrupted Lewis, with a forced laugh; "you are skilled in disputation on moral sciences, but I fear your utilitarianism obscures your appreciation of morals in life!"

"I am talking sense. But there is something better still, when a man is as moonstruck as you seem to be; namely, to seek a cure in alternatives, counter-irritants."

"In the company of some confiding inn-keeper's daughter, I presume?" put in Lewis, now thoroughly vexed.

"I own you have an argumentative weapon against me." Then, abruptly changing the subject: "Now," he said, "about the news I had for you. It is really a fact that your return is a simple coincidence, or have you heard about the Gilham affairs?"

"No; what about Gilham?" asked Lewis, his mind still running on ruffled thoughts.

"Why, this simply," said Charlie. "In March last Guy, the youngest, you know, who was wounded in South Africa, died on his way home. You know that, of course? Well, about a week ago the news arrived that Bob, the eldest, who was yachting with a friend in the Pacific somewhere, had a sunstroke, and died in two days. But when I asked what had brought you back, I thought you might have heard of it yourself. Now, do you begin to understand?"

"Great God!" cried Lewis, who, with undefined insight into vast possibilities, sprang from his seat in great agitation.

"That is not all. By the by, where is that *Post?*" Charles stepped across the room and took up the paper, which he unfolded. "Hallo!" he cried, in astonishment; "why, here is the very thing itself marked out for you, and in red ink. Who could have sent it?"

Lewis eagerly seized the newspaper, and, with knitted brow, sought for the marked paragraph:

"On the 16th inst., at Gilham Court, Yorks, suddenly, William Kerr, Esq., D. L., J. P., aged sixty-three."

"On the 1st of June, on board the yacht *Daphne*, Robert William Kerr, eldest and only surviving son of the above, from the effects of sunstroke, aged thirty-two."

Lewis looked up with wondering eyes.

"Yes," said Mr. Hillyard, in answer to the look; "the old man himself had a fit on hearing the news, and is now lying dead in his bed at Gilham. Now, you know the tenure of the estate, no doubt. This is the news I had to give you."

Lewis stood staring at his friend. The latter examined him anew with a strange smile.

"This is a kind of clearance which it would hardly do to contemplate, as a rule," he went on, dryly; "and yet how easily it could have extended even further—had your sturdy figure, for instance, intercepted a Boerish bullet."

Lewis did not grasp the meaning in the midst of his giddiness; he was only beginning to realize all the news meant for him: "Lewis Kerr of Gilham," a fortune, one of the finest estates in the Riding; and then the old refrain came once

more to the fore. Why, Maude could be mistress of Gilham!
What a prospect open to a simple subaltern!

While the young man thus lost himself, Charles, taking
the paper, examined it wistfully, wondering whether there
was more to be seen in that unsolicited information.

"Have you any idea——" he began, looking up from the
print. But Lewis suddenly grasped his hand.

"And you, too," he cried, in an altered voice—"you, the
only one of the family who has been good to me—wherever
my home is, yours must be, too, whenever you like to make
it so. Ah, no! poor old chap, you can't!" He already saw
Maude by his side, mistress of his house. "But, never mind,
you shall have a share in this stroke of luck, all the same."

"Stroke of luck!" laughed Charles, as he threw the paper
aside. "Is that all you have to say to this decimation of
your kindred?"

"Oh, why pretend? They all hated me. The only intercourse I ever had with any of them, but your own family,
was of the angry kind."

Charles remained a moment lost in thought.

"I suppose you are not thinking of going North with me—
for it was Gilham, not Cambridge, I was bound for—and intended to do so when I met you."

"What do you think?" pondered Lewis; "I ought to go,
ought I not? Heaven knows I would willingly pay the poor
old man the last respects. I can bear him no grudge now
for all his discourtesy (to call it by no harder name) to me."

"Well, I don't know. Do you not think it might look
rather curious under the circumstances; as if you lost no
time to assert your position? However, in this matter you
must use your own judgment."

"Oh! if you think that, of course, I should not dream of it.
I rather want to be free just now, too."

"Of course, I must go. My sisters and I are his nearest
relatives—after you; moreover, the old man has been rather
good to me. And it is time I took some rest, and I shall ask
you for that promised couch. You must be anxious, at least,
to ruminate over your new prospects."

In his present state, Lewis was glad enough to exert himself in mechanical labor, and, entering the adjoining room,
he became very busy in converting that cunning article of
furniture known as a settee bedstead into a bed for his
friend.

"There, I hope," he remarked, as he finally turned down
the cool sheets with the neatness he put into everything,
"you will find the needful rest. As for myself, I prefer this."
And he proceeded to unroll a wide canvas hammock, which

he hooked diagonally across a corner of his small third apart-
ment, and arranged in it one of the pillows of the settee and
covered it with a rug.

"Now we are taut for the night!"

"So you sleep in a hammock in the heart of London! you
lunatic you," laughed Charles.

"Judge not without experience," returned the host. "A
good hammock is a very nest for unfeathered bipeds."

"Well, why don't you get into it?" said the other, as his
friend prepared to leave the room.

"Oh, I could not sleep! I must go out and walk a while
and have a good think. Have you all you want? Yes?
Well, I shall not wake you when I come in."

For a long while, however, Charles heard his steps through
the open window on the flagstones, diminishing in the distance and returning regularly. Dawn had made way for
sunlight, and the busy hum of the thoroughfare was rising
up to the dormer windows before the noctambulist returned
to his suspended couch.

He stopped a moment to gaze at his friend, who, though
still awake, was feigning sleep. Then he proceeded to en-
sconce himself in his paragon hammock, to which he im-
parted for some time a soothing oscillatory motion. To
neither of them did restful sleep pay a visit, for all their eyes
were closed. But the thoughts and schemes that were revolving on the pillow of the couch would no doubt have
jarred considerably with the equally fleeting but more harmonious plans and hopes which succeeded each other as dis-
solving views in the hammock. Both hailed the time for
rising, with pleasure.

After attending to his friend's comforts and seeing him
off, Lewis returned to his room with a sense of relief at being
alone, and fell into a deep reverie.

The meeting with his old chum, so long looked forward
to, had proved in some occult manner thoroughly disappoint-
ing. Had it not been that the new "squire's" head was so
filled with the strangeness of his unexpected position, he
would have been much troubled. As it was, however, he
could think of nothing but Maude.

In two days, perhaps, he would again hold that little hand
in his, look into the depths of those wondrous blue-gray eyes;
at length pour into her woman's ear the endless tale of that
love she, as a little maid, had tacitly accepted.

Visions of youthful love—only the few who have not early
squandered the freshness of life can realize their glory!

The fever of departure seized him. He again packed some
of the luggage he had so carefully unpacked the day before,

sat down to write sundry directions to the family solicitor and give his address as Homburg, Poste Restante; dragged his portmanteau down-stairs himself, and, after hasty injunctions to the astonished porter, jumped into the first hansom that passed before the gates. Not an hour later he was steaming away from the turmoil of London, in search of the lady of his thoughts.

CHAPTER VII.

"QUI PART TROP TOT REVIENT TROP TARD."

On his arrival at Homburg, thirty hours later, Lewis, after a hasty toilet, sallied forth into the sunshine of the little town. He did not wish to seek Maude at once; he felt too much like a man in a dream, too confused after these long hours of ceaseless thinking, to venture entering at once into her presence.

Dreamily, he turned his steps toward the Kursaal Gardens, whither all Homburg goes to listen to music. The sky was tremulous with the light of the August sun; but there was a sort of sparkle in the air which redeemed it from oppressive heat. The band was playing a swinging waltz tune as he came up under the shade of the linden trees, and took a seat in the most secluded corner within view of the promenade and its moving stream of young faces, fluttering muslins and gay colors. In some strange way, the merriment had an instaneously depressing effect upon him. His heart sank like lead as he gazed from face to face. Oh, for the wide horizon, the green, still fields of Woldham!

And then the troubled heart gave a great leap. Not ten paces away, her delicate head dominating the crowd of smaller womankind, was she—Maude, his love!

She was advancing with that free, well-poised gait he remembered so well. Under the shade of a wide straw hat the pure oval of her face shone out a little palely, yet "divinely fair." She came past, and the rays of her blue eyes illumined the shady corner as she glanced in his direction. She did not recognize him. How could she? he asked himself, to stifle the unreasonable pang that sprang into life under the gentle indifference of her look.

He would have known her anywhere; and yet how different! The full-grown woman, in the warm richness of her young and powerful life, in delicate loveliness of feature, was not the thin and girlish being of his memories. And yet the face bore the old look. Thank heaven! She was his Maude still.

A little disdainful, she moved through the throng, suiting her pace to the slow gait of the feeble woman who leaned on her strong young arm. A heaven-blue Uhlan and a pink-cheeked boy, English, every inch of him, were pressing after her. The attention she vouchsafed them was so detached and coldly courteous in its impartiality that even the watchful lover could behold their proximity without heartburning.

And, with white drapery fluttering in the breeze that fanned his face, she, all unconscious, stepped by. A great rush of tenderness swelled his heart. Was such happiness to be for him?

Four years ago, when they had parted, under the snow-bound sky, and she had slipped her little fingers, warm from her muff, into his cold grasp, how frank and firm had been their pressure, how they had quivered under his passionate kisses! She had loved him then! But now? What right had he to expect this child's love to have lasted?

Madly as her exquisite womanhood set his heart a-beating, he could wish to have her less beautiful; to him she must ever have remained the only woman in the world.

Again she passed; again the glamorous blue ray swept him with unseeing sweetness. Poor fool! with his heart in his throat, shaking now as if with palsy!

The very ease with which the longed-for opportunity came robbed him of all courage. For a few hours, at least, he would hug his dream of bliss.

Before the burnished twist of hair, that flashed gold in the sunlight, had been lost in the crowd, the music ceased. Lewis rose from his seat to follow Maude to her residence, a purpose he successfully accomplished without attracting attention. He fell to reconnoitering the neighborhood, with a view to engaging quarters in the immediate vicinity. He had not far to seek; a minor hotel directly faced the more pretentious building that sheltered his love, and therein he straightway secured a front room.

The rest of the day and the long hours of the night he passed in a kind of waking dream.

For night had descended, with a purple moonless sky; odors of earth and leaf rose from the cooling soil. One by one the noises ceased, the townlet was lulled to a restful silence, broken toward midnight by a sudden brief exodus of merry, bed-going groups, passing from the Kursaal under his windows.

Half unconsciously Lewis noticed the solitary figure of a

traveler, who followed by a porter in charge of a much-belabeled portmanteau, crossed over to the hotel opposite.

The stranger stood a moment on the steps before entering, and, taking off his hat, turned as if to welcome the breeze that stole fresh from the plains. It was a keen, grave face in profile, sharply defined against the dark shadow of the wall.

It was well that Lewis could catch no glimpse of the light form that next slipped in so quickly, it had been sweet to think of his darling safe in her virgin sanctuary. Yet it was Maude who stood in the tiled hall of the hotel, watching with wide-opened eyes, brilliant with surprised recognition, the vigorous figure of the gray-clad traveler as he slowly followed his portmanteau up the stairs.

And late into the night, by her open window she, too, sat dreaming, so near and yet so far from the poor passion-tossed watcher who could not sleep for very love of her.

At length, as the dawn of day crept over the heavens, Lewis flung himself on his bed. But there could be no sleep for so busy a brain; burning with fire of hope, chilled with present-iment of evil.

Toward seven, when Homburg was already astir and abroad, he was glad to rise once more; and though depressed, he could not fail to be cheered by the beauty of the day that was to make or mar him. With courage renewed, he bathed, dressed, and drank his steaming coffee with a grateful sense of invigoration. As he stopped on the doorstep, Maude herself, the very embodiment of summer sweetness and morning freshness, came quickly out of the opposite house and turned up the street. And then he thought that fortune meant to favor him indeed.

Avoiding the fashionable throng the girl struck into a solitary side-alley that led to the pine-woods, and Lewis, with a leaping pulse, doubled his pace, and in a few strides had overtaken her.

She did not know him; not even when he addressed her in the old familiar way, and held out his eager hand. Her first look of surprise changed to a wondering perplexity at the sound of his voice, as if it struck some chord in memory, but which aroused faint associations. He had to name himself. He had not forgotten her, changed as she was. And then, at the easy warmth of her greeting, the growing possibility of that contingency he dared not contemplate came upon him with misgiving.

"Lewis!" dropping her sunshade to stretch out both hands to him; "actually, really you! Where do you spring from? and what are you doing here? You have not come for the

waters, surely?" This with a merry laugh. "Well, I am
heartily glad to see you. But how you have changed! I
never should have known you again."

Each sentence was emphasized by a shake of the hand;
not a change of color on the smooth cheeks nor the flutter of
an eyelid over the frank scrutiny of her gaze. No old comrade could have been more cheerful in his greeting.

Her careless, friendly self-abandonment, at a time when it
required all his power of control, under the touch of her
hands, filled him suddenly with a sort of anger.

"I am home on leave," he said at last, white to his trembling lips; "when I came to London, three days ago, I heard
you were here, and so I followed."

The girl gave him a quick, puzzled look; then the bright
smile wavered and faded; she slowly drew her hands from his
grasp.

"Maude," he cried passionately; "it is no use beating about
the bush. I must speak to you to-day."

"Dear Lewis," she answered in soothing tones, "of course I
will listen to you. What has happened?"

It cut him to the heart to see the uncomprehending kindness of her lovely face; he could not speak, the words refused
to come. He could only look at her with his poor, hungry,
clenching hands and trembling as he stood before her.

For a minute she waited; then, light seemed to break upon
her, and she flushed crimson.

"I think," she said very gently, rather as if in pain, "that
it may be best, Lewis, for both of us, that I should not listen
to what you have to say."

He knew thus, before she had spoken, what his fate was;
but he must speak the pent-up love.

"Maude, I have loved you since I first saw you. Surely
you knew it. You must have felt it. My only thought
since then has been of you. I dreamed of winning fame that
I might win you; I turned soldier that I might fight myself
to the front, achieve something for you. . . . Do you
remember when I last saw you? Did you not know that I was
tearing myself away from the land where you lived, only to
make myself worthy of you? I thought—God help me!—
that if I were to do some brilliant deed for you, there might
be hope for me. I tried hard, but the fame I longed for falls
to the lot of those who command. I came home as obscure
as when I left—but loving you, Maude, more madly than
ever! When we parted at the gate four years ago, I told you
of my love, you answered nothing; but your sweet eyes! I
saw a light in them that has been my beacon, my guiding
star, ever since. I came home to seek from the woman the

mute hope the child had not refused me, and then, with fresh courage, to take up the battle of life again, to force fate to make me worthy of you. If you were willing to wait, I knew I must succeed in the end. On my return I learned an overwhelming piece of news: I was rich, Maude— I was somebody at last; Gilham and all that great estate was mine! My only joy in it was that it, might be yours; I am rich enough for my own wants. God forgive me! I was mad with joy when I thought of you. I started that very day to seek you, to lay it all at your feet; what did I care for it except for you? Maude, I must hear the words from your lips; tell me yourself that I must kill that hope, grown to become the very life of my life."

There were tears in her eyes. "Dear Lewis! it can never be."

"At least you loved me—then. Tell me, you loved me then."

She hung her head, faltering: "What could such a child know of love?"

For a second it seemed as if the earth gave way beneath him.

A look, five minutes together on that sunny morning under the trembling shadow of a white-faced aspen—and it was done.

"I am so grieved," came the soft, grave voice, once the dearest sound on earth, now the most acutely painful. He glanced down at her flushed face, at the tender mouth, drawn down at the corners with the pitiful, helpless expression of a scolded child, at the eyes brimming with grief, and thought the cup of bitterness was full indeed, and that her compassion he could not bear.

"Good-by, it is good-by, Maude. Do not fear that I shall ever bring such trouble into your life again."

Mechanically he raised his hat, and, refusing to see her timidly proffered hand, hurried away along the green avenue that led to the pine-trees. Before his inward vision stretched the prospect of an aimless life. How was he ever to have courage to go on with it?

CHAPTER VIII.

"A TAVERN ACQUAINTANCE."

Late in the evening of the same day, David Fargus and Lewis Kerr—well-intentioned hunter and unconscious quarry —distant from each other by some twenty paces only, were strolling along the ill-condition pavement of a narrow winding street in the old university town of Heidelberg.

By dint of relentless inquiries, Fargus had discovered his son's hurried flight from Homburg, and puzzled to account for it, and upset in his calculations, started in pursuit. On arrival at Heidelberg, after engaging a room at a hotel, he straightway sallied forth again on his carefully arranged plan of reconnoitering. It was his intention to make the round of all places of entertainment, inquiring for a suppositious English friend—a device which he calculated would secure him an inspection of the visitors' book.

At the very first halt, fortune had favored the amateur detective. A talkative waiter suddenly pointed out through the glass door a stalwart, tweed-clad figure rapidly passing toward the street.

"This is the only gentleman who has come here to-day. English, too, I will show you the book; you can see for yourself the last entry—Mr. Kerr, from Homburg."

And thus it happened that a few moments later, David Fargus found himself dogging the erratic wanderings of Lewis Kerr through devious by-lanes and up the High street.

It was a long and monotonous way, scantily lighted.

By-and-by Lewis, who up to that had walked aimlessly, dived down a side-alley, Fargus, guided by a glimpse of the broad back under the shine of a rare lamp, sometimes only by the ring of the clean thread, roamed in pursuit, in and out lanes through the labyrinth of the older quarter.

Then the footfalls abruptly ceased; there was the sound of a swinging door. Rounding the corner, Fargus found himself in an empty street, before an old-fashioned house.

This house was studiously "Gothic," ancient. Wrought-iron work, grotesquely carved wood, gave it fantastic attractions; a hinged signboard, proclaimed, by the light of a small green lamp, in bristling, curveting black letters, that within were "Old German" wine-rooms.

The laying out of a wine-room is the object of much attention. The *"Alt Deutsche Wein Stube,"* to be found in almost every German town, is usually a place of moderate

dimensions—for the consumers of the noble wine do not
come in throngs like the daily beer-swillers.

Fargus had come to a standstill, and now remained lost.
At last he made up his mind and plunged within the lighted
recesses.

In a far corner of a deserted room sat the object of his
pursuit. From the threshold Fargus looked keenly at him.

Square-headed, square-shouldered, bearing the stamp of his
nationality as unmistakably as the stamp of his profession,
the young man sat, gazing in gloomy abstraction at the am-
ber-filled goblet. He raised his head at the sound of the
opening door, and Fargus recognized, beyond hesitation the
original of the much-studied portrait.

With an inward start, the father met the gaze of two
somber yet brilliant eyes. How often had not the George
Kerr of old, during those last unhappy days of his existence, a
quarter century back, beheld just such another haggard young
face, whenever he had chanced to meet his own reflected image.

Maintaining his outward placidity Fargus silently sat at
the nearest table; watched, under cover of his shading hand,
each action of that scowling man who was his son.

Lewis tossed his glass, filled it again, and again emptied the
brimmer. Then he relapsed into his former heavy reflection.

Fargus felt a sharp pang of disappointment; the shaking
hand, the flushed face, and brooding eye were signs that he
had learned to read but too well.

Under the sting of that first impression he now thought of
abandoning this time the creature who had been his sole
thought for so many days, lest the knowing of him should
prove a bitterness. But there came to him a curious, unwonted emotion which warned him that Nature was determined to assert her rights, however late—then the remembrance of all the information, collected with so much difficulty, concerning his son's past, information which tallied
so ill with the dawning suspicion.

A few minutes of silent watching, and it did not require
his knowledge of physiognomy to discover here was no ordinary case; some unusual agitation was at work behind the
young soldier's determined potations.

Lewis refilled and emptied his glass, and called out, in
German:

"Herr Wirth, another bottle of the same!"

There was fever in the young man's excited manner, and
Fargus began to feel a new solicitude.

"He is battling with some terrible thought. What can it
be? If I could help him . . . if I only knew!"

The host bustled in upon his reflections, and, after placing

the required flask and a dish of meat—evidently some previous order—before Lewis, turned, smiling and apologetic, to
the late-comer and requested to know his pleasure.

Fargus seized upon this opportunity with beating heart.

"Forgive my troubling you," he said; "I fancy I am not
mistaken in taking you for an Englishman, and, as I hear
you speak the jargon, may I beg you to interpret me to this
fellow?"

Lewis looked up at the speaker, who, with his peaked beard
and the great scar across his face, did not at first sight look
like a countryman.   But, falling under the spell of kind eyes
and a sympathetic smile, he suddenly recovered understanding
and courtesy, and rose to his feet likewise.

"Do you want supper, or merely wine?" he inquired.
"There is not much choice of the former in a place like this,
but the wine is good.   Perhaps you will do me the favor to
taste this; you might like to have the same—Herr Wirth,
another glass."

The pleasant, refined voice fell gratefuly on the father's
ear.

Accepting the offer, Fargus came and sat down at the same
table; the glasses were filled.

There was a desultory interchange of remarks on the qual-
ity of the beverage.   Then a not unnatural silence fell between them.

Awakening to the fact that the ice so happily broken was
fast setting again, Fargus took a plunge.

Leaning forward and fixing the moody face across the table
with a look of unconscious but compelling earnestness: "I
hope you will forgive my intrusion," said he, "on your
privacy; but when I first saw you it struck me that I knew
your face, and now, on closer examination, I feel almost sure
I do.   May I ask if I have the pleasure of speaking to Mr.
Lewis Kerr?"

Called from his far abstraction, Lewis seemed irritated, but
again became subject to some subtle, pleasing influence.   At
the last words he turned round and surveyed his interlocutor
with curiosity.

"That is my name," he answered wonderingly.   "But I
cannot remember ever having seen you before."

"You are right," said Fargus, with a smile; "but I was
looking at a portrait of you, and that quite lately."

"My portrait?   And where?"

"At Woldham Hall."

The wound was yet too fresh to bear even so slight a touch.
It was a minute or two before he became aware that the
stranger was still speaking.

"And so, as a two months' tenant of the Lone Grange, I consider myself quite an old inhabitant. I knew your late uncle slightly, and am a warm admirer of that fine old house, the present master of which, I believe, I am now addressing."

Lewis winced. Once more Fargus racked his brain for a solution, trying to ward off a dread of some hidden disgrace.

"He cannot bear the thought of his home or his old friends! And yet how well they all spoke of the lad! the General seemed to love him like a son."

"And so you know the Woldhams!" said Lewis abruptly. "How curious! Woldham Hall was as nearly a home as any place has ever been to me; it is four years since I was there. The general was very good to me. I suppose he is growing an old man now?"

"It is a green old age; he looks good for many years to come. His daughter is beautiful; I hear she is at Homburg."

As he spoke these words the meaning of it all flashed upon the father's mind. The surmises he had made regarding a romantic attachment between the fair mistress of Woldham and his son had been correct only as regarded the latter, and the young dragoon had dashed in pursuit of his old sweetheart only to be refused.

Thereupon ensued silence, this time a fairly protracted one.

The lad was hard hit, thought Fargus. No wonder the thought of his splendid inheritance now brought nothing but bitterness. "But luckily," urged the wisdom of years and experience, "it will not last."

Soon Fargus found himself wondering, and with hot indignation, what in the world that girl could mean by rejecting his son—manly, good-looking fellow as he was—and next there came a creeping satisfaction in the connected thought that the all-absorbing interest of happy love was not to come between the son and his unknown father—at any rate, for a little while yet.

Throwing all his will into the intensity of his desire, the father made another determined effort.

"Our meeting to-night," he remarked, "in this quaint tavern—ancient, at least, in intention—in the heart of a seventeenth century town, and my recognition of you over a glass of wine, might form a good opening chapter in a novel of the old-fashioned school, might it not, Mr. Kerr? . . . Of what thrilling events and adventures would not this occurrence be the starting point! In real life, who knows if we shall ever look upon each other's face again?"

Lewis turned his eyes toward his companion with a grateful sense of restfulness upon the calm, kindly face before him; but he did not speak.

"Yet I am wrong," began his companion once more, with quick perception of the young man's unconscious sympathy. "We are destined to be neighbors for a goodly time to come, and, I hope, destined to be friends. May I introduce myself to my actual landlord over there in Yorkshire?—for, strangely enough, it is now your old manor-house of which I am the tenant. David Fargus, citizen of Washington, in the United State, at your service. Shall we not shake hands?"

Lewis extended his hand to find it quickly inclosed in a warm, firm clasp and gently retained.

"Here is the birth of a new day," said Fargus, glancing with a smile at the high clock, which now pointed to the twelfth hour. He retained his son's hand till the last vibration of the twelve strokes had died away, and then, with a half-laugh, released it.

The young man brushed his forehead with the gesture of one awakening from a dream.

"A most extraordinary thing!" he murmured, staring at his acquaintance with undisguised wonder. "While my hand lay in yours I seemed to forget how dead tired I am and all about this splitting head of mine, just as though you actually mesmerized me. I had a puzzling sensation, too, as if it were quite natural to have you there—as if your touch and presence were both familiar and pleasant. I am afraid I cannot boast of being altogether in my sound sense to-night."

Stopping short to look more closely at the clean-cut profile he cried suddenly:

"I have seen you before; yet I cannot think where. I know now. It was last night; you landed at the hotel at Homburg —you stood on the steps, thinking; I saw you from my window in a little inn opposite—only last night; it seems years ago."

He felt overcome with great weariness. For three nights no sleep had descended on his eyes; now nervous strength was failing. Fargus' strong, vigorous presence seemed to uphold and master his mind.

"I am tired out, tired of life. I desire nothing but forget-fulness. I tried to find it in wine; it was worse than all. There is but one way to find it, that is in death."

Strange, thought the father, kind were the workings of fate which had brought him to his son's side at such a moment. Laying his hand on the other's wrist, he spoke gently but with an earnestness born of his own keen sense of the danger of his utter mental breakdown.

"Rouse yourself; I do not know what is on your mind, but you have let yourself run down too low. Think. There is always plenty left to do in a young life, and ultimately to enjoy. Only cowards shrink from the battle's outset. With a fair name, a good conscience, there is something worth living for in every life—you are exhausted. Eat."

The anxiety of the elder man's eye relaxed when he saw Lewis draw his plate before him and obey. Tracing the potency of his influence, as much to the young man's condition as to his own singleness of thought, Fargus watched its working with satisfaction.

When the last morsel was finished, the father, quietly proffering a cigar carefully selected from his case, the young man in the same obedient manner kindled the Havana at the match that was struck for him.

The American followed suit, and there ensued a few moments of silence, in which both lay back in their chairs, slowly inhaling and exhaling the fragrant smoke; Fargus keenly watchful, under his half-closed lids, Lewis absorbed in his new-found, dreamy placidity.

This pleasant state of things was soon disturbed. Boisterous laughter and a rattling of canes in the quiet street heralded the appearance of three hilarious youths, students, as their colors proclaimed, which gentry burst into the room and began clattering with sticks on the nearest table.

The hellish clangor broke the spell which seemed to bind Lewis's thoughts.

"I do believe that you did take me away from myself. I seem to have been in a dream—during which I see I have contrived to make a very substantial supper. Was it not you who ordered me to eat?"

"I suggested it; you required it. How do you feel now?"

"Better, thank you. Actually as if I could sleep to-night."

Here the laughter and witticisms round the table where the cavaliers had settled became so uproarious, that unable to hear himself speak, Fargus broke off in his talk and half-turned on his chair to look severely at the delinquents.

"Where do these creatures, in caps so much too small for their fat heads, come from?" he asked in a low voice, bending closer to his companion; "the University is not sitting now."

"Students on a tour," said Lewis in the same tone.

"How absurd they look with their seamed faces and that painful rotundity of figure!" He was about contemptuously to turn his back upon the group, when he became aware that its largest and most obtrusive member was now engaged in staring at him with as much insolence as two excessively heated eyes could convey, and paused to return the look with placid disfavor.

"My dear sir," said Lewis, "allow me to entreat you to be-

stow your attention elsewhere for the moment. Corps students often make it a point of honor to be actively imperti-
nent to those outside their order, on the slenderest pretext."

As he spoke, silence fell on the couleur-party, all three of
which looked solemnly toward Fargus; then the first berib-
boned individual rose, with unsteady dignity, and came forward. He stopped within a pace of the Englishman's table,
closed his high heels with a bellicose tap. "Sir," he said in
German, "why did you fix me? I cannot allow you to do so!"

The admirable correction of this challenge was lost upon
Fargus, who had to address himself to Lewis for interpretation.

"What does this gentleman say?"

"Oh," cried Lewis hurriedly, anxious to gloss things over,
"he wants to know what you are looking at him for. It is
part of their system to resent being 'fixed,' as they call it.
Mein Herr," he continued, making a slight bow to the corpsman, "this gentleman is a stranger, and speaks no German.
He did not intend to fix you, but regarded your party with a
traveler's curiosity." And, bowing again, he sat down, in
hopes of having concluded the episode.

"Very well, sir; tell him, then, not to look at us again."

"That I shall not do!" retorted Lewis, stung to anger.
"What the devil do you mean by offering such impertinence
to strangers—guests in your land?"

The Bursch wheeled round, and petrified himself into an
attitude of the most rigid dignity.

"Silly youth, I must trouble you for your card."

Lewis pulled out his pocket-book and tossed a card on the
table; the German became preposterously courteous. He
took the card with much apparent satisfaction, touched his
cap, first to one, then to the other, and swaggered back to
his companions, who had looked on in solemn approval.

Though unable to understand a word, Fargus could not
misinterpret the student's tones, nor the anger with which
Lewis had flung his card down.

"What is the meaning of all this? You are not going to
take a challenge from that sodden fool?"

"If he is not too drunk to forget all about it, it is probable he will send some one in the morning to request the
honor of a fight with me."

There was a long silence. Lewis yawned and leaned again
on the table. "If I could only sleep to-night, the chance of
meeting the great Amadis would tempt me to get up again."

The students retired almost immediately.

Fargus resolved to see his boy back to his room, and endeavor, without seeming indiscreet, to induce him to lie·down to rest.

When once more left to themselves, he laid his hand on the young man's shoulder.

"Come, it is time for you to have some sleep. Where are you stopping?"

"Where am I stopping? Where? I forget; I will sleep here."

And stretching his arm forward, laid his head on the table.

Fargus quickly made up his mind. He called the landlord, and naming his hotel, made it understood he required a guide thither.

Lewis got up when Fargus took him under the arm. The hotel soon appeared in sight, when the American dismissed his guide and hurried his stumbling charge into its shelter.

CHAPTER IX.

THE "COMMENT" OF HONOR.

Disdaining the grin of the night-porter, Fargus conveyed the young man to his own quarters.

He locked the door, perceiving an adjoining bed-room was vacant, and resolved to usurp it for himself, abandoning his own bed to his son.

As for Lewis, with a few words of thanks, he flung himself on the couch.

The elder man stood gazing at him, immersed in thought.

In the relaxation of sleep the young frame looked broad and powerful. With head thrown back the muscular column of his throat showed, deeply sunburned. His arms were folded above his head; this Fargus noted, for it had been a habit of his own youthful days.

He caught himself sighing, and at length roused himself from his contemplation, to bend over the reclining form and loosen the collar and tie, unlace and pull off the boots. Then he carefully covered the sleeper, drew the blind and curtains, and after one last look at his son, retired to the next room and closed the door.

The sun had crossed the meridian before Lewis awoke.

He lay still, enjoying the sensation of lazy well-being in every limb. Then a curious sensation of unfamiliarity with his circumstances began to wax disturbingly; and presently there was the shock of the discovery that he had gone to bed in his clothes.

He sat up, bewildered, struggling to piece together the confused scraps of last night's proceedings. It was in vain he strove; he could not recollect how he had gone to bed.

"Confound it!" cried Lewis aloud, tossed petulantly back his covering, and curved his long legs over the side of the bed, in which position a knock at the door arrested him.

"Come in," cried he. It was the stranger of last night who stood on the threshold of the adjoining room, and smiled upon him with that odd gaze which had bewitched him in the tavern.

"Well, and how do you feel after sleeping the round of the clock?" just as if it were all the most natural thing in the world.

Lewis stared hard, and then rubbed his eyes.

"What are you doing in my room?" was a counter-question that not unnaturally rose to his lips. But almost at the same time his irritated glance fell, and, when he spoke, the words came forth wonderfully modified, almost apologetic. "May I ask why you are here, what you are doing in my room? I beg your pardon," blundered he, abashed all at once, and with a confused, humiliated consciousness of the contrast between his own unkempt condition and the perfect appointments of his visitor. "I have the vaguest recollection of what took place last night—I do remember meeting you. I hope I had not too much wine on board?"

"It was not so much a case of too much wine, as of too little food, I should say, and over-fatigue," answered Fargus kindly. "Perhaps, also, too much worry in your head."

At this allusion the black cloud settled back on Lewis' face.

The father, turning to draw the curtains and admit the warm sunlight of a perfect day, went on easily:

"Pardon me for coming in upon you in this manner; I heard you move first, and call, I thought. I should not have disturbed that good long sleep of yours. But I must tell you that this is not really your room, nor even your hotel. You were too sleepy last night to remember where you lodged, and so I took it upon myself to bring you back with me."

The young man flushed scarlet.

"Was I so bad as all that?" he asked quickly, and looked so aghast that the elder man's heart went out to him.

"No, my dear fellow," he answered, gently. "Some people might have put it down to wine; but I knew better."

Lewis fixed his eyes on the speaker, who returned his gaze with one of benevolent amusement, through which the young man felt an earnest scrutiny which puzzled and embarrassed him.

"It was really good of you," he said at length—"devilish

good of you!" with a sudden appreciation of his obligation. "I have been trying, ever since I awoke this morning, to remember how I got home. I had no idea I was trespassing upon your kindness. I don't know why you took the trouble."

"More surprised would you be if you did!" thought the father, while aloud he genially remarked:

"Any one would have rendered you the same service. I was very glad to be of use to you. And now may I beg you to make use of my traps, exactly as you please. You will find no razors, but I daresay they can provide you with some sort of implement in the hotel; and as to other things, the contents of my portmanteau are at your service. Seeing you have unwittingly partaken of my hospitality, will you give me the pleasure of extending it at least until after the luncheon I have just ordered?"

Lewis hesitated, then eagerly accepted—anything to hush, for the moment, the clamor of his pain.

"You will find me on the terrace," added Fargus.

Half an hour later they were once more seated opposite each other on the creeper-hung terrace, some savory dishes and a long bottle of Rhenish between them.

Lewis would have been other than human not to feel cheered by the influence of these material things, no less than by his entertainer's extraordinary gift of pleasant conversation.

The crusty bottle was near emptied. Lewis suddenly realized that he and this man of many travels and experiences, soldier at least in knowledge, and sportsman unmistakable, were old friends already, and that he did not even know his name.

His growing attraction toward this strange being, and his simultaneously growing curiosity, prompted him now to frankly admit his ignorance and beg enlightenment.

"I should so much like to know your name," he said naively.

"Fargus—David Fargus," answered the latter, smiling.

"A proud name for an American to bear," cried the young soldier, who was an eager student of military history. "Are you any relation of the famous Colonel Fargus?"

There was a moment's pause. Lewis looked up, to see the stranger's face flush darkly under its bronze, the immense scar on his forehead standing out lividly against the tide of generous blood.

"Why, good Heavens!" exclaimed the young man, with lightning intuition, "I believe you are the very man himself!"

For the first time in his life Fargus felt an exquisite pleasure in his fame. Hitherto he had accepted its advantages as his due. Now he was tasting all the satisfaction it is capable of giving. When he spoke his smile was very sweet.

"So you have found the old soldier out. I had hardly thought a young blood like you would even know of such ancient history. Yes, it was a curious time, one that brought to the fore any man with capacity for the art of war. You have seen service, too, if I am not mistaken?"

"I was in Afghanistan, and also through that unsavory Boer business; the latter not one we English like to talk much about," answered Lewis briefly, taken aback to find the tables turned upon him. "And is this your first visit to Europe, sir?" with a pretty, unconscious lapse into the subaltern fashion of address to soldiers of standing.

"No," answered Fargus, "I am an old traveler in the Old World as well as the New. My impression of Heidelberg, for instance. will, no doubt, be limited; nevertheless a picturesque, withal a pleasant one. A remembrance of a tavern scene, very full of light and shade; of a young Englishman, immersed in thought, seeking rest and oblivion in the companionship of some excellent Steinberger; three highly objectionable roysterers—have you forgotten them?—on whom the noble wine seemed to have had a very different influence. produce a bit of local color in the shape of a challenge, of which I fear I am the unwitting cause. So much for the picturesque. Next the remembrance of an excellent lunch under the veranda of a hotel, the name of which I shall probably forget, in the congenial company of my new acquaintance. A pleasant picture to remember, and especially to sit in! Will you take another cup? Here is one of last night's cigars."

Lewis, every moment sinking more under the charm of his host's geniality, gazed with admiration.

He was growing talkative himself when their *tete-a-tete* was abruptly disturbed.

A waiter came up with a rather dirty card, and asked whether this was the gentleman's name? "For," said he, "two Herren Studenten were without and anxious to see the gentleman."

Lewis recognized his own card. Throwing it back on the salver, "Yes, that is my name. Show the gentlemen to a private room, and say I shall attend to them. How silly of me to give them my card!"

"So they have really come with the challenge," said Fargus. "You are not going to take it up?"

"If I had not given them my card, I certainly should not trouble myself much about the fellows."

"It is absurd. And it further appears to me that I am the right person to speak to these youths."

"Oh, I have not the slightest doubt that you could be accommodated with a duel also! Such creatures are simply insatiable of honorable quarrels. And, by the way, I should not wonder if it was the appearance of that scar on your face, sir, which made them think of you as a person addicted to that sort of amusement. But, even were you to dream of favoring them in that preposterous manner, you must not think that it would release me from my liability; the challenge was addressed to me personally."

There was a fairly long pause.

"What is it?" asked Fargus, suddenly bending forward to smile into the thoughtful eyes.

Lewis laughed, but with a slight embarrassment. I am almost prompted to ask you for another favor."

"If it is feasible, it is done," was the simple answer.

"It is a favor which, among Englishmen, one would hesitate to ask of one's best and oldest friend. It would take me out of a fix if you had no objection to be my second."

"Why, of course; and I shall have the pleasure of seeing you chastise the fellow, I hope."

They both laughed, Lewis with a rising spirit and a certain pleasurable excitement.

"That is wonderfully good of you. These students would be proud if they knew who it was that condescends so far to patronize their tinsel chivalry. I shall not betray your incognito, of course, but mean nevertheless to be worthy of my second. And now," said the young man gayly, "I must go and interview the gentlemen. Would you care to be present?"

Fargus emptied his glass and followed in silence.

When they entered the private room the two Germans rose solemnly, and the ceremonial began.

After the exchange of bows, precise on the German side, sketchy on the English, Fargus sat down and surveyed the scene with critical eyes. Lewis, with his hands behind his back, leaned against the high china-stove and waited.

One of the visitors, who would have been handsome under rational conditions of life, whose features were almost obliterated by the white puffiness and the interlacing scars which proclaimed to the world his untiring devotion to beer and honor laws, advanced, halted, closed his heels, braced his knees, made another bow, and observed:

"Herr Kerr, of the English army? Lieutenant, I presume?"

Lewis nodded assent.

"Herr Lieutenant, I have the honor to introduce myself:

Karl von Plöss." He placed a card on the table, whereupon ensued a third exchange of bows. "I have also the honor to present my companion, Herr Ulrich Meyerhoffer, candidat philosoph."

The philosophical candidate, a square, squat individual, came forward and likewise saluted.

Then proceedings came to a standstill; the two academic persons looked in the direction of the sofa, and Lewis recollected himself.

"Mr.—ah—Ferguson?" with an inquiring glance which Fargus returned acceptingly. "Allow me to introduce Herr von Plöss and Herr Meyerhoffer. Meine Herren, I present Mr. Ferguson, my friend. Now we ought to know each other," he went on in English, with an irrepressible boyish wink.

"Herr Lieutenant," said the first student, with increased severity, "we are sent by Herr Graf von Löwenstein to ask whether you will revoke the expressions you made use of when addressing him last night."

"Indeed!" returned Lewis, affecting surprise. "Is that all? You may tell Graf von Löwenstein that I will do nothing of the kind."

The German bowed again.

"When and how will it then please you to meet the Count? We are only passing through the town."

"As I, too, am only a visitor here, I should say the sooner the better. Shall it be to-morrow morning. But since I am willing so far to honor Count von Löwenstein as to meet him on account of his own unwarrantable behavior last night, I shall insist on two or three conditions. As the challenged party and as a stranger on your land, I have the right to stipulate my own convenience."

The student, rather taken aback, acquiesced.

"Being a soldier and not a corps-student, I take no pride in scars cheaply earned on the Mensur," with an unequivocal glance at his interlocutor's scarred and furrowed countenace. "I, therefore, decline to fight with scratching rapiers and in mattresses."

Herr von Plöss flushed violently to the roots of his pale, plastered hair. "What do you say to sabers, then?" trying to hide his anger under a sneer. "Officers, even English, can have no objection to using their swords."

"Sabers, by all means," retorted Lewis, with great deliberation; "I have not the slightest objection to meeting your principal with them—without active seconds, of course. I have one more condition to make: your side must undertake the management of every detail concerning the encounter.

You are experts in such matters, while my only friend here is, like me, a stranger."

The ambassadors retired to a corner for a rapid consultation, exercised in their minds to find a mannerless outlander ready in matters of honorable difference. "Nil admirari" is one of the canons of gentlemanly behavior in their order, and they allowed no word or look to betray their feelings.

Lewis exchanged a friendly look with Fargus, who appreciated the authoritative manner in which his son had assumed the conduct of affairs.

"You seem to be as much at home in German disputations as these fellows," he remarked; "how do you know the language so well?"

"I spent two Semesters here during my undergraduate days, and have kept it up with a view to the Staff College."

"Herr Lieutenant, we have agreed, unless you should have objection, that the duel shall take place in a certain inclosed field behind the Philosopher's Walk. You know the Philosophen Weg?"

"I do," said Lewis shortly.

"We will bring the necessary attendants and the doctor. I am Graf von Löwenstein's second. Herr Meyerhoffer is umpire. Yonder gentleman is to be your second. Is this understood?"

"Quite," replied the Englishman, and the deputation withdrew.

"Is not this idiotic?" laughed Lewis. "Can you conceive how level-headed people like the Germans cannot only tolerate, but be proud of, the peculiar ethics of the corps-student? For if one broaches the subject of the 'Duéll' with them, they have scores of reasons in its favor."

"It seems to me," returned Fargus, "that the chief result of that tender solicitude for their honor is to turn your corps-student into a highly objectionable rowdy."

"Oh, I must admit you have seen a bad specimen. Most corps-students are gentlemen."

"You have had no practical experience? Are you anything of a swordsman?" asked Fargus.

"I am reckoned rather good at that," replied the young man. "Our last colonel ranked sword exercise next only to riding in importance. I have had some practice also in German play. I think it would not be amiss were I to put my hand in again. Have you a mind to walk with me as far as the fencing-room?"

There was no trace of last night's depression left on Lewis. Fargus felt almost disposed to rejoice at a cause which had produced such results.

CHAPTER X.

"You are a good swordsman. I am glad of that," repeated Fargus, musingly. "How do you come to be a fencer? Most of your countrymen now look upon scientific fencing as an un-English pursuit."

"That is a John Bullish idea which is fast disappearing from the army. In olden days we had the best broadswordsmen in Europe. With me sword-play of every description has always been a special taste; I began to cultivate the science at the early age of twelve. I was brought up by my Spanish grandparents, partly at Seville, where I was born, partly in an old, very dilapidated family place they had, near Ronda—a sort of half castle, half farm, where we used to pass the summer. There was a large loft in one of the towers, where old rusty odds and ends of arms and armor and torn books were stuffed away—a favorite haunt of mine, whither one day my grandfather traced me unawares, to find me practicing by myself. It seems he watched me with delight, as I pinked and hacked the back of a fine old Cordova leather arm-chair in the true orthodox style. The old man was so pleased with what he considered an innate taste for gentlemanly accomplishments that he engaged a man from Seville to give me lessons. Dear old unsophisticated grandfather!" Lewis continued. "He little thought what a deal of trouble it would give me, in after days, to unlearn all the antiquated passes and tricks. It was the same with my riding. It was old General Woldham who initiated me to the easy comfort—to man and beast—of a hunting-seat. Good old soul! he was much kinder to me than my own kin!"

"I liked what I saw of him," said Fargus. He had been greedily taking in every word which unveiled his son's past, and his pleasure in him grew as he listened; but it was almost with a sense of jealousy that he heard of all those who had taken the father's place, and among whom was divided that gratitude which might have been centered on him.

"Please forgive my garrulity," cried Lewis, with a quick blush. "You should not have let me go on prosing about myself. Here is the University Fencing School. I hope this does not bore you."

"I have neither found you garrulous nor tiresome," responded Fargus warmly; "and I am prepared to derive much interest in watching you wield the saber. Do you lead the way."

Being vacation-time, the Fechtboden seemed deserted. There was none of that busy uproar of clinking, rasping blades in opposition, of thuds loudly sounding on padded arms, of monotonous commands, varied at intervals by high-pitched words of encouragement or objurgation; which in term-time proclaims academical activity.

Lewis rang, and sent his card to summon the master.

This jovial personage, to while away the hours, had evidently been solacing himself, in the company of congenial spirits, with a deep after-dinner draught of Bavarian, made his appearance in his shirt-sleeves.

The man of the sword at once recognized an old pupil, of many years back, and was much delighted, from a professional and artistic point of view, when he learned the immediate cause of the call.

He introduced the visitors into a large room, the vaulted ceiling of which was supported by pillars.

"Well, Herr Kerr," cried the master, after suiting his visitor with saber, arm-guard and helmet, "I hope you have not quite forgotten our old lessons in *echt Deutsch* fighting. Now, take your measure; on guard—good; straighten your arm and brace your knee more—good; and now beware of the Manchette.

"Remember, Herr Kerr, that, among us, the dictates of manly honor prohibit any retreating; the left foot remains firm, as by the measure. Cut, parry, or countertime if you like, redouble, always give and take; but never stop, hesitate, fall back, or retire the body, after your foreign custom. That is not correct here. Now straight the arm, brace the knee, hard with the thumb. And, Herr Kerr, remember the Manchette."

A flicking cut over the young man's guard, which sounded grimly on the gauntlet, emphasized the caution.

Fargus watched with satisfaction. Lewis' play was sharp, decisive, and neat—severe, as one conversant with the schools would have called it—and he was in fair condition; the master, on the other hand, although naturally superior in point of hits, breathed stertorously after ten minutes' play, and perspired to confusion.

"You must also beware of lunging too wide, worthy sir," he remarked, coming with evident relief to a standstill, and mopping his good-humored face; "you might find it dangerous on the grass. When is it to be; with whom? You know," he added, "with one of the profession such things are honorably safe."

At the mention of the name, however, the jovial lanista was unable to suppress a whistling ejaculation, and a transient look of concern shadowed his rubicund visage.

"Graf von Löwenstein, of Munich! *Donnerwetter*, Herr Kerr, for your first duel you have found a right doughty opponent! Well, you must not tire your arm. This will suffice for to-day. You will do; you have improved since you used to come here. Now, my last counsel: keep your hand warm before coming on the ground; a thick glove, for instance, will keep your wrist subtle—such details have decided the fate of many an encounter."

"What do you think of the Krummer Säbel, as a sport?" inquired Lewis of the Colonel.

"I know so little about it. We in America trust more to lead than to steel. All this appeared very scientific; but it seems to me that a young man should make more use of his legs."

"That is the very essence of the *echt Deutsch* play—every cut is to be stopped with the blade. Here they look upon all dodging and springing as derogatory to a gentleman."

"A likely explanation," said Fargus, smiling; "though it seems rather absurd that people who are not walking beer-barrels should be expected to forego their natural advantages. At this well-regulated game there is little danger of severe cuts."

"Oh, the German saber can wound with quite sufficient severity, as we shall perhaps see to-morrow. And this reminds me that the authorities, although they wink at the Mensur in a way almost equivalent to licensing, punish all other forms of duelling with fortress imprisonment, when they can lay their hands on the actors."

Fargus strove to conceal his concern. The expression of the master's face, his ejaculation on hearing the name of the adversary, haunted him.

"They would not imprison a stranger, challenged by a native!"

"I rather fancy they would, and be only too delighted to get the chance. This reminds me, that since you are so good as to stand by me, it would be better to make your preparations for leaving early to-morrow. These people recognize no distinction between seconds and principals. I should have told you of this sooner. Did you contemplate stopping long?"

"No; I am as free as possible, and have not the least anxiety as regards the fortress business—for myself, that is; but what if you should be wounded?"

"There is little about my pocketing something in the scrimmage. If there is a redeeming point in this whole foolery it is the unflinching pluck of the corpsmen. They will do their best to keep everything secret, for their own sakes; and I have no fear but that I can either be hidden up somewhere, or able to make 'tracks.' I shall get ready to be off early to-morrow; my business and I have to return to England."

"Listen, my young friend," said Fargus, after a moment's silence. "I am sorry, now, to have countenanced the affair; if you will allow me, I shall not leave you till you are through it. Meanwhile, you had better make my hotel your head-quarters."

"I shall be very glad," said Lewis, "and am much obliged for your kindness. Now, what shall we do—walk about?"

"Anywhere you like," answered the American. "I shall enjoy the stroll in your company. I should congratulate myself on our chance meeting, did I not feel I have been the cause of bringing this unpleasant affair upon you!"

Lewis walked on in silence; then, with some hesitation:

"I am nothing if not indebted to you, Colonel. Should matters prove serious—though it would be affectation to intimate that there is any great danger of that—I should still have reason to be glad of your appearance. I believe you have saved me from what would have been far worse. Owing to the utter destruction of hopes I had cherished for years, I felt last night as if the springs of my life were broken. The thought of self-destruction was gaining the mastery over me. Your company did me good. Though, naturally, at the time I should have preferred being alone, it was a very black spell that you broke."

Fargus' mind wandered back to the old days, when he, too, had known the grim fascination.

"I would not presume to moralize," he said; "but I am glad the spell is broken. Never allow yourself to become familiar with the demon of self-destruction."

"Never fear. Indeed, I feel now quite ashamed of my mawkishness. I have no mind to desert my post in this world," he suggested, changing the subject; "shall we turn in this direction?" And he led his companion along a narrow lane which wound its abrupt, pebble-paved way up the flank of the Castle hill. "This town is full of reminiscences for me."

Fargus assented willingly. Little conversation was attempted until they reached the terrace gardens of a well-known tavern.

There for a time, standing by the parapet, he seemed lost in the contemplation of the smiling panorama shimmering in the hot, sunny air beneath him. The gray-brown roofs of Heidelberg spread in length between the hillside and the strand where the Neckar lazily rolled its yellow course, with now and then a mild foaming over shallows or weirs. Beyond, the mellowing vineyards to the south merged into the pine-clad slopes.

"It is strange," he said, sitting down on the corner of a table under a tree, and still looking wistfully out across the land, "to see so little change in the old scenes, when we have changed so much."

"Dear me!" said Fargus, sitting down in his turn, as, with a flourish, the waitress placed on the table before them two tall glasses of amber beer brimming over, "have you changed so much since your student days? How long ago may it be?"

"It is seven years since I sat in this very place, not a very long time, but the cycle required, as the physiologist tells us, to renovate every atom of man's physical being. And it seems to be much the same with the mind," he added.

"You talk like an old man," put in Fargus, willing to humor his companion in a vein most likely to lead to personal matters.

"I do not know. It seems to me that the final change, which really constitutes old age, is one of indifference, that with it comes a greater state of serenity—a soothing sense that the battle of life, whether lost or won, is over—that the days of eagerness are too remote even to be regretted."

He drank half the contents of his frothy beaker, and continued:

"This is good. I saw you smile indulgently when I spoke of disappointment. Have you not found most of the rungs in the ladder of life more or less a disappointment? Is it not a fact that whenever you are brought back to the feelings of old times, you awaken to the discrepancy between anticipation and reality? We look to the moment when we shall have achieved cherished objects of ambition—meanwhile, the very contemplation of a desired future robs what might be an admirable present of its real savor. When the achievement has taken place, why is it that we then look back with unavowed melancholy to the period of our illusions? For, when it has been secured, the slowly achieved position has lost its satisfaction, our pleasure has been blunted by the gradual process."

Lewis halted, lost in reverie, and Fargus watched him.

"This is a curiously contemplative frame of mind for a sunburned dragoon, just home from the wars! It would seem as though this German drink had infected you with the dreaminess peculiar to the lank-haired German student."

Lewis came back from his distant thoughts and smiled.

"You are right, Colonel; I was again living in the days when discussion took more willingly a contemplative turn than it would in the ante-room of a cavalry mess; but this return to bygone haunts has brought back the past days. Did you chance to meet Charles Hillyard at Woldham?"

"A handsome, pale university lecturer?" asked Fargus.

"The same. Did you see much of him there?"

"Not very much; the little I did I found interesting."

"There was one of my disappointments," Lewis went on. "I wonder if it is he who has changed, or I? In the old days he was one of my stars. There is very little I would not have done for him. We had a room in common under that mossy roof yonder. He was a good German scholar and I was a poor one. We were inseparable. This tree was our rallying point for the morning draught. Before going, would you like to see a students' Kneipe? Ours, the Carolina, used to be here."

They emptied their glasses and moved toward the house.

A few words to the landlord, who soon recognized one of his former patrons, induced him to open the sacred precincts of the Carolina, which, it being vacation-time, now rested in darkness.

A long, rather narrow room, warmly lighted by stained glass windows, the rich colored, but highly incorrect, heraldic panes of which brightened the severely solid furniture. A ponderous oak table, much rubbed and dented by endless courses of disciplined compotation, crossed at the honor end by another, smaller and slightly raised; two formal rows of hard carved wood chairs, and a dignified presidential throne. On the table, between a couple of drinking-horns, elaborately archaic and unwieldy, a heavy wooden tobacco casket. A large special panel fixed to the wall was devoted to the heavy china pipes of the members, almost every one of which was inscribed to its owner by a brother Carolinian; over this hung a trophy of flags, devices, and club colors, emphasized by a pair of crossed rapiers. Numerous photographs of individuals or groups dotted the walls. To one of these Lewis straightway drew near.

"There we are still!" he called out, pointing to a group which showed the Carolinians in a forest excursion, seated or standing in various picturesque attitudes round a very prominent beer-barrel, each man holding his covered glass or his long pipe in one hand and with the other clasping, in pointedly devoted manner, some special comrade by the shoulder or the arm.

"What a ridiculous pair we did look!" laughed Lewis; "though no worse than the others, of course. And yet we did meet here, almost every day: and Hillyard—Tipp—was actually the soul of our parties, though he worked eight hours a day and accumulated knowledge without ever talking about it.

I used often to think of the contrast between the student of Heidelberg and the University lecturer, when, on our return to college, I watched him from the body of the hall, dining at the high table—grave, reverend, as befits a Don, and no doubt talking unimpeachable sense. Now there no longer seems to be such enviable superiority on his side. I regret our old relations."

Talking in this strain, they sallied forth again, toward the pine woods. Fargus, who felt his curiosity increase, led him gradually on. And a delight it was to the father to hear the story of his son's assimilation to England and things of England, at a time when a boy's character and tastes are already formed; to hear how he struggles and the unhappy sensitiveness of the first years gradually gave place to the pleasures of independence and of well-earned success. And it stirred him strangely to learn how strong the love of his father's country had grown in the boy's heart.

They spent the remainder of the afternoon in an invigorating walk through the peaceful, romantic scenery of the Neckarthal. Occasionally, Fargus found himself led out of his depth on literary excursions. But he enjoyed the converse perhaps the more for the contrast between what he had the right to have expected in his son and what he actually found.

And by the time the sky had grown purple and golden over the pine-bristling hills and they were tramping homeward, the mutual sympathy had ripened on each side into genuine appreciation.

And thus, at the end of the first day spent together, Fargus, filled with warm and proud satisfaction, hardly knew what he liked best in his newly-found son, the manly, soldier-like bearing, or the scholarly refinement.

CHAPTER XI.

"PASSES, FINCTURES, AND COUNTERTIME."

Lewis slept soundly, with rambling dreams of old times.

Fargus spent the night in wakeful cogitations, and at dawn arose and made ready for the eventful morning. When the first stir of life in the house became evident, he summoned a servant and ordered a substantial breakfast; then he aroused his neighbor.

"Everything is in full swing," he said briskly, as Lewis put in his head at the door; "we have a couple of hours before us; make haste, that we may start early and have time for a walk before your fencing bout; it will invigorate you and put your circulation in order."

The untidy brown head disappeared; in due course Lewis emerged from his chamber as neat and trim and generally polished as beseems an English officer of dragoons.

After a leisurely meal, and armed with a couple of cigars from Fargus' case, they sallied forth into the freshness of the morning. The father's sole thought being now to keep Lewis in his present collected and cheerful mood, he allowed no trace of his own misgivings to appear in look or word.

"What a delicious day!" said he, as they swung along. "In face of scenery like this, under such a sky, does not the errand on which we are bound seem incongruous?"

"Yes; the surroundings are more suggestive of an aubade than a trial by battle," said Lewis.

"Well," he resumed, "I should have scoffed at the idea of such an enterprise a few days ago; but now, somehow, I rather enjoy the excitement."

They crossed the Neckar bridge and ascended the right bank of the river, discussing as they went the question of single combat; first, the institution as it now exists, then from a historical and ethical point of view.

"It seems to me almost inconceivable," he remarked at length, "that, with such a very well-digested system of opinions, you should now find yourself on the way to put your honor to the test of fencing skill."

"Oh, Colonel," put in Lewis, "do not believe that I consider my 'honor' engaged in the least. It is a mere matter of convenience. I do not hold with the gentlemen who, by the way, I now hear are coming up behind us—a man's honor to be such a delicate, fragile entity that death or murder is preferable to the risk of its being doubted by the first bully. Far less do I believe that there is only one kind of honor, namely, a constant readiness to stake one's body, in good mediæval fashion, in support of a position assumed rightly or wrongly. For the most curious thing about the 'point of honor' among upholders of the duel is that it applies to physical courage only, never to the moral. As for these persons whom we are to meet this morning, they have even more curious tenets on this subject than other Continentals; unlike us who hold a gentleman to possess courage as a simple matter of course until he give proof to the contrary, they refuse to believe in the fortitude of any one who has not earned his credentials in that ridiculous institution of theirs—the Mensur. I, however, did a foolish thing, in a moment of mental obfuscation, in giving my regimental card. But do not believe that I should have considered. my honor attainted had I chosen to decline the encounter."

As they turned to ascend the Hirschgasse—the lane celebrated for leading to the time-honored tavern where are held, at regular intervals during the session-time, so many glorious and gory arbitraments—they were overtaken by a carriage; therein the three corpsmen, lolling back at ease, together with a bearded and spectacled· personage, presumably the doctor. Next to the driver sat a "factotum," no doubt well practiced in such expeditions.

The four occupants, as they rattled past, gravely raised their hats without turning their heads.

"I am convinced these men think it very 'bad form' of us not to have driven here in state, as they do. True, it looks as if we felt sure that we shall not require a conveyance back." Lewis spoke gayly. "Still," he continued, "it might perhaps have been wiser to have one. Now, should I be disabled, I shall have to be deposited in that tavern yonder, where you may this moment see pompous Herr Meyerhoffer entering with the servant—in quest of the weapons, I suppose."

"Please God, we shall be under no necessity of that kind."

. But Lewis laughed at his companion's serious look. His spirits rose perceptibly as the moment approached; indeed, by the time they reached the place of combat, nothing but the necessity of keeping up British decorum and a cool, gentlemanly carriage could subdue a rising sense of jauntiness.

The whole "duel company" now moved together along a by-path which, winding for a short while through the birchwood, led to a well-secluded glade. There the Englishman and his second retired apart for a last few words, while the natives proceeded to make their final arrangements. The factotum flew hither and thither, carrying water and a basin to the doctor, who was spreading his instruments and bandages in engaging array on the stump of a tree; opening the case of swords; removing with febrile activity stones and fallen branches from the spot chosen by the umpire.

Seeing his opponent stripping himself to the waist, Lewis very cooly began to do likewise.

"Business-like, is it not?" he remarked, with an amused smile, to Fargus, as the latter silently helped him.

"A business I wish were well over," thought the father, yet trying to respond with confident ease, as he glanced at the well-knit, close-muscled frame revealed, and inwardly cursing the pragmatic fooling which was bringing it into jeopardy.

At this point the umpire came up to them, and, touching his cap coldly, remarked:

"We are ready."

The count had already assumed the two protective bandages which German custom prescribes, even for the more severe saber duels, one to the elbow and the other to the arm-pit. The factotum had taken his post as look-out man on a slight knoll whence a view could be had of all approaches. Seeing that he alone was waited for, and not wishing to appear a laggard at the fray, Lewis was about to advance somewhat hurriedly, when the student stopped him. "I perceive you are without the requisite bindings," he said, a trifle imperatively; "we cannot allow you to proceed thus. As the gentleman with you is a stranger, I will have the honor, if you will so have it, to arrange them myself."

The Englishman surrendered his arm with courteous thanks, and the neglect was quickly repaired.

Fargus had to own that he was by far from being as cool as his boy, and was chafing under the obligation to remain passive. Why had he not taken up this quarrel himself? He might have settled that self-sufficient swashbuckler with an ounce of lead, and thought less about the matter than of seeing his brawny boy lose a drop of blood. Ah, well! the die was cast. God help the good champion!

The fever of fight had come upon Lewis as he took up and balanced the wide-hilted saber presented to him. The cool breeze fanning his bare arm and breast, and the "responsive" weight of the well-mounted saber, sharp as a carving-knife, heightened that muscular sense. There was naught in him to recall the dreamy philosopher's mood. But, for all this nervous tension, he appeared, as Fargus noticed with much approval, the very picture of self-possession as he stood to meet his foe.

It was, of course, his first encounter of the kind; whereas the pale, fat Graf—a notorious duelist—had gone through the experience many a time and at many a weapon.

They advanced toward each other on the selected spot, the German with studied coolness, even indolence—the Englishman with quiet deliberation, strangely at variance with his gleaming eyes. The seconds placed themselves on either side. There was a short pause, during which nothing was heard but the rustling of the trees and the chirp of birds. The umpire rapidly ascertained that every detail was correct, then clear rose his voice:

"Engage; are you ready?—go!"

The last word was no sooner out than the corpsman, waking up as if by magic from his deceptive impassiveness, with the speed of lightning darted two of those flicks from the wrist which are so characteristic of German sword-play at his opponent's forearm.

Had not the latter at that moment instinctively dropped into his more familiar hanging guard—when the brunt of the cut was taken up by the convexity of the hilt—he would undoubtedly have been disabled from the very outset. As matters turned out the extreme end of the curved blade reached his arm, and inflicted thereon a small cross-shaped wound. Beware of the *manchette!* the old master had warned him truly.

"Halt!" shrieked the umpire; and the combatants dropped their hands, while the doctor examined the cut, in spite of Lewis' impatient protestations, only, however, to pronounce it of no consequence, and give permission for the resuming of the engagement.

The student's white face had remained as expressionless as a mask, but Lewis' anger was roused by this humiliating hit at the very first pass. With burning eyes and compressed lips he now, once more, and this time deliberately, assumed his English guard, and, at the word of command, led off himself with such vigor as to frustrate, by forcing his opponent to use strong parries, all further attempt to score points by insidious flipping.

And now it became a fight, indeed! The German, firm as a rock, stopped and returned Lewis' fast-lashing cuts with the most admirable coolness and precision. Some twenty throws had thus been exchanged when the umpire's shrill command again resounded:

"Halt!"

On Lewis' bare chest, extending from the left shoulder to the right breast, appeared a thin red line; this rapidly widened, and numberless slender rivulets of blood presently began to descend in interlacing stripes.

Fargus came forward, deadly pale; Lewis glanced down at the wound with a careless smile, intent only on trying to hide his mortification.

"Merely a scratch, Colonel—nothing of any consequence!"

And the surgeon's verdict, after inspection, being that the wound was not disabling, the pair started off once more.

This time both seemed to have lost their coolness. The bout was short. After a moment of dead silence, during which each fixed the other with a glaring eye, and gripped his sword with twitching hand, Lewis suddenly launched forward a swinging, English cut at his opponent's body, and the latter, taken aback by his full lunge, rarely risked in German play, forgot all his caution, and attempted a counterline. The result of these unpreconcerted methods of fence was disastrous.

Fargus saw Lewis' blade bury itself deeply in his antagonist's bare flank; but the cry of triumph which well-nigh escaped his lips turned to an exclamation of dismay. His son's face was laid open from the temple to the chin. The unfortunate German dropped his sword, staggered, clutched the air, and finally collapsed in a heap on the ground, rolling partly over, and then lying motionless, and to all appearance dead, save for a slight twitching of mouth and eyelid. Staring in horror at the ghastly sight of his handiwork, Lewis stood as if spell-bound—all unconscious of being himself far more horrible to behold with his cloven cheek gaping hideously, his right arm and hand, his body down to the waist, by this time scarlet with streaming blood. Then he reeled suddenly, and, in his turn, would have fallen, but for Fargus, who, rushing forward, seized him firmly under the arm and conducted him to the doctor's tree-stump, on which, disposing with one sweep of the hand of its array of instruments, he gently pressed him down.

"Thank God! this is over," said the elder man with a dry throat; beads of cold sweat shone on his forehead. "How you are bleeding, poor boy," attempting with a handkerchief to hold together the lips of the face-wound. Lewis looked up, dimly struck by the affectionate, almost paternal, tone of his new friend's voice, but for the moment unable to speak. "Let me see," continued Fargus; "the arm is nothing, the chest not much—yet how terrible it might have been! The face-cut is bad, though. Will these fellows never attend to you?" he went on, angrily looking round; "what are they all crowding over that brute for?"

"I am afraid he is worse than I am," said Lewis, faintly and indistinctly, for, the wound rapidly stiffening, he could not move his lips without painful efforts.

"Do not attempt to talk. Hold this tight; I will go and see."

At that moment, however, the doctor came toward them.

"A bad business," he said, significantly shrugging his shoulders.

"What! dead?" cried the amateur, aghast at his success.

"Not yet, but—— We have not heard the last of this affair. And now, what about you?" he added, lifting the handkerchief. "Hum! a fine high-quart—six needles or more." And without further parley he proceeded first briskly to sew up the open cheek, then to wash and bind the other slashes.

As he was putting the finishing touches to his artistic arrangements of lint and sparadrap, the servant on the lookout was heard to give a low cry of warning, and presently a man rushed through the creaking underwood into the glade. What he had to communicate was evidently of importance, for they at once called the servant back, and the four men held an animated consultation, at the end of which he who had acted as umpire walked up to Fargus.

"Sir," he said, coldly saluting, "it will not be safe for you to return to your hotel. A messenger has just been sent by a friend in the town to warn us that the police have found out something about this duel, and are on the watch for our return."

This speech delivered, the Germans took no more notice of the adverse party than if they had not been, but, gathering round the doctor, fell to discussing the possibility of removing their unconscious principal to some place of safety.

Lewis translated the allocution, and held a council of war.

"We cannot go back—if he dies . . . fortress for us; five years perhaps—for both of us."

"What is to be done?" asked Fargus. "Can those fellows advise us?"

"They are even in worse plight, and not well disposed toward us. Only plan I can think of: find our way to some railway-station as soon as possible. Must walk, too," he added, having paused to reflect a while.

"But, my dear boy, how far can you walk in this state? Can you walk at all?"

"Must. I know the country. To-day to Schoenau, behind that hill. Let me take your arm—weak on my legs—better presently."

And without casting a glance behind, the father supporting his son in tenderest solicitude, they walked slowly away from that nefarious "field of honor"—even as the students' party, carrying the inert form of their companion, were silently leaving it in the opposite direction.

CHAPTER XII.

WANDERINGS.

For three long hours the two men tramped onward, in winding lanes, through mysteriously somber pine-woods, now on the highroad between the vineyards of the warm hillsides. But their circumstances were little conducive to the enjoyment of scenery.

Manfully did Lewis settle down to his task of covering the twelve miles or more to Weinheim, though every step throbbed responsive through each of the six needles which held his face together, and every beat of the slow pulse to that low, gnawing ache in the heart which loss of blood engenders.

Full of solicitude, ever rising and ever repressed in fear of self-betrayal, the father strove to while away the heavy time and to lighten the way by the help of his strong arm.

As the sun ascended and the air waxed sultry the calls for Fargus' brandy-flask and the halts grew more frequent; and Fargus felt his boy's arm lean heavier on his.

At last, after one of these halts he made a dead stop with trembling knees.

"You will think me a coward; I can't go another step; I must lie down."

"A coward! How can you talk so, my dear fellow! If I told you what I really think of you, it might make you vain. No, no; you cannot lie down here in this blazing sun; hold up a bit; hang on me till we get into the shade yonder."

But Lewis was past holding up. He reeled and staggered, and Fargus had almost to carry him under the spreading chestnut-tree he aimed at, which shaded a little oasis of cool, green turf, where the clear waters of a tiny streamlet sounded their welcome notes.

With a groan of relief the wounded man let himself down at full length in the shadow, while his companion moistened the bandages, noting with deep anxiety how fast they seemed to dry up again under the heat of the wounds.

"How sickening to have to give up! Ashamed of myself!"

"Now, do not fret," answered the elder man, pouring from his hat, which he used as a pitcher, a slender, grateful stream of water over the burning head. "You have nothing to be ashamed of. It is the earache that knocks you down, isn't it? Take a little more of this brandy-and-water," he continued, after holding his son's hand for a moment in his, and sliding his fingers down to find the faint, unequal pulse. "It will be easy to get something to give you relief as soon as we can get to a civilized place. Meanwhile, you must be quiet, and, above all, no more nonsense and fretting."

Lewis looked up with a sort of grateful smile.

Fargus went on. "You must stop here quite quietly and rest, while I make off to the nearest village and get a conveyance of some kind or other."

A short half-hour of hard walking brought him to a village, which, as usual in Germany, boasted a rather promising-looking inn. There, in default of any knowledge of the vernacular, his absolute determination to make himself understood, backed up by the judicious display of a gold coin, stood him in good stead.

Fargus stood over the good-natured innkeeper, hurrying him on, by gesture and personal help, till they drove away at the fullest speed the state of horse and vehicle would allow.

With a leaping heart he hailed the chestnut-tree again, and found Lewis an object of solicitude to a trio of swarthy peasants, who were surveying him with great sympathy, and who, with many gutteral expressions of good will, volunteered to assist him into the carriage. To Fargus' intense relief, the patient seemed somewhat the better for his enforced repose; and when he had installed him as comfortably as possible on the cushions of the ramshackle chariot, and pulled up a tattered hood to screen him, he gave the order for Weinheim.

Though but a few miles distant, it seemed an endless way.

It was two o'clock when the alighted at the best hostelry in Weinheim. Fargus engaged a private room for the invalid, whose condition he explained to the English-speaking waiter by a cooly mendacious account of a fall in a rocky part of the woods while on a walking expedition. Having seen his charge first dispose of a cup of broth and a glass of the best wine, the American started forth to prepare the way for their next stage.

Lewis had sketched the general idea of the retreat. Fargus now busied himself in carrying out the special details.

In an hour he returned, provided with all the necessary information, and accompanied by a porter laden with various indispensable purchases; a traveling-bag, changes of linen, a soft felt hat for the bandaged head, a straw one for himself—selected for disguise—several articles of pharmacy, lint, bandages and so forth. Then he locked himself in with Lewis and proceeded to minister to the comforts of that jaded youth.

But it was with dimly grateful sense of relief, when cleansed of dried blood and dust, and luxuriating in fresh linen, that he found himself again reclining on the bed, with cool bandages on the fevered wounds. The latter concluded his preparations with all the expedition, noiselessness and method of a professional, packing all the necessaries for the forthcoming journey.

When the time drew nigh for their departure, he came up to the bedside and gently roused his companion.

"My boy, all our arrangements are made. We start this evening ostensibly for Darmstadt, but really for Brussels. I think it safer to cover the whole journey at once, since out of the country we must. The more I contemplate the possibility of a prolonged visit to a fortress at the Prussian Government's expense, the less I like it."

"By all means let us go," said Lewis, striving to conceal by how much suffering the effort was accompanied.

"We shall have to start pretty soon. Can you stand a fourteen hours' journey?"

"Under your care I would go further," was the quiet reply.

"Remember, we are traveling under the style of Messrs.
Thomson. You are my son, Robert Thomson."

As Fargus spoke he threw a curious, wistful glance at
Lewis, but as it was, the young man's energies were too much
centered on the endeavor to carry his injured frame with
some kind of dignity out of the dangers to permit any waste
of strength in watching the outside world. With a mute sign
of acquiescence he received the suggestion and slowly dragged
himself out of the room, leaning heavily on Fargus' arm.

After a short while the sickness, caused by the change from
the reclining to the sitting position, passed away, the transfer
from carriage to train at Weinheim, as well as that from one
train to another at Darmstadt, was successfully accomplished,
as much owing to the patient's dogged pluck as to his companion's long-sighted care.

As police directions, started by the Heidelberg authorities,
were already being issued for their aprehension, Mr. Thomson
and his invalid son, in a specially reserved compartment, were
speeding toward Brussels, *via* Cologne. But the father only
drew breath in security when, on the following morning, they
crossed the frontier.

"Thank God!" he murmured, as the train at last moved off
from the station and sped on Belgic territory, and he bent
gently forward to look at the apparently somnolent form
stretched at full length on the seat opposite.

As he now glanced at the half-averted face a sudden pallor
overspread his own. Even as he looked, a heavy shuddering
passed over the whole body. The father felt his heart turn
cold. He knew the terrible menace of such signs even before
he raised the dry, twitching hand to feel the wiry beat of the
pulse: fever had set in. He had counted on his boy's unusual
vigor and health, without taking into account how highly
strung his nerves had been by mental trouble but a short time
before.

But David Fargus was not the man to waste his energy on
vain regrets. After altering the patient's position, pulling
down the blinds, opening the window to insure air, he once
more took a seat opposite his son, and, with melancholy look
fixed on the altered face, fell to considering how best to meet
the unexpected emergency.

He could, of course, stop at the nearest town instead of
Brussels, but, while only saving a couple of hours, he would
not then be sure of obtaining such good medical attendance.
And Lewis' life might now depend on medical skill. Fargus
determined to push on to Brussels if possible. At Brussels
matters would be far from being all plain sailing. Burdened
with a possibly delirious man he could not leave for a minute,

he would have to find immediate quarters, and to have to peregrinate the town from one to another might be death to his boy.

There was the alternative of a hospital. In England he would not hesitate a moment to take the sick man direct to such an institution, where he would be sure of receiving the best care. Could he be as sure in a Belgian hospital?

Fargus resolved not to let him out of his own keeping. What gold could purchase for him, gold should be forthcoming for. Luckily he had provided himself with plenty of money, and he could do no more than hope in the all-powerful persuasiveness of a well-filled purse.

But in an unexpected way the difficulty was lightened. At Liege, just as the train was moving away, a burly Belgian burst open the door and tumbled headlong into the carriage, and they were off at full speed before he could perceive that he had intruded upon a reserved compartment and an invalid. When he did so, he confounded himself in apologies. The man had a pleasant, open countenance, and positively radiated affluence, good-nature and self-satisfaction. He looked at Lewis, prostrate and speechless, with sympathy, clacking his tongue after the fashion of his countrymen.

Fargus hailed the amiable giant as a possible angel of succor. In a few words he explained the state of affairs, and begged him to suggest some hotel where they could be received, and the most skillful doctor known in Brussels.

The Fleming's eyes grew rounder as he listened, and his interest in the traveling Englishman rose to a pitch of excitement. Surveying the unconscious hero with increasing admiration, he chuckled or groaned alternately, as delight over the downfall of the Teuton, or commiseration over the sad plight of his antagonist, possessed his soul.

When Fargus proffered his request, he cried cheerily:

"As to that I should be delighted if you will allow me to offer you the hospitality of my bachelor quarters. Here is my card, sir"—fumbling vigorously in a waistcoat pocket, which his rotundity of form rendered rather difficult of access—"M. Frédéric Bocage, bon bourgeois et Bruxellois, at your service. Your son shall receive every care. I shall have the house kept as quiet as possible; but you understand, sir, now and again a bachelor establishment may be rather noisy."

"I am sincerely grateful for your kindness," said Fargus, "but if you knew of some quiet quarters, where we could have good attendance and be sure of being undisturbed, it would be better in every way we should remain independent. It is only as a last resource," he added, smiling, "that I should dream of taking advantage of your most hospitable offer, and bringing the trouble of such a serious illness into your house. I cannot be mistaken; my son is in a very dangerous state."

M. Bocage, awed by the dignity of manner which Fargus maintained, did not press the invitation further. He knew of rooms overlooking the Gardens, close to his own house, where he had no doubt they would be received, and which were comfortable, large and airy.

"If you will allow me, I will conduct you thither and go for the doctor—my friend Bertrand, a man of the greatest ability; for I agree with you your son looks very ill."

The Belgian was as good as his word, and of invaluable help at the trying juncture of their arrival. Lewis was in a state of stupor, and it was with difficulty that he was got safely to the house whither M. Bocage brought them, and where the sight of his visage and the genial authority of his cheery voice smoothed over the landlady's dubiousness. Leaving the father to see to the patient, he bustled off in quest of the physician.

Having undressed his son, and seen him stretched between fresh white sheets, with iced compresses on his forehead, Fargus sat down by the bedside to wait for the doctor, whose arrival was promised before evening.

Twilight was spreading apace, and through the half-open window came a glimpse of promised sky, in marked contrast with the darkness and repose of the silent room.

It was exactly a week since he had left the Lone Grange in pursuit of his unknown boy; only four days since he had first spoken to him; now there was not a thought, not a prospect in his life, which was not absolutely encompassed by him. Had he known him and loved him all his twenty-five years of existence, helped him, trained him to be what he was—he did not think he would feel differently now, that his anxiety could be more poignant, or his tenderness more exquisitely keen.

Fargus gently lifted the hand that lay in his own—what a strong brown hand it was! how doughtily it had wielded the sword so chivalrously taken up in defense of a stranger! Lewis' hand was a little large, and there, straight across each strong palm, amid the inexplicable and generally absolutely personal designs, ran the unusual, unbroken, transverse line, held with pride by the Kerr family to be a special characteristic of their race.

There came a pleasure to Fargus each time he succeeded in tracing some likeness to himself or his family in the stranger son. Beside the odd way in which the latter seemed to have reproduced in his own so many of the phases of his father's life, there were a number of unmistakable and interesting signs of hereditary connection about him; something in the carriage of the head and the general bearing recalling to the self-made American the personality of his own English father; such family traits Fargus had looked for and welcomed.

The smile which this last discovery had evoked ended in a sigh. To have ignored him till his brave manhood, to have found him such as he was—for there was not one point so far Fargus would have wished different in his son—and to lose him, perhaps, after all!

Suddenly the sick man began muttering to himself. Then he sat up, and Fargus could see him staring fixedly before him. Presently he spoke again:

"Hear how the seconds fly! I shall soon be there; she is waiting for me." He stretched out his hand, laid it on the watch which ticked on the table beside him. "It beats with mine! I know her heart beats with mine. Maude, I have returned! Where is she?" The words became indistinct again and died away in confusion on his pillows.

Fargus, with a heavy heart, lit a candle, placed the watch where it could no longer disturb the patient, and once more applied the iced bandages. A knock at the front door and the approach of a firm, quiet tread on the stairs announced that welcome arrival.

Hurrying out to meet him, Fargus arrested the new-comer on the landing to explain the patient's state and the history of its causes with all possible brevity, after which he introduced him into the sick-room, and with a sad nod indicated the bed where the wounded man at that moment again started to a sitting posture, and, bending forward, held out his clenched right hand, with thumb extended, as though grasping a sword.

"There—there! No? I'll get at you, though." A terrific spring would have thrown him upon the floor but for the father's detaining grasp.

The doctor, a fresh-complexioned man of middle-age, with a thoughtful bald head and practiced keenness of eye, looked quickly from the fevered countenance on the bed to the pale one bending so anxiously forward.

"Your son, sir?" he asked, as he drew out his watch; then, without giving time for a reply: "Needless to inquire; the resemblance speaks for itself."

"Yes; traumatic meningitis I fear," he said corroboratively; then, as if in answer to a sort of gray, stricken look upon the other's face: "Not necessarily fatal. Your son seems to have a strong constitution—indeed, by your account, must be made of solid material to have done what he has done under the circumstances. Of course, that forced march in the heat, not to speak of the careless, insufficiently antiseptic treatment of the wounds, is sufficient to account for the present state of things. Much will depend on constant watchfulness. You must have a professional nurse."

"No, doctor; I mean to nurse my boy myself."

"Trained nurses are best in cases like these. Your son is delirious; he may be violent; he is a powerful man."

"I have experience of such cases. I shall manage him."

"But you will have to watch him day and night; it is too much for one person."

"I shall not leave him day or night. I have no objection to a trained helper," added Fargus, "and shall be grateful if you can send one over."

On the doctor's grave face there crept a look of sympathy.

"You must have your way, I see," he said with a transient smile, as he sat down to write his prescription; "and, on the whole, it may be your son's best chance. No one ought to be able to nurse him better than his father."

After giving directions for the treatment, promising to send a hospital attendant and to call early in the morning, the physician took his leave.

As soon as he had dispatched a servant for the medicines, Fargus came back to the bedside.

The bright eyes opened and looked at him with intentness.

"I must get up," said Lewis; "it will not do to be late at the rendezvous."

With gentle force the nurse pressed him down again.

"Lie still, my boy—lie still. Rest in me."

The touch of the father's hands, the soft earnestness of his voice, seemed to soothe Lewis for a moment.

A sudden hope sprang into life within Fargus' breast. He was not blind to the danger of his boy's state, and knew that few recovered from this terrible disease. But his boy should not die. Fargus remembered the influence he had so strangely exercised over him at their first meeting; it actually seemed as if this power would stand him in good stead now.

And day and night for a whole week the father wrestled for his son's life, catching the merest snatches of sleep on his chair (always holding one hot hand in his). It was evident that the same besetting theme haunted the poor unhinged brain throughout. Its ravings took the same course day after day—eager, restless pursuit; a transient ecstasy of joy. But never, even in his most violent frenzy, did Fargus' voice, look and touch fail in the end to soothe his son. The doctor called him a born nurse.

One morning, while Lewis slept, the fever fell. Fargus, sitting at the head of the bed, must have dropped into a doze. He was startled into wakefulness by the feeling of the patient's hand in his. It was no longer burning with the dry heat, but blessedly cool and moist.

Softly he rose to his feet and bent over the sick man. Lewis was sleeping quietly, with light regular breathing, and the beard was dewed with perspiration.

Fargus had kept up while matters were at the worst without unbending; the relief shook him with emotion. He noislessly walked to the window and glanced forth, crying voicelessly from the depths of his swelling heart, "Thank God!"

When he came back to the bedside, Lewis, awakened by the slight noise, opened his eyes and raised them to his face.

"Colonel Fargus," he said, in a very weak, weary voice.

"Yes, my dear boy."

"Have I been ill?"

"Very ill, for more than a week."

Lewis closed his eyes again, while his companion measured out some medicine. Then with slow deliberation:

"You have been here all the while?"

"Yes, of course. Drink this."

Lewis obeyed, with a faint smile.

"And you have been nursing me?" he resumed, after swallowing the mixture.

"Why, certainly, Robert Thompson; don't you remember I am your father?"

The patient paused to gather his wandering reminiscences.

"I remember, we were going to Brussels; are we there now?"

"Yes; I can have no more talking, or you will be ill again."

The young man was mute for a few minutes, then the unconsciously plaintive voice was lifted in gentle persistence:

"You have been very good to me."

"Fathers sometimes are to their sons."

"Am I to call you father, then?" with another feeble smile.

"Every one believes us to be father and son; you had better do so. And now I exercise my parental authority in ordering you to silence again, and if possible to sleep."

For a few days everything went smoothly. Lewis, at first so weak, seemed to gain strength steadily. He slept much and ate well, and appeared to enjoy in placidity the happiness of returning health.

But after that there came a halt. With increasing strength came increased mental activity, and with the latter depression, loss of appetite—every night rising temperature.

The doctor owned himself puzzled. Lewis had been féverish, moody, irritable, and evidently in pain, and had at length fallen asleep with his throbbing head between his father's hands.

"I cannot make it out," said the physician. "He was on as fair a way to recovery as ever I saw. The inflammation is over, the wounds healing fast; and now these fever symptoms, this renewal of suffering—above all, his depression. . . . If we do not take care we shall have a relapse, and then— Have you any reason to think there may be something weighing on his mind?"

"He had a great disappointment just before this illness."

The doctor pondered. He had grown to take a deep extraprofessional interest in the case, and had an admiration for the devoted father; he did not mean to let their patient slip through his fingers.

"Can you do nothing to remove this mental worry?"

Fargus shook his head.

"We must change the treatment, rouse him, distract his mind and make it work in different channels. We shall have him up to-morrow, I think. A little fresh air will do him good. Mr. Thomson, you must do your utmost to keep your son from brooding. Such cases sometimes turn into melancholia."

During that night Fargus watched his son—unknown to the latter. As he heard him moan and toss in his sleep, or saw him, from his place of observation, staring with wideeyed misery into space, he swore to himself that, if human agency could encompass it, the woman whose name had been with such unconscious and pathetic frequency upon his lips should learn to love him as he deserved.

What could be her reason for refusing him? she who had known him for years. And how he loved her! In those delirious utterances of his, what a wealth of tenderness was there betrayed! what a devotion!

Where could she have found a match for him?

The more he thought the more convinced the father became there must be some misunderstanding at the bottom— that Maude, who had loved his boy in years gone by, who had seemed so heart-whole, save for her undisguised preference for her old comrade, could not be in earnest in thus blighting his life. Some mischief-maker might have come between them, and Fargus' brow darkened—serene-faced Charlie, who wanted her for himself, perchance? There was a task for the father; it was well he had returned in time to unravel the plot.

CHAPTER XIII.

"A BOLT FROM THE BLUE."

Toward the sunset hour of the next day Lewis sat on the balcony, propped with pillows, enjoying the evening breeze. The patient had been declared convalescent; the change from bed to armchair seemed to have been successful. There was no return of fever. Fargus' determination to keep him from brooding had been so delicately manœuvred, it was impossible for a sweet-tempered nature, like Lewis', not to be beneficently influenced by it.

M. Bocage, who had kept the sick-room supplied with fruit and every kind of delicacy, had begged for an interview to say good-by before leaving on a journey. The Belgian's jolly presence, hearty laugh, cheerful conversation, never devoid of mother-wit, had amused Lewis and shaken him out of himself.

The day had passed well; matters looked promising again to Fargus.

"It is cheerful to see your head out of its swaddling bands."

"By the way," interrupted Lewis, "did I rave at all?"

"Of course you raved," replied Fargus. "A good deal about fighting, as far as I could make out."

Lewis heaved a sigh of relief.

"I suppose I shall be plagued with questions about this face of mine."

"You are not, I hope, thinking of returning to England too soon. It will take you some time to recover completely; remember, it has been a touch-and-go business with you."

"I should like to get back in a week. There are things I must see to: that succession so unexpectedly devolving on me. And this reminds me, by the way, that my solicitors were to keep me acquainted with the progress of affairs. I wonder if they have written to Homburg."

The latter, resolved to keep the conversation off the unfortunate topic, answered without the slightest curiosity:

"Shall I write and have them forwarded?"

"That would be good of you. I must keep myself acquainted with the development of my fortunes, and whether my presence is required over the water."

"I hope it is not," said Fargus, forseeing that an early return might put a stop to the intimacy which had grown so precious. "You know," he went on, "I do not want to let you out of my supervision until you are really restored."

"Unless it be quite necessary, I have no wish to move. I have no superfluity of energy, and I shall inflict my company upon you as long as you will tolerate it. The debt I owe you is great already, yet I mean to eke it out still further."

Part of the pleasant hour was allowed to glide by in silence, as they watched the gorgeous copper sunset. By-and-by Lewis, who was languidly stretching himself in his armchair, went on again, as if in continuance of a private strain of thought:

"Convalescent after a dangerous, exhausting illness must be a delicious period when there is no canker of the mind to poison every thought of the future."

"That," said Fargus, in a quiet authoritative manner—"that is a thing, if you like, that I will not tolerate. Brooding is an indulgence it is your duty to deny yourself. You have been disappointed in one direction, in a matter near your heart, as you said, and as, indeed, your every look and word betrays. Do not think I have no sympathy there; I have had myself at least one such experience in days of old, and I don't mind telling you that I allowed myself to sink deeper than you under the discouragement. But man's fate is to struggle all his life for happiness. And, my dear boy, forgive me for telling you that it is unmanly to give up the struggle because a particular happiness appears unattainable. To a fellow like you, is there nothing in the world but a woman's love?"

Lewis looked up hastily, but Fargus went on steadily, never removing his firm, kindly gaze from his son's face:

"I know it is a woman who has caused this sorrow. I may say I guess who she is—is there nothing else in life to look to? Duty, for instance, which men like you can so well fulfill; study, which one of your attainments should prosecute to ever greater extent; fame to be achieved while you have still the spring of youth within you. Such things, I know, will not replace the love that is lost; but, still, they are worth living for. She who is truly loved can never be replaced, for she has been invested in our eyes with everything we look for in woman. But it behooves a man to remain worthy of the one he has chosen, although he may have given up all hope of winning her. I would not even urge you to try and forget. You have much that you cannot lose —a good name, a past honorable achievement, as I heard before I met you, and in attainments, as I found out for myself. Is it worthy to give yourself up to profitless pining?"

Lewis had listened with a dreamy look.

"You are right," he answered simply, glancing up with a

grateful smile. "I have been hard hit; all I can undertake is to try. It is good of you to speak to me like this. Forgive me for asking, but what is it makes you take such interest in me? Why are you so kind? Our acquaintance is of short standing; outside events have made it intimate, thus far all the services have been on your side."

A shade came over Fargus' face. But he answered with resolute cheerfulness:

"I might reply that, having found in foreign parts a pleasant companion, I naturally learned to take an interest in him. But when I find in that companion a friend of friends, and one of the few relatives I know of mine in England— for my family, Mr. Kerr, is a distant offshoot of yours—one whom I expect to see much of later as a country neighbor, my interest in him becomes even less wonderful. Now let us, if you will, come to an agreement, and then drop the subject: for the time which we are destined to spend together, never ask me why I wish to be kind."

Lewis extended his hand silently, and the other clasped it with warm pressure.

The invalid took his lecture to heart, and made persistent efforts to respond to his companion's bracing cheerfulness. The latter kept the tenor of the conversation on vigorous subjects—army matters, travels, adventures and sport, the qualifications, duties and responsibilities of a landed proprietor, and all other topics he could think of with so much tact and variety, that Lewis never suspected he was being kept in intellectual leading-strings.

On the morning of the third day after that evening conclave Lewis was in his room dressing. He was sitting in his shirt-sleeves, taking a rest and looking more placid than he had ever done since their acquaintance, when Fargus brought in a letter.

"Just the one I expected," said Lewis, glancing at it. "I dare say you will have to help me to make out its meaning. Legal English will be more than I can master at present."

He leisurely opened the envelope, while Fargus remarked, after scanning the heavens, that it would be a perfect day for their first drive; that the carriage would come round in an hour.

Receiving no response, he turned round to find his son, with ashen lips, staring, as if in petrified amazement, at the open letter. Then blood suffused the young man's pale face; he started to his feet with a strangled exclamation of anger, only to grow white again and stagger back with a sudden failing of strength.

"What is the matter?" cried Fargus, rushing toward him

and seizing his hand, which was cold and clammy. "Here, take some brandy," hastily pouring a little in a glass and forcing it to his lips.

Lewis drank the dram and seemed to recover himself. Putting Fargus away from him with a mechanical sweep of his arm, he began to peruse it again with the most earnest attention.

After a little while Lewis looked up with dazed eyes and seemed to catch sight of Fargus for the first time.

"I can't make it out, all the letters jump about so. Will you please read it to me—slowly."

With a vague presentiment of evil Fargus picked up the letter.

"'From Perkins and Stubbs, Lincoln's Inn Fields. *Re* Gilham Estate. Private and confidential.'

"'DEAR SIR: We think it would be strongly advisable for you to return to England as soon as you conveniently can. Circumstances have come to our knowledge with reference to the above which we feel certain will cause you as much surprise as they have to us, and which we think will require your immediate attention.

"'Mr. Charles Hillyard called on us this morning to obtain our advice on the question of heir-at-law to the late William Kerr of Gilham. It would seem that he is in possession of documents which he strongly believes must establish his claim to the succession, by entail, over your head, on the plea . . .'"

The steady voice faltered as the meaning of the words was borne in upon the reader; he broke off with a deep exclamation.

There was a silence. Lewis muttered without looking up:

"Go on, I am beginning to understand. I must hear it all."

Fargus clenched his fist. It was a rare experience for him to be strongly moved by anger. But an almost murderous fury against the man who dared to cast such an insult at his boy shook him to the very depths of his being. "Oh, to have him by the throat, kin though he be, within the grasp of these strong hands!"

"Please go on," said Lewis again.

It required all the elder man's force of will not to betray himself now. With a wonderful mastery over his voice he began once more, glad that his boy, absorbed in his own turmoil of thoughts, could not notice the change which he felt on his own face.

"'. . . of illegitimacy on your side. We had to inform

Mr. Hillyard that as we had hitherto always acted in your interest, and especially as you had requested us on the death of your uncle, previous to your departure abroad, to watch over your affairs, we could not undertake to act for him in the matter. We informed him we should communicate with you. We gather that Mr. Hillyard is anxious to come to an amicable settlement by private agreement. More information we cannot give you, as Mr. Hillyard was naturally very reticent.

" 'Hoping to hear from you at your earliest convenience,
" 'We are,' etc."

He read on to the end without faltering. Here was a Nemesis indeed! The sin of his selfish youth had found him out at last.

Who would believe him if, as a last resource, to prevent a flagrant injustice, he were obliged to come forward and tell the true history of David Fargus and George Kerr? What a train of miserable, humiliating, ridiculous litigation, if nothing worse, such a course would entail, and with what slender chance of victory! And if it failed, how ignominious, how dishonoring! nothing short of criminal conspiracy in the eyes of judges and laymen, between two men hitherto held as models of honor!

"Thank you," said Lewis in a loud voice, after a while, lifting his head again and looking at his companion.

It was a haggard, drawn face, with the stamp upon it of his recent fight against death; but the father's heart swelled as he marked the look of proud composure it now bore.

"Thank you; I wish you would be so good as to leave me to myself a little. I must think."

Fargus, with a sad look, was about to comply in silence, when Lewis, struck by the alteration of his features, caught at his hand.

"Why, you seem quite upset yourself! You are very good to me."

Fargus wrung his hand.

"You mean to fight it out, my boy?"

"To the last penny of my fortune," answered Lewis.

When Fargus returned he was calmer and more hopeful.

Scanning the past in minutest detail, he could not recollect anything, save the unfortunate fact of his reputed suicide to support the extraordinary charge. On the other hand, the position his son had always had in the Hillyard family, his nearest relatives, would be strong presumptive evidence in his favor; that none of them had doubted his right to the name until it became profitable to the next-of-kin so to do—one who had always up to this cheerfully claimed cousinship with him—might go some way toward shaking the latter's credit, whatever "proofs" he might have collated in his greed.

It was balm to Fargus to see his boy determined to take up the fight for his own and his father's honor.

When he came back to Lewis' room, and found the young man bent more doggedly than ever on resistance, more sullenly fierce against the treachery that cast the slur upon him, there was also a new satisfaction. The shock seemed to have had, on the whole, a bracing effect upon the sick man, by instilling a healthy combative tone into the brain. There was some color on Lewis' face; he walked his room with head more erect and a firmer tread.

"I have no proofs to stake against Charlie's documents, whatever they may be—curse him!" he cried, stopping in front of Fargus, and striking the letter as he spoke. "What proofs can a man have whose father died before he was born, whose mother died in giving him birth? I am George Kerr's son, and my mother was as pure as yours."

"I know it," said Fargus, looking deep into his eyes.

Lewis was too much comforted to notice the strangeness of the words.

"Ah, Colonel Fargus! what should I do without you? Yet I have no right to weary you."

"Lewis," said Fargus, "you are my fictitious son, remember, so forgive this familiarity, and I do not conceal from you that you have grown dear to me since we two have been thrown together. I am a lonely man—there is no being in this whole world that David Fargus can claim kindred with—and you, not so desolate, stand likewise somewhat strangely dependent upon yourself. Let me see you through this new trouble. I have a cool head and a free one, while you must not overtax yours, as yet, and a man will require all his wits to unravel Master Hillyard's tangle."

Lewis' hesitating expression vanished under the deep sympathy.

"You heap benefits upon me. I can not refuse the offer of your help and friendship at such a moment. You are right, Colonel Fargus: I am alone in the world—utterly alone. I thought I had lost so much, I had at least a trusty friend left. What a fool thing he has turned out to be!"

"Perhaps," suggested Fargus, "we are making mountains out of mole-hills."

"I have no doubt it is trumpery," said Lewis abstractedly; "but clever trumpery, coming from that quarter; and trumpery carefully elaborated in the dark may be difficult to disprove. I believe I had lost everything when—when we first met. Now I find I had still to lose the only real friend I ever made. In your case, the kindness has been all on your side. Charlie and I were chums for years. Curse that succession, it has lost me my old comrade, and may now lose me my name—the name I have been so proud of.

"Now I understand the change I found in Charles when I met him, though he tried to blind me to it. Let him look out; I have a greater stake than he: he fights for money, I for my name."

There was a long silence in the room.

After a painful spell of cogitation, Lewis spoke again:

"Yes, I will fight it out, were it only for my dead mother's sake. I must return to London as soon as possible."

"I cannot think of letting you travel for several days. Correspond with your lawyer from here. Write to-day, stating your determination, announcing your return for next week. Shall I pen it, and you will sign?"

"Yes," returned Lewis, after consideration; "I shall require strength and all the wits I possess to fight a man like Charlie—amicable settlement, forsooth! It makes me sick at heart to think of the fellow I had placed on such a pedestal plotting against me above-board, since he, who was the first to announce to me the turn affairs had taken at Gilham, never gave me the slightest hint of his intention to try and ruin me—worse than ruin me! I don't feel very strongly about the estate, but I will not have my mother's good fame sullied. And, above all, I will not have my father's name taken away from me. I never knew him; but my grandfather, and, later on, my father's sister, taught me to be proud of him; and pride in my name has become a sort of religion with me. I will tell you some day all I know about them— meanwhile, you must help me to get strong again. I am not yet fit to undertake business."

"No," said Fargus, with renewed concern; "to-day is devoted to fresh air, and I hear the carriage at the door. We shall be back in time to write to London."

During this constant companionship Fargus had ample opportunity to learn more about his son's affairs, and, incidentally, something about those of his other relations.

The father, as soon almost as he had read the letter of ill news, had come to the conclusion that here was the clew— here the reason of Maude's incomprehensible repudiation of her old love. Charles Hillyard had remained at Gilham; he was to have dined at Woldham the very night of the funeral; as the elder man remembered now he must have been quick indeed to work his evil purpose for the news to have reached

Maude so soon. Yet it was like the general's impetuosity, more especially if artfully worked upon, to lose not a second to write in warning to his darling.

Meanwhile Lewis, on his side, had drifted toward deeper suspicion of him. Was it not possible, even probable, that Charlie—since he was capable of double-dealing at all—might have played him false in other quarters? The strange discovery on the night of their meeting had forced a portentous confession out of him. Since he could lie at all, he might have lied about Maude—ay, and to her!

The more Lewis thought of her sudden coldness—that coldness tempered with compassion which had struck him as so hopeless—the more he came to fancy he saw through it the handiwork of his false friend.

And thus, contrary to Fargus' first misgivings, the shock of this bad news did not retard the progress of recovery. Day by day the doctor was able to report progress, and at the end of the week felt justified in sanctioning the return home.

"I can only offer you a little room in an old, rather dilapidated Inn," said Lewis, while his face brightened at the prospect with a look of pleasure; "but I undertake to supply you with good books, good wine, and good cigars, and you will see London from a less conventional point of view than from a West-End hotel. I can make a show of returning your hospitality."

"It will be a fit sequel to my journey in search of novel impressions," replied Fargus, hugging with delight the prospect of a prolonged course of intimacy.

CHAPTER XIV.

DEA EX MACHINA.

London again, on a tawny September afternoon. Beautiful, at least to the two travelers whom a hansom has just disgorged in front of the massive gateway of Staple Inn: to Fargus, filled with the memories and emotions which a return to England each time awakened; to Lewis, who had a cat-like attachment to his old haunts.

The friends felt nothing but a healthy hunger as a result of the short day's travel, and had agreed to proceed at once in quest of food, after depositing their luggage at the inn. But on their way out Lewis paused a moment to give directions to the jovial, red-faced, red-waistcoated porter anent the preparation of his rooms.

The young man, having concluded his instructions, was about to hail his companion, when the porter stopped him, and, looking full of importance and mystery, observed in a confidential whisper:

"Beg pardon, sir, I don't know if you'd like the other gentleman to hear, but there has been a lady here twice already to inquire after you."

"A lady? What sort of a lady?"

"Young lady, sir, smartly dressed—that is all I know, sir," said the porter, with just the suspicion of a twinkle in his eye. "She wanted to see you *most* particularly."

"Why—who on earth— Did she leave no name?"

"No, sir; said you would not know it if she were to, and wanted to know when you'd be back."

"This is mysterious. You are sure she meant me?"

"Oh, no doubt about that, sir; she said Mr. L. G. Kerr."

"And you are sure it was a *lady*? What was she like?"

"Tall, well dressed; seemed a handsome kind of lady—can't tell you more nor that, sir. She called again yesterday in a hansom. I told her you would be back to-day, and she looked pleased and asked at what time you might likely to be in."

"Well?"

"That I couldn't tell; she said she would try and find you at home."

A man who consorts with a high ideal has rarely grounds to dread the specters of past pleasures. Lewis Kerr did not need to waste time in analyzing his recollections.

"Well, then, if this person calls again when I am in I will see her; if I am out, ask her to fix an hour." And turning to Fargus he took his arm, and they crossed over to the Bull Inn in quest of their meal.

"And who is she?" asked the latter carelessly.

"I really could not tell you," answered Lewis. "Some young lady anxious to meet me. I cannot think who it can be."

Fargus shot a swift, anxious look at him, but felt rebuked as he met his son's clear, straightforward eyes.

After an old-fashioned English repast they returned across the road and mounted the twisted flight that led to Lewis' *pignon sur rue.*

"Well, Mr. Thomson, father mine," cried the latter as he ushered Fargus into his rooms, "this is my English home— a poor thing, sir, but mine own—indeed, the only home I have ever known in my paternal country. Come what may, of this at least I am master, and, humble as it is, I trust you will look upon it as yours also."

Fargus crossed the threshold of his son's little home in a silence that he could not break. Then, standing in the middle of the room, he slowly scanned the surroundings with a tenderly appreciative eye. The curious retreat might have been that of bookworm, student, or philosopher, to judge from the mass of volumes that lined the walls from floor to pent-up ceiling; or of artist, to go by the quaint, motley furniture, the odd relics of antiquity, the pictures, the "curios"; but for the extraordinary order and neatness more characteristic of the soldier, with which every corner of space was utilized without crowding the modest limits. A home, thought the father, exactly fitted to its owner.

His pleased and wandering gaze suddenly became fixed as he caught sight of the pictures over the mantel-shelf. He walked across the room to look more closely. His own portrait and Carmen's. What a beautiful creature she had been! Since he had known his son, David Fargus had never had another harsh thought for his dead wife. And underneath those two well-remembered portraits, the sword, the Highland dirk and medals, and other chattels which had belonged to George Kerr.

David Fargus felt his eyes moisten as they fell upon these relics of his own past, so piously collected and enshrined in his boy's lonely home.

The young man came up and followed the direction of his eyes.

"That is my father's portrait," he explained gravely, "taken when he was about my own age. Was he not a fine fellow? And that is my poor young mother. Damn that cur who is trying to cast infamy upon her memory! Now tell me candidly, Colonel Fargus, do you see the likeness between my father and me?"

He placed his back to the chimney-piece and stood under the picture, looking eagerly at his companion. Fargus remained a moment lost in thought, comparing, with heaven knows what sadness and pride, the young, expectant face of the living with the painted image of the supposed dead. But the father was pleased to see one, and there was no mistaking the conviction of his assurance.

"You are like him—very like, dear boy."

"Not such a good-looking fellow, of course," said Lewis, with a blush of pleasure. "Still I always thought there was a look of myself there. I am glad you see it too. Now sit down in my own armchair. It is time for your smoke. Which will you have, pipe or cigar?"

"A pipe. It is more homely, and I already feel so much at home," replied Fargus, who sat down, with a contented sigh.

"Would you like this one?" he asked, producing a very black clay pipe mounted in silver and amber; "it is one of my few heirlooms; no one but myself has ever used it since I had it. I treasure it as the apple of my eye. I will trust it to your hand."

He placed the object in Fargus' outstretched palm—the identical grimy pipe, the trusty friend, under whose soothing influence that first self of his had awakened from the madness that led to death, so many years ago now, before its present owner had seen the light of day! Fargus looked down at it with dilating eye.

"It was my father's," said Lewis, here interrupting the flood of reminiscence, with a smile at his companion's mute solemnity of contemplation; "that is why it is so precious to me. It came to me with all the other things when I set up my college rooms. Mrs. Hillyard, his sister, you know, who had preserved them for me, used to say it was his favorite pipe."

Fitting the amber mouthpiece to his lips with an odd familiarity, Fargus lit that memorable relic and sank back in his chair, while Lewis rummaged about the room.

At last, when everything was again in the absolute order, of the picturesque as well as handy kind, he sat down opposite his guest, and filled a pipe for himself.

"I am tired," said he, enjoyably drawing his first puff. "I am not quite so robust yet as I might be. I am glad to think I shall have you at my elbow in all these affairs."

"So am I. I am as much interested in them as you are."

"It is very odd," said Lewis; "I am so accustomed to look to you for help it all seems perfectly natural. But, still, it is most extraordinarily self-denying of you, when I come to think of it.

"This suspense is wearing, though I try not to brood over it too much. Let us hope I shall learn something definite at Perkins' to-morrow. Hallo! who goes there?"

A smart rattle, as of some one tapping with a stick or umbrella. Lewis, full of curious anticipation, went to open the door, but the next moment, with a stifled exclamation, stepped back into the room.

A young woman, dressed with quiet simplicity in soft pale gray, with a large black Rubens hat, wreathed with many falling feathers, on her shapely head, a gray parasol in one hand and a somewhat bulky reticule in the other, stood on the threshold against the light of the stair window.

On hearing Lewis' ejaculation, Fargus rose and hastily advanced, only to halt in his turn with every sign of the most unmitigated astonishment.

"Miss Woldham!" he cried.

The visitor, who had seemed inclined to beat a retreat, on sight of the elder man, recovered her self-possession as he spoke. With great deliberation she walked into the room, looking from one to the other with a slowly dawning smile of peculiar significance. Lewis was the first to find out his mistake—he had been tricked again by that resemblance!— and frowning upon Maude's double, stood waiting with impatience for her next move, while Fargus, all at sea and shaken out of his usual self-possession, surveyed the newcomer with eyes in which wonder was now melting into joyful anticipation.

"Look again, old gentleman," their visitor said, "are you sure I am the real Miss Woldham?"

At this Fargus entered upon a new amazement, to give place to an expression of the most complete mystification. Maude Woldham never spoke with that twang, that vulgarity of diction, however strangely similar the tones of the voice might be; nor had Maude Woldham's eyes—as he examined closer—that unflinching stare; nor were the beautiful lines of her face so boldly marked. But if not Maude Woldham— who, in the name of heavens?

"This is Mr. Kerr's rooms—L. G. Kerr—ain't it? because that's the person I've come to see."

She turned to Lewis as she spoke.

"And you're the man, I take it?" she pursued.

Lewis glared at her without answering—was it a planned insult of Charlie's?

Fargus came to the rescue with a sudden intuition of some of his son's feelings. "These are Mr. Lewis Kerr's rooms, madam, and, as you have guessed, this gentleman is Mr. Kerr himself," pressing his hand in friendly warning on the young man's shoulder. "He has been very ill—is not yet strong. Will you not take a seat?"

"Thanks, I will," responded the lady, taking possession of the armchair, and tossing reticule and parasol on the couch. Once more addressing Lewis, while she proceeded leisurely to divest large but well-shaped hands of their long gloves: "Oh, my!" she remarked, "these are funny stairs of yours," bestowing pleased and smiling looks upon her astonished hosts.

Lewis and Fargus exchanged a glance of amazement; the latter was beginning to enjoy the humorous side, and a rather dry smile wandered about his mouth.

"And so you are Mr. Kerr. I am glad I have found you. You've just come back from Inja, haven't you?"

"Now that you are quite at home," with scathing politeness, "I presume I may ask what I owe the honor of your visit to? You appear to know a good deal about me; but I have yet to learn whom I have the privilege to address."

"You've never seen me before, then? Are you sure you've never known any one—something like me? Think well; that one over there seemed to think I was quite a friend of his at first."

The two men again exchanged a glance. But one thing was clear to both; the girl knew perfectly to whom it was she bore so marvelous a likeness.

"You do look cross!" still tauntingly fixing Lewis; "perhaps it was a little cool my bouncing in that way. But there's one thing I wanted to find out for sure. And didn't I do it, too? I'd rather not have found it out so true. And shall I tell you how? I saw it written on your face, Mr. Kerr, even before the old gentleman was kind enough to say it for me."

There was a pause. Lewis threw himself on his stool and folded his arms with the air of one who resigns himself to a trying infliction.

"I shan't try your patience," she said gravely. "I have come here on a serious matter to you—and to me;" this with a sudden hard compression of her full red lips. "To begin with, my name's Hilda Hillyard—Mrs. Hillyard."

Neither Lewis nor Fargus was able to restrain a movement of surprise.

The girl looked from one to the other with a bitter defiance.

"What makes you both gape at me like that? If there is any reason why I should not be Charles Hillyard's wife kindly mention it."

She waited for a reply; receiving none, broke into scoffing laugh.

"Maybe you've heard of him paying his court elsewhere?" —her lips trembling as she spoke. The friends became lost in amazement; their visitor, who had leaned forward to watch their faces, fell back with a sigh of relief. She resumed, after a pause:

"You've heard nothing? I am glad of it. You're surprised he should marry me because I'm not a lady. You're right, I'm not; now I don't mind telling you I'm not his wedded wife, though it's well-nigh four years that I've been as good as one to him."

The silence that ensued seemed to gall the reckless speaker.

"Perhaps you're that particular, you'd rather not have anything to do with me? I am afraid you'll be sold in the end."

The brazen look was as a cold douche to Lewis. He turned

away his head with vexation. Fargus, more tolerant, more far-seeing, cast a grave, not unkind, glance upon the girl, under which her eyes fell; the bold, handsome features worked with sudden emotion.

"I'm not ashamed of what I have done. There's many a fine lady, who flaunts about the court, and shakes hands with the Queen, has not as clear a sheet to show as me; many a wedded wife hasn't been as true to her husband as I have to Charlie. I don't care whether he marries me or not, but he don't leave me."

Her face set into a look of determination. She looked straight before her, dropping each word slowly with emphatic meaning.

"We are quite in the dark," put in Fargus gently. "Why should Mr. Hillyard leave you? And—forgive me if I appear rude; but what has this to do with us?"

Fargus' manner seemed to please. She smiled upon him broadly, and, with a childish change of mood, replied almost gayly:

"Why, it has a good deal to do with that young man. I've come to tell him about it; but he's cross. Come now, that's better—you look a deal nicer when you're good-tempered. And you'll live to thank me on your bended knees before I've done. But"—looking wise—"as it is something private and confidential, I'd better know who the old gentleman is. Will you introduce him?"

In answer to an acquiescent glance Lewis complied with the request.

"I'm not much the wiser," remarked the visitor candidly. "Look here, Mr. Kerr, you'll be just as much in a hat as me, if your friend was to split upon us. So perhaps you'd better send him away."

This was qualified with an amiable smile at Fargus.

The latter looked amused, but Lewis responded impatiently:

"Mr. Fargus is quite to be trusted; he is my adviser upon most important legal business at present. Anything you have to say to me must be said before him."

"It would serve you right if I were to leave you in the lurch. But I won't—first, because I believe you're a good sort; second, because I like the looks of him even better than you; thirdly, because it would not suit my book. You've important legal matters? Then, I dare say all my news won't be as much news to you as I thought."

Lewis bent forward. She surveyed him a moment with a malicious smile, and looked round the room.

"Why, I declare, if that isn't a tea-tray, with everything as handy as can be. Now, look here, you can smoke your pipes, if you'll let me have a cup of tea. I'm just dropping for it."

"It is not made yet," groaned Lewis. "I can get you some before long. In the mean time, perhaps, you will be kind enough to state your business."

"Now, don't you bother," said the damsel, rising. "You sit down there; you don't look over-well. I'll cook the tea." And with much neatness she proceeded to arrange the cups and light the spirit-lamp, perfectly at home. "This is like the place Charlie has at his college," she remarked.

"You have been to Cambridge, have you?" said Lewis, becoming rather tickled.

"Yes, once. He don't like my being seen there. They won't have ladies about the colleges—so he said."

As she stood up, leaning on the back of the chair, her hands behind her, the careless attitude displayed the magnificent lines of her figure in all their warm, firm perfection. Fargus stood watching the scene in silence.

The girl glanced over her shoulder and met Lewis' burning glance.

"You look as if you could eat me!" she cried. "Well, is that Miss Woldham better than me?" And with a bold movement she drew herself up and turned slowly round. After a second devoted to the enjoyment of the impression, she sat down by the table, and pursued with great composure: "I don't think she is. She may be a lady; a lady is only a woman; I know what sort of a woman I am, and I'm as good as her."

Then, with her broad smile, that displayed teeth of the most perfect regularity and whiteness, she again looked from one man to the other in that self-satisfied and good-tempered way, poured out two cups of tea, and handed them graciously.

"I wonder, now, if you think me cheeky to call on you in this way," she remarked, sipping her own portion.

"We are delighted with the visit," said Lewis gravely; "but I own I shall feel a desire to hear more of its purpose."

"Well, one of my purposes was to see the effect of my appearance upon you—it beats all I expected. You must be as bad as Charlie himself about that girl. That was one of the reasons why writing would not do. Now, to come to the other: I think you expect to come into a certain property?"

"Perfectly. I have come into one."

"Well, Charlie thinks he has found means of coming in for it."

"But if you can tell me how he hopes to keep me out, that would, I confess, be news, as you have it."

"It would be silly to ask," replied the girl, after the manner of a humorous proposition, "if you are really anxious to get that fine property, I take it."

"I mean to get it," Lewis replied, "for more reasons than one."

"We are of a mind on one point, because I mean not to let him get it, if I can prevent it."

"But," interposed Fargus, "what are your reasons? I presume he believes he has a good chance of success."

"My reasons," cried the girl, "is that I have found out his little game—I'm not going to be given the slip in this manner. I've been as good and faithful to him as any wife. I've always put him first and foremost. I've given in to all his fancies, and what do you think those fancies were?—why, to make me look as much as possible like that girl of his. What do you think his little plan now is? Why, to pension me off—who would have given him money if I had had it, earned it for him, if he would have let me—pension me off, that he might go and play the squire on his land and marry her; that's all. Now, so long as he has only his college-money to live on, she won't look at him; nor would he marry her on small means. And ladies, you know, ain't as easily satisfied as one like me; now you know my reason for wanting to keep him out of the property. I don't want none of these changes."

Lewis had grown crimson. "That girl of his" in connection with Charles, made him shudder. He rose and paced the room uneasily, for the first time dreading Charlie as a rival with burning jealousy.

"I won't let him go," she pursued doggedly. "Just fancy, making a dummy of me. But, won't there be a jolly row when he finds the papers gone!"

"What papers?" cried Lewis, coming to a standstill.

"Why, them papers I have brought to you. Just hand me my bag there, please." She tugged out of the reticule an immense envelope, bulky with inclosures, and tied together with string, and placed it on the table. "Now listen to me," she went on laying her open palm over the bundle. "It's a good turn I've come to do you, and before I let you have them—which I think you ought to be pleased to have—you must swear never to let on how you came by them."

"I don't know that I can in honor take advantage of this. How did you come by these documents."

The girl arched her straight eyebrows and looked at him, but aloud she ejaculated triumphantly:

"What! Not if they are actually addressed to you?" holding up the bundle so that Lewis could read on the envelope

his own name in the clear well-remembered handwriting of
his old guardian.

CHAPTER XV.

SUDDEN DEVELOPMENT OF BRAIN IN A DUMMY.

"My God! Uncle Robert's writing!" exclaimed Lewis in
fear and anticipation, and stretched forth his hand to seize
the parcel. The visitor enjoyed the situation too keenly to
relinquish it so promptly. She whipped the papers behind
her back.

"No, you don't, my lad; till I've had my say. Besides, you
want to know how I've come by them, first. If I can't show
you I've come by them honestly, perhaps you'd rather not
have them, though, if nicely cooked and dished up, I'll be
bound they can be made to prove that you've no more right
to the estate—nor to the name of Kerr, for all that—than
that gentleman yonder."

Quivering with impatience, Lewis turned to Fargus, and
the latter came forward and addressed the girl with gentle
authority.

"You are keeping my poor friend in cruel suspense. I
am certain that nothing you can have got hold of would
ever prove what you suggest, but you understand that those
letters must be of great importance to Mr. Kerr, as they are
addressed to him. Will you not give them without delay?"

"I won't tease him any more," answered she, "and he don't
seem strong enough to bear it. I'd like you to hear what I
have to say, first. I'd like to tell you how I came by them.
I don't care that you should think too bad of me. If I don't
have my say before you get hold of this, you'll be far too
busy grubbing at what's inside to listen to me. Now, don't
go on so, Mr. Kerr; it's as well, as I'm sure your friend will
agree with me, that you should learn what that cousin of
yours has been up to. May be, too, I'd like you to hear how
clever I've been, and how I've circumvented him. But first
of all, you won't split on me?"

"One instant," said Fargus; "will you allow me to speak
apart with my friend for half a minute?"

Receiving a careless nod of acquiescence in answer, Fargus drew his son into the inner room.

"You have confidence in me; leave me the management of
this. You do not realize what an extraordinary piece of
luck this is; a positive godsend! Let the girl have her own

way. The more she says, the more shall we learn of what might have remained sealed to us. She will prove an all-valuable ally."

"I hardly know if I am justified."

"Can you not trust your honor in my hands, Lewis?"

The young man winced under the glance of reproach. All he knew of his kind friend's honored past, rose up before him.

"Forgive me, I put everything without reserve in your hands."

"I accept the charge," answered Fargus.

They re-entered the room where Miss Hilda sat awaiting them.

"We give you our word of honor, as gentlemen," said the American, "that no one shall ever hear from us that you have been mixed up in this business. Does that satisfy you?"

"It'll have to do. I'll trust you, though I've small reason to believe in a gentleman's honor. Well, my name's Hilda Wren. For four years I've lived as Charles Hillyard's wife. The first time I saw him, up the river, I thought he was so handsome he looked like a prince. I said to myself, 'That's the man for me.' I loved him then, and I've never changed. I love him still, for. all his black falseness to me. He said he could not marry me, because the old fools at the University had made a law against Dons marrying. I know it's no longer so; I found that out too. He took a house for me in Vincent Square. Do you know the place? Anyhow, I've made him a nice cosy home there all these years, though it was dull to be so much alone. I'd have been glad to help him more; I could have earned money easy; there is not a swagger shop in London that wouldn't pay high to have me about. He wouldn't hear of it. I was to live like a lady— slow work enough I found it; but I saw him every week. We'd go out a drive together, go to the theatre, or a day in the country; and I was happy, and never a suspicion came till a fortnight ago.

"It was a small thing put me on the scent. I set to work then and made it out; my eyes are well opened now."

Despite the men's eagerness for their visitor to have said her say, with the unread bundle of papers and its contents hanging, a sword of Damocles over their heads, they could not help feeling sympathy with her.

"In August, Charlie had told me he was off a-yachting with a friend; I hadn't seen him for nearly a month. It wasn't true—he was at Gilham; I found it out afterward. A lonely month for me; no letters, not a bit of change. We used to go away somewhere at that time, the happiest bit of the

whole year to me. I thought he was having a holiday after
his hard work. As I'm telling you, it passed the middle of
the month, and Charlie turned up unexpected. Wasn't I
glad! When I think of it I could beat my head against the
wall! He looked ill, I thought, and worried like. It was
hot. I didn't mind his being grumpy, with the joy of having
him there. After tea, he went sound asleep on the sofa; I
didn't mind, either. I thought, 'He's real tired!' and went to
put a pillow under his head. I saw his pocket-book sticking
out of his pocket. A thought came over me I'd like to see
if he'd got my photo safe where we'd put it together in a kind
of secret place. He never felt me touch it, and I pulled it
out."

She caught her breath with a sort of gasping laugh.

"There it was, sure enough! I was pleased, and then I
had another happy thought. I'd had my photo taken while
he was away; an uncommon good one. I said to myself it
would be fun to put in one of the new ones instead of the
old thing. I pulled out the old photo from under the slab.
Guess what I found! Another photo underneath. I thought
it was one of myself, I never saw anything so like; but I
couldn't be such a fool for long. Well, I thought that he
kept it there just because it was so like me. Silly thing to
think. But I couldn't make it out; I thought he was still as
fond of me as I of him. I pulled it out; on the back of it
was written: 'To darling Susie from Maud Woldham, September 14, 1876,' the photographer some man in York. That
minute he stirred in his sleep, just as I was going to have a
look at the papers. I stuff everything back and lay the case
on the ground beside him, to look just as if it had fallen out
of his pocket. I went back to the window to think. I
didn't want him to know I suspected. If he thought I was
watching him, he'd be close as wax, he's so clever, I'd never
have a chance against him. I soon settled in my mind I'd
not let on, and there were three or four queer things about
it. First of all, the photo was given to his mother—I knew
her name was Susie; then, it was taken in York, and Gilham,
where his mother lived, is near there; so I said to myself,
'It's clear the girl comes from that part, too'; the date was
before he even met me; the girl's hair was done just the
same way he made me do mine when he knew me first. That
last set me thinking. After a bit he wakes up; when he finds
the book on the floor he gives a sharp glance at me; I was
smiling at him quite cheerful; he puts it in his pocket without a word. 'My girl,' says he, 'go and put on your bonnet
and we'll have some dinner. I've been debating whether I'd
start on a journey to-night; the business is important and

I've made up my mind it's better to go to-night.' 'Where are you going?' 'I'm going to Southampton,' he said, scowling at me, 'from there to the South of Spain.'"

"To Spain!" interrupted both men with a cry of amazement; Lewis looked across to Fargus with a bitter smile, and said:

"He is determined to leave no stone unturned."

Miss Wren caught up the remark and pointed it with characteristic directness:

"No, that he won't!" she cried. "Your mother was Spanish, wasn't she?"

"Yes," answered Lewis, reddening again with indignation.

"He's gone to rake up something about her. Don't take on like that. Who cares about what he may try to do—so long as he don't succeed? It's uncommon lucky for you I had my finger in his pie. You're beginning to find it more interesting than you thought. I begged hard to take me along with him to Spain, partly to see the face he'd make. I didn't believe a word about his going. I thought he was off again to Gilham. He said he couldn't. I asked him what he was going for. He said: 'Business, money matters. A relation of mine's dead. If I find out what I want, I ought to have his money.' I noticed he was in mourning. I began to think he *might* be telling the truth. 'Go and get your bonnet on—we have just three hours left together,' pulling out his watch. All my doubts of him came back. So when I came down-stairs to go out I listened outside the door, and peeped through the key-hole, before going in, and I could just see him as busy as possible stuffing letters and papers into his dispatch-box. When I turned the handle and came in he gave a start, shut up everything and quickly locked the box. 'Hilda,' he said, 'you see this box. It contains papers regarding that inheritance; they are very important; you must leave it at my solicitor's to-morrow. I am going to write a letter for you to take to him. I meant to leave it myself, but it was after hours; if I wait I'll miss my boat.' 'I'll do it,' says I. Then he wrote the letter for me. Then we went out for dinner. He was very nice. During dinner he pulled out his pocket-book to get a banknote, and laid it on the table. I took it up careless-like to look at it, to find out if he'd got my picture still, and pulled it about as if to set it straight. The other photo was gone. I knew then there was something behind it."

The narrator paused. Fargus, looking kindly at her, thought her face seemed pale.

"You are tired," said he; "you had better rest a little."

"I've not told you the half yet. I'm not tired; you don't

fancy these have been pleasant things for me? Not that a woman who has loved and trusted a man with her whole heart for years can find out he is a villain and feel none the worse for it! I love him; if I didn't I wouldn't be here. He'll always be the one man for me, and I mean to keep him. But it's been cruel hard. You haven't heard the worst, nor how I found him out. That girl's photograph, and the hurry he had been in to shove in the papers and the photo didn't let me sleep that night, after he was gone—it was to Southampton, after all. I went to the station and saw his ticket. The next day I couldn't eat, read, walk, work, or think of anything but that box. I sat down and stared at it from morning till night wondering what was along with that photo. I could stand it no longer. I fetched all my keys and tried them. Trust Charlie for a good lock on his secrets! Not one would fit. I thought I must find out, come what might. So I go down to the landlady, a shrewd body, and I say, over a cup of tea, in a careless way: 'There's a dressing-case of mine got locked with a snap and the key inside, and I've tried every key in the place. It's a Chubb lock. I'll have to break it open.' 'Don't you do that; take it over to the shop, they'll open it for you. We did that and got a new key and no trouble.' 'Give me the address and I'll go.' I took it coolly, never pretended it was anything of importance. As soon as I could I made off up-stairs, and off in a hansom with the box. To cut it short, I was that grand and airy at Chubb's the smart young man never dreamed of suspecting my story, but opened the box and measured the lock for a new key. I had to order a new one for appearances' sake. The lock does shut of itself. Back I got into my hansom. I couldn't keep my fingers out of the box, but rummaged in it all the way home. One thing I made out—the girl's photo was not in it; he had taken it with him; a bad sign.

"Soon as I got in I turned all the papers on my dressing-table and sat down. There was a big envelope tied up with your name on the top, Mr. Kerr, and lots of letters about business that looked dull enough; that was all. Nothing about the girl. I began to think I was sold; I turned over every nook. Then I took up this here envelope: 'Lewis Kerr, Esq.' 'Now, where the dickens have I heard that name?' Then I remembered you were that cousin he used to be such chums with. I used to wish you to Jericho, when you kept him away from me. That was in the first year I knew him. I could see nothing in these stupid lawyer's letters, so the papers he spoke of as so important must be in that packet, yet it was addressed to another man. I got curious and untied the string. There were a lot of letters and things inside;

you'll see it for yourself. I couldn't understand what there was so precious about them. One never knows what a man like Charlie can make of things. It didn't seem a bit interesting to me. What could it matter to Charlie about your father and your mother? The letter to you at the top said itself the papers were of no importance. So it was all queer he should be that anxious. I thought I'd read the business letters. I read them. They did tell me lots. The first thing was Charlie might come into a grand fortune. So it was true what he said. 'Now he can marry me.' Simple of me. Then I wondered why he hadn't wanted me to know. 'Hilda,' said I, 'read on before you make a fool of yourself.' The next thing became clear to me was it was your fortune he was after. That's how he comes to have the letters addressed to you. And yet I felt as if things weren't quite on the square. 'If he can play hanky-panky with his chum, it may be a bad look for me.' After that I opened the last lawyer's letter; I've got it in my pocket. I'll read it to you now, if you will give us some light."

Lewis rose to obey, and Miss Wren, who had been impatiently tapping her foot during this delay, spread out a crumpled letter under the light, and once more raised her voice with sarcastic emphasis:

"'Dear Sir: We think that it would be better if you would let us have the safe custody of the documents, as on them depends everything. It is advisable you should investigate yourself the registers of birth and baptism in Seville. Although we may look upon the proofs already in your hands as practically sufficient if utilized to their full powers, the matter would, of course, be settled beyond the possibility of dispute, should the date of the claimant's birth be found not to tally with the requirements of his case.

"'With reference to the young woman in question, we certainly opine that, considering the very handsome compensation you would, in case of success, be willing to offer her, you need anticipate little trouble. Meanwhile, we agree with you that the sooner an understanding is come to the better, and we shall be happy to undertake the necessary negotiations should you feel sufficiently confident of success to venture on the expense.'

"That is all; though my head went round as I read it, I said to myself: 'That's about that girl.' You may well look at each other; to think of me, such an innocent! 'That's all right,' I says; 'it's that girl.' I put up the papers and closed the box and went about the room singing, all the time I kept saying: 'It's that other girl he wants to get rid of.' All at once I knew I was lying to myself. 'I must find out for certain, or I shall die.' I made up my mind to open the letter he had given me to take with the box to the solicitor's. So I light my spirit-lamp and boil my kettle and hold the letter over the steam and open it as easy as anything, and after I'd opened it I stood staring at it, and, Lord bless me!

"I know that letter by heart. It's short. It went on this way:

"'DEAR SIR: I was not able to leave the documents with you, of which you have the copy, this afternoon. I steam to-morrow morning for Gibraltar, my dispatch-box, containing, among other things, the papers in question, will be left at your office. In default of a better messenger in my hurry, it will be brought to you by the young woman I spoke to you about. It may be as well that you should see her. In great haste, yours;' and so on.

"When I read that I seemed to go mad like. I rolled on the ground; I could have killed myself, only that it would have made things too easy for him. Then I read everything over again. I thought of everything. That Woldham girl was a grand young lady, for wasn't she his mother's friend? When he found he couldn't have her, he finds me, and I'm so like her, he takes me instead. That's why he made me do my hair so, and dress so particular—now like this, now like that; he never went yachting at all. All those letters were addressed to Gilham, and there he was, seeing her again, and making up to her. When he finds he can do a friend out of a fortune, and step into riches and grandeur, he'll cast off the wretched dummy, and get the real one! That's where he's wrong. I've sworn I'll keep him, and I will!"

Panting, she walked the room in a fierce manner, clenching her hands as she went, while the friends heard the sound of a suppressed sob. When she returned, and stood again within the circle of the light, she was dry-eyed, and the magnificence of her beauty struck them with fresh force.

"Did you ever see that Woldham girl in a dress like this?" she asked sharply, "or a hat like this?" sizing the black-plumed headgear that lay on the sofa, and planting it roughly on her head. "Answer, can't you?"

"I have only seen Miss Woldham for three years or more, and that only for a short while," answered Lewis.

But Fargus was more willing to humor the girl, the reason for which was so pathetic. He shifted the candles to examine her by a better light, and exclaimed in tones of surprised conviction:

"I do remember, now that you ask, I have seen Miss Woldham dressed just like you at Woldham. I used to think it looked as if it had come out of an old picture."

"I knew it," cried Hilda Wren, stamping her foot. "All along he's made me dress like her. I'm a dummy, I tell you— a blessed dummy! But I'll make him smart for this," resuming her pacing about the room. "He always pretended to care so much about fashion. I was to wear this, that; one wants to look nice, and I never thought of anything except: 'Isn't Charlie proud of me!' Oh, what a blasted idiot I have been! I'd have torn the cursed things to bits and dashed it on the floor. I'd have torn the rags off my back, rather than have done it, if I'd known."

She paused, and suddenly her tragic airs fell from her.

"It was a good idea to put on those clothes he made me get last, and let you see me in them. Mr. Kerr seems bad; head aching, eh? I shan't be long finishing. I made up my mind to play a big game to prevent Charlie dropping me. 'I may whistle for him, if he gets the fortune, so I'm determined he shan't; nothing worse can happen to me; if he can't have her, he'll come back to me, sooner or later! There was a chance that way, and none the other. I thought it well over, and how I'd bring you the papers. My first idea was to burn them, when I'd reflected the papers were yours by rights, then I wanted to find out quite clear about that Woldham girl. So I had to go to the lawyers first, with the empty box. That old duffer, that was so free with his good advice about getting rid of troublesome young women—may be I'll worm something out of him, too. After a week, I'd everything clear in my head, and I began to think it time to settle my fine young man's business, when I got a letter to spur me up. It was as cold as you please, saying he hoped I'd done his commission; that he couldn't tell when he would be back—not for ever so long. That letter told me something else. He wasn't pleased with the way things were going over there. I knew by the crossing of his t's that he was fit to be tied when he wrote; I guessed that he was safe to be coming home almost immediately; and wanted to blind me, he did not mean to come here; it was plain that he was beginning the cooling-off business. My blood was up, and without any more ado I clinched the matter. I took out the packet of papers that meant a fortune to Charlie, a slap in the face for you, and the sack for me, and put them carefully in my hand-bag, locked the box, and buried the key in the garden. Then I fastened up the letter I was to bring to the lawyer; you'd never have known it had been touched. Well, I got there in time.

"'Mr. Hodgson in, young man?' says I. 'I'll see, madam,'

says he; 'what business, may I ask?' 'Say it's Mrs. Hillyard, please,' says I, 'and give him this,' and handed him the letter. Presently he comes back and says Mr. Hodgson would see me. And up-stairs I went, him carrying the box for me. There was a little old gent sitting at a desk; he was as like a weasel as ever I see. 'Sit down, madam,' says he. 'Is that the box? Put it down, William, and leave us. So you've brought this from Mr. Hillyard. I see this letter's dated a week back.' 'Couldn't come sooner,' said I, smiling at him. He frowned, but didn't seem to have a word to say. 'He gave it to me,' I said (talking of the box, you know), 'the day he went off. I didn't know it was so pressing till I got a letter from him this morning, saying he hoped I'd done his commission. He wrote from a place called Sevilla.' I thought, 'If I want him to speak up, I'll have to improve a bit.' So on I went again: 'I'm to call on you for something concerning myself besides—I'm sure I don't know why.' At that he was really taken in, as he was humming and hawking. That seemed to touch him up. 'Have you that letter here?' he asks, as dry as can be. 'No, I haven't,' says I; 'if I had, you shouldn't see it. I don't mind telling you that Charlie seemed uncommon jolly over his business there—and he says great things is coming.' I knew I'd have to tell a lie or two."

The girl's mimicry was marvelous.

"You'd have laughed a bit if you'd been there, especially if you'd known what I was up to. Then I went on: 'I haven't come here to be snapped at with cross-questions, and it's a pity for me to waste this lovely afternoon in this stuffy little hole of yours. I've done the job as Charlie told me. If you've nothing to say, it don't matter. I suppose I shall hear all about it when he comes back.' I jumped up and made believe to go. 'Wait a bit, madam,' says he, waving his hand. 'I have something to say, rather of a delicate nature, so I must beg you to listen to me quietly. When I have done, you will see it is all to your advantage, on the whole.' 'Now for Charlie's handsome compensation,' thinks I. 'The case is this,' says the old man. 'Mr. Hillyard has explained to me the nature of his relations with you. You know they are such as cannot last forever.' 'No, I don't,' said I. 'You should know it, madam. Mr. Hillyard's connection with you is not what his family or friends would approve of.' 'You mean,' said I, 'that I'm only kept. I'll have you know,' I said, 'that Mr. Hillyard would have married me years ago, only he'd lose what he calls his fellowship if he did, and that's worth a pot of money to him.' 'My dear young lady,' he says, 'it would be false kindness to allow you to mistake your position, but it's more than a year since that regulation's been done away with.'

I couldn't speak, for that came hard on me, I own. 'Without any further beating about the bush, Miss Wren, I must inform you Mr. Hillyard's life is about to change. He has come, or is about to come, into some landed property. He will have to reside in the country and undertake the duties of his new position.' I knew right well what he meant. 'Well, I don't quite see what that's to do with me; I don't mind—I was brought up in the country myself.' 'This is wasting my valuable time, Miss Wren,' said he. 'Mr. Hillyard has been some time in coming to his resolution, but has made up his mind, and he has charged me to let you know it, that there might not be too much sentiment.' I kept up my part well. 'So he has made up his mind to drop me, has he? Suppose, now, I mean to stick to him.'

"The old man told me I'd be a fool for my pains, for I'd lose the compensation Charlie was ready to give me, and he jawed a lot about the impossibility of my being able to bring in a breach of promise (as if I would try such a thing!) after living with him four years. Well, after a good deal of talk, he tells me the compensation Charlie 'll give me is three hundred a year, as long as I never come near him, or write, and I left him, saying I'd think over it all. He stood looking after me, grinning and rubbing his hands, and thinking himself so jolly clever. And me going off with the papers in the bag on my arm!

"Don't you think I am a fool not to take that compensation? Do you know, that lawyer fellow said I could make a real good marriage with such a fortune?"

She sprang from her chair and flung the papers across the table to Fargus, who caught them between his hands.

"Now you can have them; I've done with the things. And I'll make off with myself; it's getting late."

Brave as she was, her voice broke a little.

"Don't look at me like that!" turning on Fargus; "don't pity me—I can't bear it." But before he could answer she had recovered herself. "Not a looking-glass in the place," she observed, planting her hat on her head; "just like a man's room? Good-by, Mr. Kerr; I'm real sorry to see you look so ill. And good-by, Mr. What's-your-name. I believe you have the brains of both of you under your hair, for I am blessed if that young friend of yours seems to know if he's standing on his head or his heels. Perhaps you won't mind dropping me a line some time to say how the whole affair goes off, and what Charlie's up to. He'll be fit to murder me."

"I shall certainly write if you wish," answered Fargus, shaking her warmly by the hand; "but where to?"

"Send your letter to the Keppel Head, Vauxhall Bridge Road, care of Miss Polly Evans. I've your word you'll never let on to Charlie? Sooner or later he must find out it was I who took these things; but I'd as lief he never knew of this visit of mine to you."

"He never shall know from us. You have laid my friend under great obligations, Miss Wren. If ever I can be of use to you in any way, do not hesitate to write. I will in my turn give you my address in the country. Mr. Kerr," he added with a smile, after penciling his direction, "is rather too young to be able to befriend you. But an old man like me has his privileges."

She took the card and gave the speaker a grateful glance.

"You're real kind," she said. "I trust you a long way, for all I've only known you a couple of hours. You have a true friend there, Mr. Kerr; you're in luck. Good-by. I'll get a cab for myself."

The door closed after her.

CHAPTER XVI.

"LITERA SCRIPTA MANET."

The father and son stood facing each other, too full of thoughts for speech. Fargus broke the silence.

"A strange turn in our affairs," he said, "but one which will wonderfully simplify matters."

Lewis sat down with an unconscious gesture of bewilderment.

"The whole business is sickening. I seem no better than Charlie. We should have told her that we declined to have anything to say to such underhand ways."

Fargus held the papers in his hand, with a troubled eye. Was that sensitive honor of his boy to be now another obstacle to overcome? Difficulties lay on every side.

"Lewis, this is overstrained. Are not these papers addressed to you? Are they not yours by right?"

"Give them to me, then. I may as well know the worst at once. I make a poor return to you for all you have done to me."

"You are weak and ill," said the father, "and sorely tried, or I confess your want of confidence would be wounding. Come, my boy; leave the perusal of these documents to me."

Lewis rested his throbbing forehead on his hand;

"Let me see my uncle's letter, at any rate," he said doggedly.

"You could not read it. I can see by your manner that you are almost blind again with headache."

In compliance with a nod of assent from his companion, Fargus pulled the letter out of its envelope. "What if the elder Hillyard were to bring the same indictment as the younger?" It was impossible further to combat Lewis' feverish determination, and he began to read aloud in a voice that grew firmer as he proceeded. The letter was dated a couple of years back, and ran thus:

" 'MY DEAR LEWIS: It is nearly two years since you passed out of my tutelage; but, knowing that it was your wish, and especially that of my wife, I have continued to look after your interests in general. The hour is now drawing very nigh, however, when I shall have to resign all earthly charges. My doctor here, as well as the specialist I have consulted in London, both admit that my time is likely to be limited, and when this is received by you the great change will have taken place for me.

" 'Business matters, however, are not what I have now to write about; you will find, I trust, that all your worldly affairs are well cared for and managed by Perkins.

" 'After accepting the medical men's verdict, I set to work and put all my papers into final order, and in so doing I came across a bundle of papers, some of which concern you directly. These are the letters and other documents which came twenty-four years ago, before you were born. I considered it my duty to gather and to retain (for my own safeguard and justification), when, on your father's death, at my wife's request, I undertook to assist his helpless widow in her trouble, and began those relations by correspondence with your grandfather, Don Atanasio de Ayala, which ultimately led to my undertaking the duties of guardian to you.

" 'I have thought of destroying these papers. But I was restrained by scruples of conscience. Rightfully they are yours, and now my purpose in writing is to advise you strongly to burn this bundle unread. No good can come of raking up old family misunderstandings, the last effect of which has been visible in Mr. Kerr's persistently hostile attitude toward you. You will do wisely in leaving the past undisturbed.

" 'I cannot even send you this, as I hear with satisfaction that you have been allowed to volunteer for active service in Afghanistan. You will receive the packet, therefore, when you return to England, as I sincerely hope, safe and sound.

Let me say, ever since your grandfather on his death asked me to take an interest in you, I have watched your career with no feelings but those of satisfaction; I feel sure the rest of your journey through this life will be marked by the same sense of duty and moral refinement I have observed in you. In this hope I must say, what is beyond doubt, a last adieu to you.   Yours affectionately,

                         "'ROBERT HILLYARD.'

"My dear boy," said Fargus, looking his son full in the eyes, and throwing into his gaze and voice all the intensity of his desire, "you hear what this message from the grave tells you. Will you burn at once, or trust me to examine, these relics so unfortunately preserved. And if, on examination, I agree with your guardian, will you let me fulfill his wishes? Let us settle this business now and forever."

Lewis returned Fargus' gaze with a sort of fascination, and then slowly extended his hand as if in token of acquiescence. Without delay he withdrew into the other room, and, lighting a candle, perused the papers hurriedly. Every word of that farewell letter to Carmen was branded in his mind, but now, the plausible constructions which might have been put upon every bitter sentence seemed to flash out portentously.

He turned to the brief lines in which William Kerr repudiated his brother's widow, and his face burned with indignation at the brutality of their barely-veiled insinuations. What sudden working of fate, having brought back from the grave, by an extraordinary malice, this damning circumstantial evidence, now placed it within the grasp of the man who had been the unwitting originator of all the mischief?

These papers formed a chain of evidence almost complete against Lewis, and, aghast at finding that his own rash acts had, in the old days, forged the first and strongest links, David Fargus was seized with a perfect frenzy of impatience to destroy them while he had the power.

Beginning with his own and Carmen's letters, he held the yellow leaves to the flame and watched their glowing annihilation. The last blackened scraps of the squire's letter were vanishing under a licking tongue of fire, when Lewis entered the room.

"Colonel Fargus," he cried sharply, "what are you doing?"

Holding a crumpled bunch of paper over the candle Fargus restrained Lewis' hasty approach with an iron grip; then, the destroying element having invaded the last corner of the last writhing sheet, he turned to him with undisguised elation, and answered:

"Carrying out your guardian's direction. Listen, Lewis Kerr of Gilham; your case is as clear as the flame which has now consumed all this folly. Don't look at me with that stupefaction. These papers should have been burned long ago. I have done what it would have been your duty to the memory of your father and mother to do yourself."

"Oh, why did you not let me see them?"

"There was nothing but the history of a quarrel and of the circumstances which attended the death by drowning of George Kerr, your father. The reason I have burned them is because, morbid as you are, after your illness, you would have pored over those old letters till you made yourself ill again. I have burned them to keep them from you, as well as to insure their not falling into Charlie's hands again. Do you doubt me now? Do you doubt your mother, after all?"

Lewis' brow cleared. How could he have doubted, even for a moment?

He said so aloud with a shaking voice.

"Not mad, but upset by all this."

"Thank God, all's well that ends well, and your future is bright once more. Now," with a cheery change of manner, "it is past nine o'clock. It has been a long, eventful day. Let us go out and dine, after that to bed. Your head will rest the better for some supper and a good glass of wine."

CHAPTER XVII.

SCYLLA.

In that queer old attic, which to Fargus had already grown one of the pleasantest spots on earth, the two men sat the next morning over a late breakfast.

Outside the world was gloomy. The rain was dropping from the gabled roof and beating the casement.

Inside the quaint bachelor home looked the very shrine of comfort, and such had been Fargus' first thought as he emerged from his bed-room and found Lewis leaning against the chimney-piece quietly scanning the morning paper as he waited for his guest. Lewis Kerr, rich enough to gratify all his peculiar tastes, was pleased to surround himself with household items attractive to the eye. Tea was fragrantly brewing in a silver pot, which Fargus suddenly recognized as one of George Kerr's wedding presents; a rye loaf stood crustily inviting on an ancient and precious oaken platter; bacon and eggs reposed crisp on a Dutch plate. Lewis had slept soundly, and had awakened strong and refreshed to find life decidedly brighter and more interesting, in spite of damp and gloomy weather.

Fargus, on his side, perceiving the beneficial change in his son's mind, was not slow to respond to it. The morning meal was thus a cheerful one.

"I feel a different being this morning," observed Lewis, as he sat down to the breakfast table. "Upon my word, Colonel, though I was very angry, I quite see now how wise you were to keep those papers from me just then. You will have to tell me what was in them."

"Of course I shall," said Fargus, quietly sipping his tea. "It is necessary you should know all the facts of the case, for your adversary is pretty sure to introduce them to you under some vivid artificial light whenever he tries conclusions with you about this intended amicable arrangement."

None could have guessed from the speaker's manner how sorely his spirit quailed from the prospect. It was inevitable that on him should devolve the duty of preparing Lewis against the forthcoming revelations of Charles Hillyard. The night had been spent thinking over the simplest way of dealing with the case—to tell his son the story of George Kerr's suicide as set forth by these letters. But best that he should learn it from the lips of him who could argue with absolute conviction the falseness of Charles Hillyard's interpretation. The burden of the father's secret anxiety could not but be lessened to find Lewis in such healthy frame of mind that morning.

"I see no reason to repent my decision of last night. What was it Talleyrand said about letters? 'Give me three lines of a man's handwriting, and I'll hang him.' This shows what his masterly cunning thought of the capabilties of 'black and white' for being twisted to any purpose. Your cousin's scheme for utilizing these letters was too clever to justify me, as your adviser, in leaving them in existence an hour longer. I might have had a fit in the night, gone mad, or broken my neck; and, however sensibly you may be disposed to look on things this morning, I had good reasons to mistrust your quixotic turn of mind, not to foresee the possibility of your being tempted by specious arguments to give them up again. A soldier is notoriously a bad business man."

Lewis smiled at this lecture.

"I grant you," answered Lewis, meditatively, "you would prove a far better match than I for Charlie. Indeed, the gusts of anger I cannot restrain every time I think of him paralyze my common sense. I ought to thank Heaven it has been settled as it is; I can hardly imagine how I should have come out of it."

"I am deeply curious," said Fargus, "to see how Mr. Hillyard's game will go on now that the trumps are all in our hands. That young man is clever. He would play, I am sure, an admirable hand at 'poker.' I met him, as I told you, several times at Gilham, and noticed his striking face, though I cannot say I felt much attracted by his cold, calculating character, which for all his polish of manner, I could not help finding out somehow. As for you, all this business has been a rude awakening to the fact that a few friendships can stand the test of clashing interests. And yet yours was a friendship of more than usual closeness, was it not?"

"I can answer for my side, at least," said Lewis. "I looked upon him as the Breton knight of the legend might have looked on his *frere d'armes,* as the gold digger, your Bret Harte tells us of, looks on his partner; and besides this, to his influence I attributed whatever success I had at college. He was, in fact, my high ideal of the Englishman, in those days when all my eagerness was to make myself worthy of my country, I would have done anything for him. And now here I am, face to face with the fact that Charlie, for self-interest, steps from his high pedestal to the low level of pettifogging schemer."

"And this youthful fascination of yours," asked Fargus, leaning back in his chair, "this romantic affection, was it reciprocated?"

"We were great friends, though his liking for me was, of course, of a different kind; such as befited a coach toward his pupil, a thoroughbred Englishman toward a semi-foreigner, a man of standing toward one decidedly his junior. I really believe he would have gone out of his way to do me a good turn. And I have come to the conclusion," continued Lewis, "that money considerations alone could not have induced him to act so dishonorably. There must have been a stronger lever at work. Yesterday's revelations confirmed much that before I had only suspected. Colonel Fargus, it is useless for me to try to conceal what you know already, though I have never told it to you in so many words. I had reasons to think Maude Woldham might love me as I loved her. It has been the aim of my life to try and win her. When I heard of my accession to the Gilham fortune I started off after her to Homburg, at once, full of not unjustifiable hopes. I asked her to be my wife—and was refused. I believe that, had it not been for that slander on the question of my birthright, Maude might have remained true to her tacit pledge to me. How could she think of mating herself to a poor devil

whose very name is supposed to be his own only on suffer-
ance? There was pity in her eyes when she recognized me;
but that pity only accentuates the insult and the grief."

"All this may be true," said Fargus, quietly. "But instead
of fixing the past, fix the future. The elaborately-con-
structed plot which was to deprive you of the woman you
want, the name that belongs to you, and the fortune that
awaits you, falls to pieces now that its main prop has been
removed. What follows? You become one of the great landowners, the head of one of the oldest families in that part of
England which Miss Woldham brightens with her presence.
And with reference to what has taken place between you and
her, don't you think it better that she should have refused you
through some hidden reason which she could not tell you to
your face—perhaps, acting under some order written to her
by her father—than that her motive should have been mere
indifference? Her sense of generosity (I know the girl's
charming nature, for all that our acquaintance is but of a
few weeks' standing) when she learns the truth, will warm her
heart toward you more than the knowledge of your prosper-
ity. As for the father, from the drift of the conversation we
have had together, I know his dream would be to see his
girl happily married, if marriage did not take her away from
him."

"My dear Colonel," cried Lewis, "what good your talk does
me! I declare you are a very alchemist of the mind."

"By the way," said Fargus, smiling, "I came last night to
the conclusion that it really seems a pity to waste these autumn days in London. Our reason for remaining on here
has been happily removed, the best thing we can do is to
take a train for Yorkshire to-morrow or the next day. Moreover, it is time you should make act of presence on your
estate. If you do not care for the lonely splendor of the
Court, my shooting-box will give you the warmest of wel-
comes. I propose, then, to start myself to-morrow, and that
you should follow in a day or two. You must consult Perkins, and best by yourself, though all you need say is that
you believe your cousin's claim will come to nothing, and
that, since no active steps have been taken by the other side
as yet, you, at any rate, will quietly continue to act as if you
had never heard of it."

Lewis looked as if the proposal were tempting enough.

He said, after reflecting a while: "And if you will be so
good as to have me, I should rather go to you. I shall see
more of you; and, besides, I hardly like to go to Gilham until
it is evident that Charlie has abandoned the field."

"There need be no fear about that," answered Fargus, when

the sound of a letter falling through the slit of the letter-box attracted his attention.

"By Jove!" said Lewis, looking at the clock, "we are late this morning. Probably Perkins' missive to fix an hour for our interview."

Lewis proceeded in quest of the letter. When he returned he was holding the still unopened envelope in his hand.

"From Charles Hillyard," he said, briefly.

He tore the cover open and studied the communication for a few seconds, then tossed it with a dry laugh across the table to his companion, who sat watching him with some uneasiness. The letter contained a few careless lines in the small cramped handwriting peculiar to many scholars, and merely begged the recipient to fix the earliest date possible for an interview on matters of the utmost importance.

"Cool, is it not?" mused Lewis. "Not a hint of what he is up to, though Perkins told him he would write to me about the business."

"There is no need for you to see him, surely," urged Fargus. "This letter was written last night; he evidently knows nothing of the loss he has sustained. When he finds out that he has lost the trick, his rage will be fearful for a little while; and you, my boy, have got a hot temper of your own, too, and are not especially disposed to be deferential with him just now. I confess I am of opinion that it would be better to wait a while, and exchange your ideas by letter for the present."

"No, no," cried Lewis. "You have been right and wise in all your advice, but I cannot agree with you there. Why, Charles would think I am shirking the ordeal. Since I must see him, the sooner this hateful business is over the better. Besides," with a half-malicious smile, "I should rather like to see him before he makes the discovery of the empty dispatch-box. I am curious to hear his version of the case. I should not be sorry to give him a bit of my mind, either."

Fargus looked at his son, and there was a somewhat perturbed speculation in his eye.

"Excuse me," Lewis proceeded with great briskness, "there is the morning paper—I shall send a telegram to Charles to say I shall be ready any time after three to-day."

And, without waiting for an answer, ran out of the room. The well-assumed placidity of expression departed from Fargus' face. Charles Hillyard, whether cynically self-confident or maddened by disappointment, might say things to Lewis which might be as hard to disprove as they would be cruel to hear. And it rested with the father to try and explain away to his boy in some plausible manner all the mis-

leading evidences with which that friend of his was waiting
to buffet him—doubly hard in the face of Lewis' susceptibil-
ity on matters that had been a source of pride to him, and
one the success of which was problematic. Yet it had to be
undertaken, and Fargus accepted it as a first expiation of
his past selfishness.

When Lewis returned from his errand and the two sat
down opposite each other by the blazing hearth, the elder,
feeling the uselessness of delay, plunged into the heart of the
business with all the facility he could summon.

"Now about my report," said he, "concerning the relics
which I cremated yesternight. I must ask you whether you
ever heard any theory advanced on the subject of your
father's death, other than what you have told me?"

Lewis frowned; then he answered slowly:

"Never. I must own since all this ado on the subject has
been raised, I have been going over what I know of the past
in my own mind; and I have more than once thought that
the other side may possibly wish to make out that he committed suicide. It seems absurd, but the idea has haunted
me of late."

"As it happens," replied Fargus, "my dear fellow, you have
made a shrewd guess; that is one of the chief points on which
your cousin bases his plan of campaign. And in fact it appears it was generally rumored at the time that your father
did commit suicide. It was not set afloat by your relations,
for Mr. Kerr, who had quarreled with your father on his marriage, was never heard to speak of him. Your uncle Hillyard, on the other hand, was far too discreet and conscientious to ventilate such a theory. George Kerr—who set out
one evening to take a solitary sail round Portsmouth Harbor—never came home again."

Lewis was the first again to break the silence.

"I never knew, I never dreamed of such a thing till the
other day. Were the gossips busy about my mother, too?"

"No," cried the father emphatically "No, Lewis; that was
left to your cousin, when he found it suited his interest. And
now this brings me to the papers. You heard from your
uncle's words, the first and most important, you know, is
the last letter of your father; that letter points to a very
angry quarrel between him and your mother. Do you know
anything about their short married life?"

"The only person who could have given me any information was Aunt Susie Hillyard," Lewis answered. "And she
was always so frightfully cut up when she talked about her
brother that I never liked to broach the subject; but I do remember her saying that my mother was a spoiled beauty, and

my father a wild, irrepressible boy, and she feared they often fell out; but she was sure they loved each other, all the same. But please go on, sir; what about these letters?"

"It is not likely," Fargus went on—"it is not likely, I say, that she could have made him happy in the long run. It is probable that they fought desperately, and that is just what the letter in question seemed to point to. At any rate, when your father wrote from Portsmouth, there is no doubt he was in hot anger. He bade his wife farewell forever, telling her he was glad they had no children. It would seem it was suicide he meditated, for he added 'Every one will believe in the accident you will hear of.' Now, Lewis, be calm. If it be true that your father meant to do away with himself, if the only deduction one could draw from his letter in conjunction with subsequent events is that he did do so, that is the worst that can be said. It may be a source of grief to you, but, reflect, the man who contemplates suicide does so, in nine cases out of ten, in a state of mind akin to insanity. A young man of no occupation—I believe you said your father gave up the army to marry—may well fall into that state which culminates in the madness of self-destruction; you know how near you were yourself to it, and from how inadequate a motive. I am beginning to think, after all, I need not have mistrusted your common sense."

Lewis gave a faint smile; and Fargus, taking up the cold pipe, puffed at it with a great appearance of content.

"The first most obvious thing to be noted is that your father makes absolutely no accusation which could, except by the most gratuitous implication, be looked upon as affecting your mother's honor; moreover, if his angry departure from his home, and his threats of self-destruction had been brought about by the discovery of some shameful misconduct on her part, that would have involved the existence of a third person, to whom there was not even an allusion in the letter. I think this is a circumstance which would have gone some way toward demolishing Mr. Hillyard's theory. In the second place, concerning your father's belief in his own childlessness—which, no doubt, would have been used as one of the claimant's strongest arguments, it can prove absolutely nothing one way or another; your mother herself could hardly at that time have known of her condition. You think things are beginning to shape themselves, do you? You begin to understand how it is that these letters, conveying to any right-minded person none of the evil meaning your cousin would fain find in them, could make a pretty case against you."

"You put things very clearly, Colonel. What of the other letters?"

"Oh, the others," returned Fargus, "the others are of small importance compared with that letter of your father's which was evidently the pivot on which turned the whole scheme; they are only important as connected with and corroborative of it. Your mother, on receipt of the same, wrote in great distress to your father's sister, imploring her to come and advise her. This, in itself, is not the act of a woman who has sinned against her husband and been found out. Nevertheless, this incoherent scrawl, in which the writer childishly announces she has had a 'dreadful letter,' that her husband means to kill himself, that she does not know what to do—in which she blames herself, yet calls him very cruel in the same breath, might easily have been utilized to its fullest extent by the counsel for the claimant, as implying a full confession of guilt."

"And is that really all?" asked Lewis at last, with a sigh of relaxation. "Is it really on no better grounds than those that Charles is trying to impeach my position?"

"That is all," answered the father; "insufficient grounds, indeed, to convince a man of honor, but quite sufficient for a petifogging lawyer and an unprincipled claimant. The rest of the papers consisted of a letter from the squire of Gilham. He stated that he saw no reason for departing from his determination—taken on the occasion of your father's marriage. It was a churlish letter, and revealed all the bitterness of an old grudge. There were the Portsmouth letters and the newspaper paragraphs relative to your father's mode of death, which, if suicide, was so cleverly contrived to seem accident. They were of no value to Charlie, save in connection with the rest."

The young man remained plunged in reflection. He knew the worst, that was a relief; and the worst, after all, resolved itself into two facts; that his parents had quarreled, and that his father had committed suicide—painful facts for their son to have to learn, but by no means such as could, without willful distortion, be made to impugn his mother's honor and his right to his name.

"Thank you," he said at length; "you have been as frank as you have been kind. I do not deny that, however great a blow the story of my father's death must be to me, I am relieved to find these proofs of Charlie's contained nothing worse. Indeed," he added, smiling, "I have had so many blows lately that I think I am rather hardened to them now. We had better go out and get our lunch over, or we shall not be back for the claimant. I say we, though I really do not know, Colonel Fargus, if this time the interview had not better be a *tete-a-tete* between the princpals."

"What, discard your legal adviser already?"

"I should like to have you. I was only thinking of expediency."

"Do you think your cousin would absolutely object?" asked Fargus. "I do not mind that in the least. If Mr. Hillyard is ashamed to say before a third person what must be blazoned before the world if he gain his object, down goes that in my black book as another mark against him. Lewis, I cannot abandon you at this moment. You will scarcely be able to meet that cold-blooded relative on an equal footing, though you have the whip hand of him. Impulsive natures are at a disadvantage on such occasions. Therefore, unless you say in so many words that you have a personal objection to it, I shall see you through the business to the end."

"Very well, then—that is settled," said Lewis, simply.

As the father and son were entering the coffee-room of the Bell, in quest of the midday meal, Charles Hillyard, sitting in that sanctum of legal learning, was concluding, for the benefit of its owner, the account of his recent journey.

"No doubt," remarked the solicitor after some reflection, apparently devoted to the unsatisfactoriness of the narrative, "we cannot blind ourselves to the fact that we have as yet failed to get hold of the proof positive we wanted, however morally convincing the evidence you possess is. All things considered, if you feel yourself equal to carrying it through with the necessary ease, that personal interview you spoke of undertaking to-day might lead to a private agreement which would simplify matters. You can represent to the young man how immensely to his advantage it will be to avoid the scandal of a public trial.

"We received your dispatch-box. Do you contemplate taking these important documents with you this afternoon?"

"Of course not," answered Charles. "I have with me the copies I made myself and which I showed you, which will be quite sufficient for the occasion. But I suppose Mr. Kerr will want to satisfy himself as to their genuineness, and that he must do here."

"I am glad to hear you say so," said the lawyer. "I confess that I was surprised to find that you could confide a matter of such importance to a person like Miss Wren. She placidly admitted that it was only when you wrote again from abroad that she was reminded of her promise."

Here the old gentleman suddenly came to a standstill, and gave a puzzled, not to say anxious, look at his client's darkening face.

"This is very odd!" proceeded the legal luminary. "I never thought of it till this moment. Miss Wren certainly gave me to understand that in that very letter you expressed yourself extremely satisfied with the progress of your business in Spain."

Charles started from his abstraction and shot an angry glance at the speaker.

"That is impossible! I never mentioned about it."

"I cannot have been mistaken," murmured the other. "Am I not correct, also, in believing that you desired me to take the opportunity afforded to broach the subject it was arranged I should settle with her?"

"Certainly not," replied Charles, with increasing surprise.

"My dear sir," said the lawyer, "allow me to remark that it is you who have been premature in your manner of dealing with this person. Whether she had some inkling of your proposed generosity to her and wished to secure it, she told me that in your letter from Spain you had most expressly requested her to come to me."

"I told her to go to you with the box, of course," said Charles, "nothing more. So you told her all about it. Well, you had no end of a scene."

"She took the news with perfect composure, and seemed, indeed, very much gratified and impressed by the figure of your intended annuity. Of course, she knows that nothing is yet settled, but she left with the promise to think over the matter on her side."

Charles Hillyard's face, instead of clearing during this soothing speech, grew blacker and blacker as it proceeded. "So she agreed?" he asked abruptly at its conclusion.

"Practically, my dear sir."

"Without a protest? Without wanting to see me?"

"With the most absolute coolness."

For a minute or two the young man remained absorbed in thought. Then he seemed to come to some settled conclusion, and suddenly his scowling brow lightened.

"Well, perhaps it is as well so; I am surprised. But the deed being done beyond undoing, I hope I may find it for the best, after all. It had to be done some time. I confess," he went on, with a short laugh, "I expected more trouble than that; but, as you remarked with true wisdom, there are few wounds to people's feelings which money cannot heal. And now," he added, taking up his hat, "I see your clock points to the quarter; I must be off—I am due at Staple Inn at three."

"Then you do not wish me to accompany you?" asked the lawyer.

"I think not; I know my *soi-disant* cousin by heart, and I shall be able to lay the siege against his weak side all the better for being alone. I hope to let you know to-morrow that he has proved amenable to reason."

Thus spoke Mr. Hillyard with careless confidence.

But when he had reached the top landing of the set of stairs leading to Lewis' high-perched chambers for a moment he found himself wishing that he had indeed deputed the disinterested man of law to manage this cold business now with friend, even as with mistress. But with Charles Hillyard hesitation was a weakness of invariably short duration.

He knocked, and following the invitation to come in, opened the door and was confronted by Colonel Fargus, who greeted the visitor with a cold, dry smile.

CHAPTER XVIII.

CHARLES HILLYARD EXPOUNDS HIS CASE.

The meeting was so absolutely unexpected, withal so particularly undesirable, Mr. Hillyard halted in blank amazement.

"Colonel Fargus!" he ejaculated in tones too spontaneous to express aught but the most unmitigated surpise and annoyance.

Fargus met the suspicious glance which accompanied his handsome nephew's exclamation with one in which a certain enjoyment of the situation was blended with very distinct disfavor.

"How do you do?" he said quietly, crossing his arms as he spoke, as if to obviate the necessity of offering his hand.

The occasions were few, indeed, on which Charles Hillyard had ever been discomposed by such keen yet seemingly foolish vexation. The unreasoned antipathy he felt for the transatlantic lion whom his simple Woldham friends had promoted on so short an acquaintance to so high a place in their esteem was unaccountable, even to his most secret self, but none the less real.

As promptly discarding all outward semblance of perturbation, he was inwardly resolving to get rid of the unwelcome third as speedily as possible.

Lewis had not spoken. Leaning against the high mantelpiece, he stood motionless, sternly facing the visitor, without attempting the smallest advance.

Charles, though he had, of course, realized that, warned of the object of his interview, Lewis would meet him in no conciliatory mood, was not prepared for such determined enmity as was here displayed. Without other reason than his prejudice, he connected this unexpected dignity of anger with the presence of Fargus.

Nodding to Lewis, he addressed him with a coolness born as much of his habitual and almost unconscious contempt for him as of the combative feelings caused by Fargus' proximity.

"I understood from your telegram that you meant me to come here to-day, Lewis; and I thought I would find you alone. I fear I have disturbed you *tete-a-tete* with Colonel Fargus," turning to the latter with that affection of pleasantness which is popularly described as "from the teeth out."

"Not at all," quietly answered the person referred to.

"I must say it is most curious," proceeded Charles, bestowing a keen look on the mysterious American, "to meet you here, Colonel, with Mr. Kerr."

"Really?" queried Fargus, with gentle malice.

Then there followed a silence in the attic room, which, as neither Fargus nor Lewis was willing to break it, fell awkwardly upon their visitor.

After standing for a minute or two gazing from the former's placid countenance to the latter's irate face, he again lifted his voice with a show of insolence that betrayed his irritation.

"Well, since you are so pressing, I will take a chair. Thanks." And sitting down straddle legs on one of the old oak seats, he folded his arms across the top of its straight back, and, looking up scrutinizingly at his cousin, proceeded pleasantly: "What have you been about? Where did you get that slash?"

"A duel in Germany."

Nothing repressed by the tone of the reply, Charles gave a short, contemptuous laugh, and went on in the same bantering manner: "It is in your Southern blood, and you cannot help it, I suppose—but I didn't think—no, I did not think you were quite the donkey to go on the Mensur. But there is one thing I am even more curious to learn, and that is how the dickens you come to be acquainted with our colonel. Have you been to Gilham since your return?"

"No," answered Lewis, again with the curtness that would not waste a word. "I met Colonel Fargus in Germany."

"In Germany—in Germany! . . . Oh, I see, at Homburg, of course." There was a cold smile on Charles' lips, a slight arching of the calm brows, as he spoke, sufficient to point his meaning; and Lewis, more galled by this than by an open taunt, flushed crimson, but could not at the moment trust himself to speak, for the fierceness of his resentment.

Once more there came an irksome silence, and Charles, for all his well-tempered armor of self-control and self-esteem, found it difficult to oppose an impassible front to the undisguised hostility of the two men.

"At any rate," he began once more, this time with some sharpness, "it cannot matter to me much, either how you have contrived to bring back such a 'Schmiss' from your wild expedition to Homburg. But as I am here on business of importance to myself, as well as to you, Lewis, it is, I think, better that we should soon settle down to the discussion of it."

Neither Lewis nor Fargus offering any deprecation of this statement, Mr. Hillyard pursued, after a marked pause: "However, I do not offer to withdraw, considering that I am here by appointment, and that I have already lost twenty minutes in waiting for your leisure."

"I beg to state," said Lewis, "that it is I who am waiting."

Charles' nostrils dilated, and the crimson mounted to his face.

"You force me, then, into the position of begging you to dismiss your guest. Pray forgive me, Colonel Fargus, for a seeming discourtesy."

Despite his hard judgment on his nephew, Fargus could not but admire, if only from an æsthetic point of view, the determined self-control of the young man's manner in the face of such odds. "What a pity," thought he to himself, as, merely bowing in reply, he now, at a sign from his son, advanced to the table and took a seat thereat.

"Whatever you may have to say to me, Charles," said Lewis, without stirring from the position he had taken from the first, "say it now, before Colonel Fargus, who has my full confidence in this matter, and upon whose advice I am determined to act in all that regards it."

Charles' brow darkened. His weak-minded cousin acting under the advice of this impenetrable, unaccountable American! What might that portend?—no good, certainly; no help to the easy settlement of this disagreeable business.

"This is folly, Lewis," he cried, in a hard tone. "I must decline to discuss intimate matters before an absolute stranger."

"Colonel Fargus acts as my legal adviser for the present," reiterated Lewis. There was an ominous gleam in his eye.

"Your legal adviser!" repeated the college Don, with another of his quick, contemptuous laughs. "It is as like you to make an American colonel your adviser in a matter of this kind, as it is, when returning unscathed from serious warfare, to seek the adornment of a Schlaeger cut."

"You lose," thought Fargus, as he quietly watched the scene and forebore to take notice in any way of the disparaging allusion to himself, "all your advantage, my friend, as soon as you release your grasp on your temper."

"I do not suppose," resumed Lewis doggedly, "that your purpose here to-day is to discuss my mental weaknesses. I tell you Colonel Fargus remains by my wish; I give you the opportunity you desired to speak with me upon matters you state to be of importance."

"You are a fool, Lewis!" pronounced Mr. Hillyard slowly. "You are aware, I know, of the present state of affairs, yet would make a man who can only be the most casual acquaintance of yours privy to what I must say to you to-day."

"I am aware of the true state of affairs."

Lewis spoke quietly enough, though his mouth quivered with anger.

"You will repent your unwarrantable offensiveness to me, and this absurdity in dragging a third person into our business. I warn you fairly what I must speak upon to-day will be no pleasant hearing for you. However, a willful man, I suppose, must have his way."

Still Lewis remained silent.

After a few minutes' impatient waiting, Charles carelessly turned his back on Fargus, and observed in his old patronizing manner: "Seeing your present mood, it would be idle, I presume, to try and convince you that in this errand of mine I am really actuated to a great extent by friendly feelings."

"It would," interrupted Lewis, with a sweep of the hand.

"Quite so. Yet it remains a fact that in seeking a private interview I have been prompted mainly by the desire to spare you as much as possible, under the circumstances."

Again Lewis vouchsafed no reply; but a tightening of the lip and a red flash of the eye betrayed how intensely his cousin's words and manner tried his small remnant of patience.

Charles paused as if to select his words, while his eyes musingly wandered over the quartered coat-of-arms wherein Lewis' family pretensions were blazoned above the portraits of his father and mother. At length, with a certain effort, he began to expound his case with that thoughtful choice of language so familiar, and once so pleasing to Lewis.

"It may be as well that I should first briefly recapitulate the main points in the family history of Kerr of Gilham which have led to the present deadlock. Mr. William George Kerr, my grandfather, whose death occurred in '46, had issue: by his first wife, William, the late head of the family; by his second, George, who died in '57, and Susan, my mother, who died two years ago. Mr. William Kerr, who died last July, had then no issue living. The estate is entail on the heirs male. The question now is, who is the heir-at-law? I think this is the case in a nutshell."

Lewis nodded impatiently, and Charles proceeded: "This question of heirship unfortunately raises a point, which, but for the unforeseen contingency of the untimely death, without issue themselves, of the late squire's two sons, no one would have had any interest in investigating. And it is the strange irony of fate that the task of lifting the veil which covers the parentage of my old friend and pupil should devolve upon me."

Tumultuously Lewis' heart began to beat; the sickening slander was coming home at last.

"I need hardly say, Lewis," proceeded the speaker, with an unconscious deepening of his voice, "that it is serious grief to me to have to say all this to you. The name which you bear is yours only by prescription, so to speak, and it is my painful task——"

"Oh, for God's sake," interrupted Lewis, stamping his foot furiously, "a truce to your hypocritical sympathy! Since you could turn traitor to friendship, have the courage of your opinion—say your say, at least."

"This anger is futile," answered Charles, "and unjust, too. I may appear selfish in insisting, as I mean to do, on my legal and moral right. Granted. It is, I repeat, almost entirely for your sake I wish the case to be kept from a court of law, where I should have to assert my claim without mincing matters, and where the fact would be made brutally public that you cannot prove yourself to be the son of the late George Kerr and that I can prove the contrary."

"Charles Hillyard, you are a liar as well as a hypocrite and traitor!"

Fargus' strong arm was in an instant interposed between Lewis' furious gesture of menace and the motionless figure of the visitor.

"My dear boy," he said, with kind severity, "you are now putting yourself in the wrong. Better let me conduct this business for you."

Charles had not stirred a muscle under his cousin's threatened onslaught, but his face had hardened into colder contempt; when Lewis, yielding to the firmness of Fargus' hand, resumed his place, he addressed himself to the latter, and said, with a sarcastic smile:

"I see now that my old pupil has done wisely, after all, in taking you as adviser in this affair. You Americans are proverbially cool-headed, Colonel Fargus. I now agree with you in thinking that it may be as well if our friend will leave you to act for him in an affair he is so evidently unfit to manage himself."

"You hear, Lewis," said Fargus, resuming his seat in the arm-chair, and half turning to his son. "Will you retire *pro tempore* figuratively into the background, and trust me to discuss Mr. Hillyard's business with him?"

"Pray do," said Lewis; "you know I have given you a moral power of attorney."

"Then, sir, I am at your service," turning again toward Charles, who promptly resumed the thread of his exposition.

"I said that I had the proofs in my possession that my friend here, Lewis, was not the son of George Kerr, and, in consequence, not the heir-at-law. Here they are." And he placed a bundle of papers on the table by his side.

"In 1856," proceeded Charles, "George Kerr married, at Seville, Doña Carmen de Ayala. They lived together, I gather from the dates, one year and a day, so unhappily that at last, after making a shocking discovery concerning his wife's conduct, George Kerr left her and committed suicide."

Lewis' face became ashen. It was hard, even after all Fargus' careful preparation, to have to hear attacked the honor of the woman who had borne him and not smite the slanderer to earth. He clenched his fist and turned his eyes slowly toward Fargus, but meeting the same grave and confident smile as heretofore, took courage from it for further self-control and patience.

"Yes?" said Fargus, as he bent toward Charles Hillyard. The latter had paused. Surprised at the silence, he turned sharply, to catch the mute intercourse between the two men.

"Yes—and then?" asked Colonel Fargus.

"Then, Mrs. George Kerr returned immediately to her country, and in the natural course of time her child was born. That child was christened Luis Jorge Kerr. The squire, at Gilham, refused steadily to recognize him. My father, moved by feelings of benevolence, and prevailed upon by my mother, who loved to imagine that something was left in this world of her dead brother, accepted the office of guardian to the young outlander, while I became, out of personal liking, as they say, his guide, philosopher, and friend."

Here Charles stopped again, as if waiting for objections.

"That is not all, surely," said Fargus.

"Of course that is not all. It is, so to speak, the broad sketch."

"Thus far," said Fargus, composedly, "the story is one of a man who, five-and-twenty years ago, is alleged to have committed suicide because he was not happy with the foreign woman he had married, and of his posthumous son, who had one bad uncle and one good one, after the fashion of fairy tales. You will be able to prove, I suppose, that George Kerr had positive cause to suspect his wife; secondly, that his death really was the result of suicide, not accident, as reported by the papers at the time; thirdly, that his suicide, if suicide there was, was brought about by horror at his wife's behavior; lastly, that the posthumous child could not by any possibility be his son. Unless you can prove all that, your story would hardly be adequate to support your important claim. You have, of course, more facts in reserve?"

"It is quite a pity you were not a lawyer, Colonel Fargus," said Charles, with mocking admiration. "I have facts in reserve. I can prove, to the hilt, almost every one of the points you have raised. Of the excessively unhappy life led by George Kerr and his wife, and of the last scene between them, evidently brought about by the discovery which led to his flying a dishonored house, I have sufficient testimony, having found some of the servants who were at that time in George Kerr's employment. But in this case personal evidence is not even required, as there is extant a letter from George Kerr himself which shows explicitly that his life with his wife was miserable, and further points to one particular, unpardonable offense, which has driven him in disgust to make away with himself. In further proof of the question of suicide is the summary of the inquiry into the alleged accident, if it be read in the light afforded by the dead man's letter. And, finally, there is Mrs. Kerr's own letter to my mother, in which, at the same time, she admits her guilt and announces it as the cause of her husband's death. There is no actual proof that Lewis cannot be the child of that union —for he was born in March, 1858, while his putative father died in the month of July preceding—but, unfortunately for him, two passages in the existing documents fill up the lacunes. In one of them George Kerr writes: 'Thank God, we have no children.' In the other Mrs. Kerr, struck with remorse, admits: 'I know I have been guilty towards him.' Lastly, I can prove from various letters written by the late Mr. Kerr to my father, that the belief in the illegitimacy of this boy born in foreign parts was shared by all his English relations, except, as I have said, my mother."

"Before I ask you, Mr. Hillyard," said Fargus, "how these

documents—the most important of which undoubtedly should, by rights, have been surrendered long ago to my friend— have come into your hands, I should like to know how you propose to prove their authenticity?"

"Upon my word, Colonel," exclaimed Charles, with a laugh, "one might almost imagine that you had prepared the defense at leisure, so methodically do you survey my means of attack."

Fargus answered with a grave inclination of the head.

"You have not answered my question," said he.

"Your objection was so very obvious. Their authenticity can, of course, be established beyond doubt. My uncle's handwriting and my father's are easily verifiable. There was at first a certain difficulty in connection with that of the late George Kerr; but it was found that his last will was holograph, that it was proved, and 'is, of course, accessible to experts. As to Mrs. Kerr's letters, I will now inform you that I have just returned from Spain, whither I went to verify certain data—among others, the handwriting of Lewis' mother. I obtained leave to take away sundry old letters, photographs of which I can let you see whenever you wish."

"What would those courteous Spanish people say to that sample of an English gentleman's conduct," put in Lewis, scornfully, "could they but have known your purpose?"

"Their thoughts on the subject would cause me little concern. Does not your church teach that?"

"Your knowledge of the rules of my religion is as insufficient, Charles, as your conception of the rules of honor," said Lewis, in icy tones. "You have obtained some of my mother's letters by means of lies worthy of a private detective, not of a gentleman; just as you have retained, for your own purpose, papers which belonged to me—which, plainly worded, is theft."

"Lewis," said Fargus, "let me again entreat you not to speak another word. This is a consultation. We shall waste much of our purpose if you condescend to angry recrimination, however true what you say may be, and however justified you may be in saying it."

Charles felt the backhander more keenly under the dispassionate form in which it was administered that the angry insult of his poor cousin; but, without changing his manner, he said very quietly:

"After this little expression of opinion on my character, I should be quite justified in abandoning my present friendly intentions, and in letting matters go through the regular channels, with all its consequent publicity. But, having gone so far through an exceedingly unpleasant ordeal, I consider it worth my while to see it to the end."

"I am glad to hear you say so," said Fargus; "but as the unparliamentary expressions were on our side, would it not be advisable for you to explain how you have come into the possession of things which we might claim as our own?"

"I have no objections," said Charles, carelessly. "My uncle, William Kerr, gave the papers to me, or, rather, directed me where and how to get them, before he died. He recovered consciousness toward the middle of the night," he added to Fargus, as if anticipating an objection, "for half an hour or so. He was terribly babbling, but he was able to make his meaning clear through sheer determination. I confess I had been thinking somewhat of the succession myself, but there was no mistaking the emphasis with which he said, 'No bastard here.'"

"And how could the squire come into the possession of these unlawful goods?" asked Fargus.

"The squire was my father's executor, and must have found this bundle among my father's papers. They were addressed to Lewis, with a letter in my father's hand, but unsealed. He always had a deep resentment against Lewis, and it was a sore point with him that my father and mother should receive him as they did."

"May I ask," said Lewis, in a low voice, "if you consider you have also a right to your father's letter to me—whether you read it, and mean to keep it to use against me?"

"I most certainly read the letter, and I should use it were it likely to prove of any use to me. I do not in the least attempt to deny it, but I am quite certain, on the other hand, that, could he have foreseen the death of both the direct heirs, he would have felt bound to make use of them himself and assure the succession to the legitimate heir."

"Surmises as to the probable conduct of Lewis' late guardian are useless as evidence," interposed Fargus, anxious to forestall his son's reply; "and it remains a fact, Mr. Hillyard, that you have unlawfully appropriated letters for the purpose of damaging their rightful owner and advancing your private interests. You are wise, certainly, as far as your own interests are concerned, in desiring to avoid publicity."

"My dear sir," returned Charles in a bland voice, "I am not in the least afraid of the world's verdict any more than of the jury's. But I believe," he added, wtih a cynical smile, "the world would not be hard on the successful claimant."

"At any rate," said Fargus, feeling an uprising of anger hard to conceal, "I am one with you in desiring to avoid the open scandal. I presume that you have now adverted to every proof you possess of the irrefragable character of your claim."

"I have."

"And you hold there copies of all important documents?"

"Yes," said Charles after a pause, devoted to the endeavor to understand the drift of this question.

"Very good. What have you got to propose to him?"

"First," said Charles, "that he should read the attested copies, which I shall have prepared and sent to-morrow. Then, if he should wish to see the originals, that he should call at my solicitor's and satisfy himself, and if he comes to the conclusion that his chances of establishing his legitimacy are too slender to justify his risking an action in defense, that he should come to an agreement, resigning his claim. I may point out how excessively damaging such a public trial would be to him in his regiment if he fails."

"Thank you for your forethought," said Lewis, endeavoring to conceal, under an ironical smile, how sore a point this reference to his beloved regiment touched upon. "Let me repeat your own words, and that with a clearer conscience. I am not afraid of publicity."

Fargus, with a warning glance at the young man, again interposed his quiet voice:

"You have no objection, I presume, to allow me to examine these wonderful documents?" he asked of Charles, who in reply handed him the parcel.

Fargus withdrew near the window and silently proceeded to read them. Lewis watched him at first in some surprise, but remembering the promise made to Miss Wren, and thought he understood the menœuvre, though it somewhat grated upon his particular ethics.

At length the reader looked up. His task was completed. The papers contained an accurate copy of those which he had destroyed the night before; there was nothing new in them save some marginal hieroglyphics in shorthand, evidently added by Charles as memoranda for his own use.

"Did I understand you to say you had no other copy?" he asked.

"Yes," answered Mr. Hillyard; "this is the only one for the present. You would, I suppose, like to keep it, but I should prefer you to have one that is properly certified."

"One moment," said Fargus, reflectively, and he walked across the room to Lewis, who made way for him on the hearth.

"Lewis, you have deputed me to act for you," he said, gravely, to his son.

Then, as both men stood watching him with some surprise, he deliberately turned round, threw the parcel at the back of the grate, and planted himself before the fire, in an attitude which seemed quietly to defy interference, while the leaping flames toyed with and licked their new prey, and, soaring, flashed with it into nothingness.

Lewis who had made a quick gesture as if to prevent the deed, at a look from Fargus restrained himself, and took a hasty turn round the room in a high state of perturbation. Charles remained motionless, but the first unmitigated astonishment upon his face merged into open and somewhat irritated contempt.

"This behavior, Colonel Fargus, I might have expected from one of Lewis' stamp, but hardly from you. Did I not distinctly state that these papers were only copies? If, indeed, I had been foolish enough to bring the originals, such a stratagem would have been treacherous, but at least comprehensible."

"Mr. Hillyard," answered Fargus in his tranquil way, though there was just the suggestion of an irrepressible twinkle in his eye. "I never pretended to be other than mortal man, and mortal man, you know, is liable to error. I regret to have fallen in your estimation. May it console you, for having had to behold such an instance of human weakness, to reflect that, at any rate, it has been futile as far as you are concerned."

Charles now got up. There was an ugly look on his face.

"I do not understand you, Colonel Fargus," he said insolently. "Good-by, Lewis. Take my advice: to-morrow you shall have these papers; read them yourself and judge for yourself, and do not hand over your will and conscience into the keeping of this"—here the speaker measured Fargus with a cold, challenging glance, and paused—"this disinterested, brand-new friend of yours."

"Good-by, Mr. Hillyard," said Fargus. "We shall meet again, I daresay, when I hope I may not have the misfortune to find so much disfavor in your eyes. I go back to my Lone Grange to-morrow. Perhaps we may meet down there."

CHAPTER XIX.

CHARYBDIS.

The sun had just cleared the golden belt of mist on the horizon; emerald-tinted gleamed the crest of the wooded slopes of Gilham, while the hollow folds of the land still lay in glaucous shadow.

Alone in the midst of his lonely demesne stood Fargus, and watched with delight the secrets of morning unfolding, and blushing, and ripening. Unable in his solitude to use that precious power by which man can relieve the over-pressure of his mind, and communicate of his joy or sorrow to fellow-man, he had risen with the birds to seek the ever-ready companionship of nature and the freedom of air and space.

He had taken his gun, almost mechanically, from the rack as he passed out, and swung a cartridge-belt over his shoulder. But the innocent blood of the wild things of moor and brush-wood was not to lie on his soul that morn.

Crushing the heather beneath his feet, dashing the dew sparkles from gorse and juniper bush, the man tramped on-ward, following his thought, till his aimless march brought him to the crest of an almost imperceptible rising sweep of ground, whence the eye dominated a wide stretch of country. To the south, beneath him, on ever-deepening levels, belted in by stripes of solemn firs, by rolling masses of yellowing timber, by horizon waves of faint blue mountains, lay the rich meadows of Gilham, the prosperous village dominated by the single tower of the Court, proudly upreared above the trees.

Fargus let his eyes roam from that distant joyful glint to the cold thin line of the empty flagstaff over the Court tower, and his heart grew warm with a presentiment of coming good.

Anxious to be ready with some news against his guest's arrival, anent that dear wish of his soul, the father, on the first afternoon after his home-coming, had hied him to Wold-ham, intent on reconnoitering how the land lay there. Maude was away—a cause of great regret—on a visit somewhere in the neighborhood, and not expected back for a few days; but the General was at home and unaffectedly delighted to see his friend, and in the untidy smoking-room, amid the pipes and guns and sport trophies, they had had a lengthy talk. From almost the first words spoken it had been evident to Fargus that, as far at least as the old man was concerned, he had misjudged Charles, and that no misrepresentation had been made here to blight Lewis' position. General Woldham was quite eager to speak of the "young squire," delighted and amazed to hear that Fargus had already made acquaintance with him, and excited beyond measure by a graphic account of the duel and its results. His pipe went out, his blue eyes, bright and keen as steel, sparkled and danced under the bushy white brows, while the most complete assortment of snorts and sniffs were produced to punctuate the visitor's deliberate narrative of the encounter, the flight across the hills, and the fever episode in Brussels. The old soldier, of course, was bound to some highly proper indignation on the subject of dueling itself, and vowed he would give Mr. Kerr a piece of his mind about his folly, and pished and pshawed at the description of the subaltern's scarred face; but he asked for a second description of the fight, insisted on an illustration of the bouts, to Fargus' great amusement, with the help of a crop and a walking-stick, and there was an ir-repressible chuckle somewhere subterraneously and a certain unctuous gloating over the detail of blows exchanged, and the foreigner's final undoing, which would not have deceived a child as to the nature of his real feelings.

And after that the General had gone on to talk about Lewis and the old days, and his affection for him; and roused into greater unreserve by Fargus' tactful guidance, there had escaped from his lips a phrase which caused the other father a warm pleasure. "Upon his word," he had said, "he did not know, after all, any one he would desire more as mate for his Maude."

"I used to think they fancied each other. Certainly Maude does not care for any one else—at any rate, she has refused offer after offer, and good fellows, too. I don't say that I was very sorry, for I can't spare my girl easily, you know, Fargus. But, by Jove! when I heard our fine young gentleman had flown abroad instead of coming here, as he should have done, I made sure I knew what he had gone for. But it seem's I'm all at sea. My girl came back with never a word about him, and now you tell me he was quietly re-visiting the scenes of his student days at Heidelberg. Can't make out what you were all posting-off to Germany for, when Lewis ought to have been at Gilham."

"I daresay Mr. Kerr will explain," had answered Fargus, careful to conceal the satisfaction which the beginning of the General's speech had caused him, and keeping his own counsel in face of the very natural exasperation which marked the end. "Young men are erratic at times: I do not pretend to understand them. All I can tell you about Lewis

Kerr is that I found him a plucky fellow and an excellent
companion."

After which the conversation had diverged into other channels, for Fargus was too well bred and too wise to push the
General further than he seemed inclined to go upon the
delicate topic, however tempting the opportunity might seem.
But enough had been said to confirm his secret hopes.
Whether Charles had prejudiced Maude against her girlhood's
choice, it was just possible he might have written—at any
rate, whatever may have been the influence at work which
caused her to refuse him, that must Lewis find out for himself. It was not for Fargus to interfere here; the coast was
clear of material obstacles, the weapon wielded by the false
friend had broken in his hand, and here was the General as
ready to welcome his old favorite as son-in-law as he had been
ready to act a father's part to him in his somewhat deserted
boyhood. This would be precious news to welcome the lover
on the morrow. Her father had as good as said that if
Maude's heart was not Lewis', that it belonged to none. Who
could know the bent of that maiden mind better than he,
between whom and his beautiful daughter there existed the
closest confidence and most exquisite tenderness? Lewis
with these odds in his favor had but to fight on for his happiness.

Fargus was a man of wide experience; his checkered life
had carried him through many strange adventures, the like
of which befall few people. He had a partly inborn, partly
acquired, facility for discovering men's inward through their
outward self, and reading with clear eye the weakness or the
vice that lay behind fair presentiments; he had a straight,
decisive judgment of conduct and events, but there was a
very important element he had never cared to study, and
which had remained in consequence as a sealed book to him.
Of womanhood—the womankind, that is, reared in loving
homes and shielded from the outer guile and the vulgar
curses of life—of the maidens that dream away their existence in innocency such as is scarce comprehensible to those
that have had to face the world as it is from childhood upward.

And now, as he stood upon the moor and sent his glance
toward that special gable in the old black and white house
which marked, as he knew, the bower of its fair mistress, he
hugged himself to think that she was destined to be the
blessing of his son's young manhood.

The day was broad when the faint clang of a church bell
in the distance recalled him to the flight of time. He glanced

at his watch—it marked the half-hour after nine; he remembered that he was hungry and had not yet broken his fast.

"Yes, Dinah," he said, looking kindly at the retriever, who, perceiving him to be awakened from his prolonged immobility, "come on, old lady; you shall have a good breakfast to make up for the loss of your sport."

With agitated tail and nose to earth Dinah bounded off in the direction indicated, and her master swung after her down the slope at a right sturdy pace. As he anticipated, there was a letter addressed in Lewis' somewhat precise and foreign-looking caligraphy. Such a thick letter! What could the boy have to say to swell his envelope to these dimensions?

Fargus weighed the missive in his hand and hesitated to open it—an unusual shadow of evil came athwart his own heart. In another minute, however, he laughed at himself:

"Positively I am as bad as a lover about his mistress over this big boy of mine. How now, David Fargus! presentiment because there is a cloud over the sun, and because a letter from Staple Inn seems too fat! You are getting old."

He broke open the envelope with a steady hand, and drew forth three closely-written sheets. The clouds drifted and drifted, darker and closer. Rain fell. Sunshine flashed out again, and the blue sky broke once more over a sparkling, dripping earth. Once Turner, the discreet, passed his head in at the door and noislessly withdrew it. Still Fargus sat absorbed over that lengthy letter, moving only to turn the sheets this way and that as he read and pondered, and read again:

"My Dear Colonel Fargus" (Lewis had written): "I fear that when this comes under your eyes your first impulse will be to mentally declare that you wash your hands of one so ungrateful and foolish. But as you have proved of more help to me in my serious trouble—been more friendly, more disinterestedly kind in every possible way—than I can express, I am emboldened to open out my whole mind to you once more and expose my present difficulty.

"It was a great blow to me to learn that what I had endeavored to drive from my mind as an exaggeration, self-tormenting fancy—the suspicion of my father having committed suicide—was actually an indisputable fact. Yet when you placed my case and Charles Hillyard's before me, I own you spoke so clearly, so plausibly, that your words seemed to carry conviction with them; and subsequently, during that first visit of Charles', my anger against him seemed to prevent me from reasoning. When I was no longer under the spell of your cheering, vigorous, sympathetic presence, I had time to reflect; and last night Charles Hillyard came again. He was in bitter anger, and said bitter things; he had discovered the loss of the papers, of course, and also knew how it happened. His very first words were so insulting to me, so outrageous about you, that, in the indignation they roused, I told him I would neither listen nor speak to him. He was obliged to leave me without obtaining any satisfaction as to what had become of the documents—though it is quite evident he believes you have them. But what he said I had to hear, and it has sunk deep into my heart.

" 'You have read these papers, Lewis,' he said; 'you have seen with your own eyes how this George Kerr you claim as a father wrote to your mother! No man can forgive her behavior, he says. He is too sick at heart even to try and punish her, but after his awful discovery he cannot live with her. But he will not ruin her in the eyes of the world. These are his words, Lewis: "I will give you your liberty and my money, but I will die!" Read that letter, Lewis— read it, if you have it, for, I suspect, your wonderful new friend has got hold of the papers, as he seems to have got hold of your conscience—for God knows what private aim of his own—but if you have them in your possession, study them alone, honestly, away from his perverting influence, then dare to say you believe your mother innocent, yourself true-born! dare to come and offer yourself as the last link of the chain of true Kerrs!' I can laugh at it now, though it angered me so much at the time that, but for that insolence, I think I could have cried out to him that he was right, that I should fight him no more. For when he spoke of that letter he had the accent of truth in his voice. And oh! Colonel Fargus, I could not turn upon him and say: 'You have twisted the words to your own evil meaning—thus, and not so, did my father write.' I could not even say to him: 'I will read, and prove you liar from your own mouth!' Why did you burn those letters? What lies before me but either to take upon me honors and riches I can never establish, to my own mind, a moral right to; or blast myself bastard, for the sake of a quiet conscience? Better, indeed, would have been the lawsuit, the open scandal, than this. At least, if by law I had been proclaimed legitimate, I could in peace of mind have accepted the position, and for the sake of my name and all it means to me I should have risked the alternative. I believe, with you, that these letters prove nothing to absolute certainty; on the other hand, I see, with Hillyard, that they lay my parentage open to strong suspicion. You, in your kindness and anxiety to befriend one to whom you had taken a liking, thought better, in the absence of any distinct proof, to spare me the knowledge of this suspicion. There are men, no doubt, who would laugh to think that on a mere suspicion I should meditate giving up name and fortune. I repeat, if I could fight it out with Hillyard in fair and open fight, I should do so, and accept the verdict of the court, whichever way it went, as final. But a series of extraordinary events have rendered this impossible. I have been legally established heir to Gilham by the revengeful cleverness of a jealous woman, and by your well-meaning but mistaken destruction of evidence against me. Can I take advantage of this? I know what you would say to me. All night, I tell you, I battled with myself, but my conscience, my honor, are too strong for me, and I have made up my mind, unless I can *prove* myself, to myself, a Kerr, I must abandon everything to Charles. I was so worn out and sick at heart this morning that I was sorely tempted to write to him and have done with it all and go back to India at once. I will do nothing without hearing from you; I hold to showing you what I fear this letter may lead you to doubt—that indeed my confidence in you is not shaken. I promise to take no steps without hearing from you, to wait patiently for your answer to this. Think for me, judge for me, and help me to safeguard my honor as you would have helped your own son; had you had one. No sacrifice can be considered when such a point is at stake; but your decision will relieve me from this constant mental conflict. I shall write to the General when everything is settled and I am outward-bound once more; meanwhile, you will keep my counsel.

"Yours ever sincerely and gratefully,
"LEWIS KERR."

"P. S.—Do you remember my asking you whether there was resemblance between George Kerr's portrait and myself? I used to think so. This morning I held it beside my face before the glass and studied both images. I could see no likeness. Everything seems to have gone from me—even the memories that have grown into my life."

A deep sigh escaped from Fargus' lips when he at length looked up from the letter, and, refolding the closely-covered sheets with almost tender care, placed them in his breast-pocket. He then rose and stood looking out across the wide prospect, checkered now with strong lights and shadows from a cloud-riven yet sun-bright sky.

So it has come to it at last. The veil must be lifted, the secret unfolded. David Fargus, the loved and admired companion, the trusty friend, must reveal himself in his true

colors. And George Kerr, whose memory, in spite of' one
supposed unhappy deed, was kept in honor by his own, must
reappear in all his deceitfulness before the eyes of the one
being he loved—with a love that seemed revengful for his
long immunity from human ties, so keen was it, so all-absorbing, so potent now for pain or joy.

How different from under the glamour of his adventurous,
careless youth did the past appear now in the garish light of
the pitiless present! Heedless disregard of another's possible
sorrow; gross egotism, which had led him to act a ghastly
lie, to desert his child, to disown his name. And from it,
behold what a train of consequences, circling wider and wider
till the lives of many innocent beings are drawn into the
spreading wrong! The death of her whom he had vowed to
guard and cherish so long as life remained; the grief and
lonely old age of her parents, who had confided her to his
guidance and keeping; the shadow across his sister's life; the
melancholy struggle of his son's childhood and youth, and
this insult to name and honor in his manhood; the dead
squire's breach of trust and dying act of enmity; the temptation to Charles Hillyard and his fall from moral altitude
to qualified dishonesty and vulgar greed; and the last wide
ripple bringing such poignant misery to Lewis, cutting him
apart from the true, sweet girl who had loved him—no doubt
loved him still—to poor, passionless Hilda, ruined and like to
be abandoned to heaven knows what unimaginable depths.

But the circle could and should be broken here, and the
happiness of two lives, at least, be saved from out of the
wreck. Thank God for that; thank God that by his own
humiliation and suffering the father had it still in his power
to save them to the son.

This was to be the expiation. What would that boy of
his, who had learned to trust him, who revered him for past
achievements and loved him for present good—what would
that white-souled man, who held honor so high that he preferred expatiation and disgrace and the relinquishing of the
woman he loved to the shadow of a stain upon it—and this
with such a simple heroism as to be fain to ask pardon for
the trouble caused—what would he think of his father when
the shameful truth had to be told? A father whom this son,
having fought his way to honorable manliness—not by his
help, but, indeed, in spite of him—owed nothing to, but
much misery in the past and in the present. A father whom
the son is never to acknowledge before the world, and whom
he cannot even acknowledge to himself without regret.
Oh, it would be hard to have to do this—to lose the esteem,
the affection so happily won, so highly prized; to feel that all

he could hope for now in their stead was anger, contempt, or, perchance—for his boy was generous—pity and forgiveness; and these were cold feelings for love to think on.

Yet, after all, as he stood there, and measured past and future with even mind, and calmly faced the coming bitterness and humiliation, a great thankfulness, a triumphant pride, rose paramount like a flood in his heart; that his son was what he was, and that he—his father—was at hand to help him in his need, and could help him at last by the sacrifice of self.

CHAPTER XX.

THE LONE GRANGE HAS VISITORS.

Holding a cup of cold tea in his hand, Fargus paced his room with heavy, regular tread, so lost to outer things that the sharp sound of the hall-door bell, the approach of steps along the flagged passage, struck indeed upon his ear, but brought no meaning to his mind; neither did he notice his servant's entrance upon his privacy, nor the subdued murmur of his voice. Indeed, he only became aware of that worthy's respectful presence when, turning in his measured tramp, he came upon him suddenly—and then with a vague memory of words still ringing in the air.

"What was that you said, Turner?"

"There is a young lady without, sir, who gives her name as Miss Wren, and would like to speak with you, she says, sir."

Fargus' face marked strong displeasure. Could ever intrusion be more inopportune. But in another minute his innate sense of justice triumphed over the natural irritation. She had been told to come if she needed help. Moreover, she might be the bearer of news—useful, if not important.

"Ask the lady to step in here," he said, thoughtfully scanning the servant's face and wondering with some annoyance what scandal and gossip this strange appearance of Maude's double would create in his bachelor household. Turner withdrew to fulfill the order, and presently, the door noiselessly closing behind her, the visitor and her host stood face to face alone.

To the latter's satisfaction, she was closely veiled with white gossamer.

"An unexpected pleasure, Miss Wren!" said Fargus pleasantly, stretching out his hand as he spoke. "What has brought you here? No bad news, I hope."

Without seeming to notice the proffered greeting, the girl threw up her veil with a passionate gesture of weariness.

"Let me sit down," she said in a sort of cry, and she flung herself into the arm-chair he was about to move toward her and turned her face, haggard for all its rounded beauty and paled from its warm richness of bloom, to look at him with fevered eyes.

"You want to know what has brought me here, and if it is bad news. It is bad news. Oh, never fear—nothing about that precious friend of yours. There is nothing new about him, it's about myself. I've been a fool, that's what it comes to. And now I have come on a fool's errand."

"What is it?" said Fargus, sitting down opposite to her, and bending forward to fix upon her a gaze full of kindliness. He felt both pity and liking for this curious undisciplined creature, child in artless impulse and woman in passionate determination.

"It's just this," she cried. "Oh, I know you'll think I am mad! I want you to give me back those papers, since it was you who took them from me. You won't, I know, but a drowning man 'll catch at a straw, they say. I had no right to have brought them to you, and they can't mean as much to you as they do to me."

Through their covering gloves the shapely hands, interlaced upon her lap, showed convulsive clutchings, and she returned his glance from hollow eyes, that looked as if they had not closed in slumber through long, weary nights.

"My dear child," he answered very gently, "have you come all this way to ask me to do an impossible thing? Those papers I saw burned myself the very night after you brought them. But even were it not so, they belonged to Mr. Kerr by right, and I could never have returned them to you for Mr. Hillyard's peculiar designs."

She listened in silence, compressing her lips till all the carmine flew from them.

"Of course," she said at length, nodding her head in dreary acceptance of his reasoning. "Didn't I say I was a fool? He has left me."

She turned her head sharply from him, for a second her whole frame quivering in a brave struggle against herself, but the next she had thrown herself on the arm of the chair and had broken into a storm of long-drawn sobs.

She was not one "of the crying sort," she had said, and in truth her weeping was far removed from the facile, elegant tear-shedding of which her sex possesses the monopoly.

Very much disturbed, and quite nonplussed as to what could be done for her, Fargus took what was perhaps the wisest course, and left her alone. She raised herself presently and quitted her chair, to walk over to the window. There she stood with her face to the breeze, and battled with her pain in silence. Then, as the feminine instinct began to reassert itself, she fell to fingering her hair and smoothing her gown, and to lay the pretty cloak neatly across a chair. She next looked at Fargus, who had noticed these signs with much relief, and a faint, melancholy, shy smile stole over her lips.

"Can I get you anything? Let me give you a glass of wine."

She looked up again, and, at the sympathetic tone of his voice, the tears glistened again under her heavy lids.

"I'd rather have some milk, thank you. I've had precious little breakfast, and I've walked a terrible way. I thought I'd get some more in the village, but there's no village, it seems."

He got a glass and filled it from his breakfast table. She sat down to it, and seizing the brown loaf in her strong hands to break off a crusty portion, fell to with right good will.

"That's done me good, I think," she said. "What a fool you must think me. But I've had a cruel time lately, and I don't feel like my regular self at all. So you've burned them papers. Perhaps it's as well. I came to make you give them back. But since you say they're burned there's an end of it. I thought to have brought him back with them, though he pretends what I've done won't prevent anything. I have been mad like ever since I saw him, and his words and his laugh when he left me have been in my ears night and day."

"You have seen him again—was he terribly angry?" asked Fargus.

"Angry! Oh, that he was, but you would not have thought it to see him. He was as cool and quiet as ever, smiling most of the time. It was the next day after I'd been to you that he came. Well, I was sitting by the window looking out, when I saw a hansom come whisking round the square. 'Lord!' says I, 'whatever shall I do if that's Charlie?' Sure enough, as it came along, there he sat, as pale as death. He looked up at me as he jumped out in a black sort of way. So then he comes in, without a word, and walks up to me, and putting his hand under my chin, looks hard into my eyes. 'It is you,' he says, and he begins to walk the room, looking nasty and damning under his mustache. I answered him back, as bold as you please. 'Yes, I know what you mean; I might pretend innocent, but I won't. You thought that you could make use of me and amuse yourself with me and drop me, just as the fancy took you; but I'm not so dense that I can't see clear through your little business, Master Charlie,' says I. 'Can you, indeed?' says he with a sort of a snarl, stopping before me. 'Well, since you've been so very clever about my affairs, tell me how you've done it, and why.' 'Nothing incomprehensible at all about it,' says I. 'I don't want you to grow so rich that I'm no longer good enough for you. I found out your game, and you gave me the chance to prevent it, and I took it.' He seemed staggered at that, and he looked at me with a funny look from head to foot. And as he looked the anger seemed to go out of his eyes, and there came into them a cold, nasty, hard kind of stare. Then he began to whistle to himself, soft and low, and I had to sit down, for my legs were shaking under me. I knew it was all up somehow, but the look of him made me feel like death."

"And then?" said Fargus, as she paused, closing her eyes and apparently absorbed in the unpleasant memory. "Did he succeed in making you confess all that happened?"

"I told him of myself. I told him all I'd done. I wanted him to know the sort of woman he'd made a fool of, thinking he could pension her off in the end. But he lay on the sofa, quite calm and collected. He would smile, now and again, to himself. But when I came to mentioning you he pricked up his ears and listened eagerly enough. 'I know the man,' he says; 'I know him well; so he took the papers, did he? So that's the game, is it?' says he, and gets up and begins to tramp about again. Then he goes back to his sofa and asks me many questions about you—every word you said, and how you looked, and where you put the papers when I gave them to you, and he seemed quite pleased like after a bit. But I thought I'd die if he left me like that. I flung my arms round him and begged and prayed him to forgive me, and only not to leave me. He stood quite still—never raised a finger to push me off—Charlie is always the gentleman; but my arms fell off of themselves—I might as well have been hugging a block of ice. 'What's the matter with you?' he asks. 'Haven't you got it all your own way?' 'Oh, Charlie,' says I. 'Have you no pity for me, that loved you all these years—will you go to that other girl, after all?' 'Why, how can I?' says he, laughing; 'don't I say you've been too clever for me? Haven't you given away the papers, and ain't I helpless without them?' And then he walks out of the room, still laughing to himself, runs down-stairs, and I hear the front door bang. I knew he never meant to come back. And I began to think, 'He's that clever, may be he'll get round the old gentleman'; and then I thought, 'If I get the papers first, I'll win him back.'

"So I looked out your station, arrived last night, and here I am. I've been beforehand with Charlie, anyhow, haven't I?"

"He has certainly not come to me," said Fargus. "But I have no doubt he will come to make the same request and to receive the same answer."

"I couldn't rest, you see," she said wearily. "May be, thought I, he's making love to that girl on the sly; may be I've not kept him out of his big fortune, and if he makes love to her how could she help herself?—she'll marry him without. I was determined," and, as she spoke, her face took that look of strange decision that Fargus knew already, "I was determined that if I found out there was talk of marriage I would go to the girl myself; for all his sharpness, he never seemed to think of how I've got him in my power there. But I've seen her," she added, more pensively, "and I own I'd rather not to have to do it."

"You've already seen Miss Woldham!" ejaculated Fargus.

"Oh, not to speak to, only as she went by; course I knew her, since I know myself. I'd have a funny story to tell her, and it would come hard on her, if she loved Charlie. But he's mine, and she shan't have him."

"Do not excite yourself," said Fargus. "There is no question of marriage between Miss Woldham and any one at present. If there were, the man would not be Mr. Hillyard."

"Think not? You don't know Charlie, I suspect; once he's set on a thing, he's a devil to get it. If you could have seen how he got round me when father wanted me to come back—poor father! Tell you what, old gentleman, you said you'd do me a good turn if you could, and now I'll claim it. You're settled down here for a bit, aren't you? Well, if you find out that this man, who belongs to me, is making up to the other girl, you'll just let me know, and I'll just hop down and spoil the little game! Will you do that for me?"

She rose and stood impatiently over him. Fargus delayed his reply.

"'Tisn't so much to ask, I'm sure," she urged at length in injured tones, plumping sulkily back into her chair.

"Come, come," answered Fargus, smiling, "I have really no business to promise such a thing. Nevertheless, I think I may promise that if such an unlikely event should come to pass I will immediately inform you of it, on the condition that you promise to come to me first."

"So that you may be sure to have your finger in the pie! Well, that's pretty good for one that doesn't like to interfere!" cried Hilda. "My! but you're a queer gentleman!"

"I confess you seem to have me there," returned Fargus. "Anyhow, I hold to my point; it is for you to decide now."

The girl's spirits had risen visibly.

"Oh! I don't mind a bit," she responded. "I've not the slightest objection to come to see you first if I do not have to come here again. She lives close to you, doesn't she, and you know her well?"

"She lives a couple of miles away, and I know her very well."

"Seems nice, sweet-tempered, I must say," Miss Wren proceeded. "I put up, you know, at that little pot-house near the station—Gilham Arms, they call it. Oh, never fear, I was all veiled up, for I didn't want to have people taking me for the other girl. So I've been precious careful that none but an idiot of a servant should see me without my veil on. I did want to have a peep at the Woldham girl, and, as good luck would have it, as I sat by the window just after tea last evening, there comes a big dog-cart rumbling down the street, a fine old gentleman, very stiff, with white hair, driving of it, and all the people touching their hats to him. He gets out at the station wonderful quick for such an old fellow, when down the steps I sees her come running to meet him. No mistake about her, either. Black hat, gray gown and all. I knew her in a moment. Kind of thing that makes you feel queerish, you know, to see your portrait running about. Well, she hugged the old gentleman—he's her father, I take it—and he hugged her back; seems as if they were desperate fond of each other. Then they both toddled up into the dog-cart, and he gives her the reins and off they whisk. A fine-looking couple, though of course it wouldn't become me to go into fits over her good looks, would it? Isn't it strange, now, to think of her, not a bit different from me, except that she was born a lady-baby, going off so happy like to her grand home, and with Charlie ready to kiss the dust off her shoes; and me, thrown aside, looked down upon, having to scheme and fight for my rights, and not a roof to shelter me if I can't keep Charlie? That father of hers seems regular set on her; so was my father on me, once, and as proud of me, though you wouldn't think it if you knew him now. My father is short and fat, though," she added meditatively, "and had a jolly red face—it was my mother had the looks."

Fargus could not help smiling at the naïveté of the last phase, but during the preceding narrative he had glanced at the clock more than once with some consternation. It was close on noon, and he had much before him. That letter to prepare him for the strange news had to be written and sent.

as soon as possible. But his garrulous visitor, lolling comfortably back in her chair, did not seem to have the faintest idea of moving.

"My dear young lady," he said at length, "it is getting late; I must point out that, glad as I am to have seen you, and much as I appreciate the value of the news you have brought me, it would be exceedingly awkward for both of us to be discovered *tete-a-tete* in this manner, and I cannot guarantee myself from chance visitors."

Hilda's lip curled with a smile of much amusement.

"Lor', an old fellow like you!" she ejaculated with a giggle.

"Supposing Mr. Hillyard should come."

The girl sprang up to her feet in blank dismay.

"Mercy on us!" she shrieked, "it's as much as my whole life is worth to meet him here! He'd never forgive me if he thought I was playing him false again. Tell you what, you'll have to hide me till it's dark."

"My dear Miss Wren, that's impossible."

There was a tinge of exasperation in Fargus' voice.

"You must, for I won't go. I'll stop in the pantry, in the box-room, anywhere you like." She stamped her foot. "Heaven knows he may be on the road already! I mean what I say; I won't go till I know it's safe. You'll have to keep me, I say. It isn't much to ask you, but it is life or death to me."

Fargus ran his hand through his hair with a despairing gesture. He knew enough of Miss Wren already to realize that he might as well hope to influence a stone by argument or threats, as to turn her from her purpose. He was himself anxious that Charles Hillyard should not discover this visit, and from Lewis' letter his appearance that day was not an unlikely contingency.

After a minute devoted to reflection, he took up a railway time-table, which he studied critically, and then:

"Listen," he said, looking up. "I am willing you should remain here till nightfall, since there seems, indeed, nothing else to be done. There is a room yonder, prepared for an expected guest; you can take possession of it, and I promise you will be undisturbed there. When it is dark my servant will drive you into Norton in time for the eight o'clock train up. At any rate, this is the best I can do for you."

Hilda was beaming once more.

"That'll do, capital!" she cried. "I always thought you were a rattling good sort," and, gathering up her scattered belongings, she followed her host into the pretty wainscoted chamber leading out of the study, already decked and prepared for Lewis' advent.

Having seen her installed in a deep arm-chair, out of range of the window, where tall hollyhocks nodded in between screens of reddening creepers, Fargus provided her with a book or two and some papers, and left her to her own devices, promising, furthermore, to supply her with food when the time came.

Once more back in his sitting-room, he sat down to indite a telegram to Lewis, which, copied at last, ran thus:

"Received your letter and fully understand your point of view; nevertheless, be of good heart. I have unexpected news for you which will completely satisfy your scruples. Letter follows to-night.   FARGUS."

This done, he rang the bell and, musing, waited for the servant's appearance.

"Turner, I want you to have your dinner early and to go to Norton as soon as possible afterward to send this telegram. Be careful that it is absolutely correct."

"Yes, sir."

"You will be back in time to catch the eight-five train for town to-night. I shall want you to drive in the lady who came this morning. You can lay out cold lunch for me before you go."

"Yes, sir."

The invaluable factotum, whatever may have been his private reflections, withdrew without moving a muscle of his face. But Fargus knew he could trust him, and was, moreover, conscious of having created a reciprocal feeling in the man's mind.

When the door had closed behind the dignified figure, Fargus once more fell to measuring the room with slow tread, after his fashion when especially absorbed in thought.

After a while he drew forth Lewis' letter, which he carefully re-read and finally destroyed with minute care. Then he sat down to his writing table, opened his desk for some fooolscap paper and began to write.

Though the shaft of light which struck, slanting and golden, through the low window, had already traveled along a considerable arc on the brick floor before he laid down his pen, sighing and stretching himself after the long constraint, his task was little more than half completed. He carefully locked the sheets he had just written in his traveling-desk, and hurried to the dining-room to repair his neglect of hospitable duties. Presently, with a well-stocked tray, he stood outside Hilda's door and knocked several times in vain.

At length she bade him come in, and, as he entered, raised

a flushed and smiling face from the soft-cushioned back of the arm-chair.

"I do believe I've been asleep," she said, rubbing her eyes like a child; "I was that tired I never slept a wink last night."

"It will do you good," responded Fargus kindly, and placed the tray upon the table. "I had forgottten all about you, and I was quite afraid you would think I meant to starve you."

"Well, I couldn't think so now, anyhow," said the girl. "My! what a lot of nice things you've brought me! Ah! I do love the country taste of things. Thank you for your trouble. I'm happier than I've been this long time: I feel I could enjoy my food now as I haven't enjoyed a bit since Charlie left. I think he can't but come back to me in the end, especially when he finds he can't have the other."

"Indeed, I trust you will have your wish," replied Fargus, unwilling to damp her renewed cheerfulness, and marveling at her wonderful buoyancy of temperament. "And now I shall not disturb you again till evening; you would like some tea before you go, no doubt."

She nodded brightly and gratefully over her glass, and he withdrew to snatch a hasty meal before returning to finish the interrupted task. This at last accomplished, he critically perused the lengthy document, folded it and inserted it in a stout legal envelope, which he next proceeded to direct, and finally to seal with a signet ring.

Then, lying back in his chair, and gazing at the envelope before him, he heaved a deep sigh. .

"Done, once for all, thank God," he murmured low to himself. "Now is the mischief at last repaired—the treacherous black and white so carelessly cast about in the old days, to be afterward so cleverly collected, is now replaced by other 'written words that remain,' and that will prove to my boy what he feared never could now be proved. And now Lewis' name, honor, fortune, even his happiness in love, please God, is secure. Better perhaps it were if Fargus died, for then this accession would not include an undesirable parent. But, oh, my son! my dear boy! how I long to see with living eyes the shadow of pain at length cleared from your brave young face. I could hardly have had the courage to tell you my shabby story with my own lips, I fear. This you will read alone"— and Fargus wistfully fingered the envelope—"and thus shall I be spared your first and natural anger. And afterward, perhaps, if the ardent desire of your heart and mine is accomplished; when Maude is your wife, and you have a child of your own to love; then, perhaps, you will come to think less harshly of the father who sinned against you so terribly—and he may see his dream come to pass, of spending some of his old age as your friend under the shelter of your blessed home at last."

Fargus fell to considering the terms of the letter to be dispatched to Lewis that night, and the subsequent course of events. He would summon Lewis to him at once; then, after breaking the seal of silence that had held his past for five-and-twenty years, after removing his son's doubts as to his parentage, he would advise him to take immediate possession of his estate. Of course, he would obtain from the young man, before the veil was lifted, a promise upon his honor to respect the secret. He would counsel him also to wait a while before again putting his fate to the crucial test with Maude; for Hilda's words that morning remained dimly haunting him: "You little know Charlie, once he is set on a thing." What if this were the true explanation of the mystery he had sought to solve by the theory of secret and premature slander? The more he thought of it, the more plausible it seemed, and he marveled that such simple explanation should not have suggested itself sooner to him. Charlie Hillyard, clever beyond the ordinary run of men, with his fine air of natural distinction, his delicately satirical manner, his high-bred refinement, a man of learning—was he not just the being to compel almost any girl to answering passion? Could Lewis but be persuaded to wait, time would soon prove to Maude that Charles Hillyard was not coming forward to take her as his wife: of that he could trust a betrayed and revengeful woman to take good care. And then would not Maude's heart again turn to the faithful lover she must naturally meet so often and learn to appreciate—and then there would be happiness, life-long happiness, for both!

At that moment a shadow fell across the bright window; Fargus looked up, and saw, with a start, Charles Hillyard, who stood looking in upon him with hard, inimical eyes.

CHAPTER XXI.

THE "SLIP," OR "HANGMAN'S" KNOT.

For a moment Fargus remained gazing at the startling apparition; but when it opened its lips to speak in mocking tones, he smiled at his own amazement.

"Good-afternoon, Colonel Fargus; you seem immersed in very deep thought. Excuse this irregular way of presenting myself."

"Oh, so you have come!" responded Fargus, quietly. "I was expecting a visit from you. Pray, come in."

"Thanks. I will come in this way," and the speaker, without waiting for reply, swung one long leg after the other across the window-sill, where he remained sitting for a moment, while Fargus, motionless in his chair, awaited his pleasure. "You have fixed upon a lonely spot here, Colonel," pursued the young man at length, as if this were the outcome of his reflections. "How easy it is to walk in upon you! Are you not afraid of tramps or burglars?"

Fargus smiled, and drew out of the drawer of his writing-table a long American navy revolver of plain and peculiarly business-like appearance, which he laid down beside him and patted with a significant gesture.

"With this in my hand," said he, "I hold the lives, or any particular limb I may select for destruction, of six men at my pleasure."

Charles Hillyard shot a look of keen scrutiny at the calm, bearded face still turned smilingly toward him, then dropped his eyes with a sudden frown.

"Will you not take a chair?" The conventional handshake had not been proffered on either side. "And do you not think you will find your hat rather warm in the room?"

Charles rose from the sill to fling himself into an arm-chair opposite the American. Silence followed, during which Fargus noticed his nephew's keen, observant glance become riveted on the long envelope which lay, its bold, clear direction uppermost, on the blotter before him. Without ostentation he took it up in his hand for a moment, then, quietly drawing the desk nearer, placed the letter in one of the inner compartments, and finally locked the receptacle with a key attached to his watch-chain. This accomplished, he turned toward his guest, to find him still intent, but smiling curiously.

"It is lucky I found you in," began Mr. Hillyard, "for I have come all the way from London to see you."

"Have you, indeed?" answered Fargus, with a gentle tone of irony. "I am sure I ought to feel greatly favored."

Mr Hillyard laughed shortly.

"As to that, I come to you because it suits my interest. I hope we may be undisturbed."

"I expect no visitors. General Woldham is the only one of my neighbors who knows of my return; and he has gone to York till to-morrow. We are sure to be left quite by ourselves."

"Glad to hear it," said Charles, who, however, relapsed once more into abstraction. Then all at once he sat up and clasping his hands round his knee, looked straight and hard at

Fargus. "Do you know, Colonel Fargus," he propounded, with marked deliberation, "that this notion of yours of coming to settle down in a solitary house four times too large for you, ostensibly for the sake of those wide acres of shooting you never shot over——"

"I beg your pardon," interrupted the host, who seemed to listen with amusement, "as a strict matter of fact, I have shot over some of them, and that only yesterday."

"Pshaw!" cried his nephew, waiving the interruption aside, "which you do not shoot over, I say; which you even leave at the very time when the only game the place can boast of is coming into season. No doubt you went to pursue your real game on the Continent"—with a scornful laugh—"but for people who are not in your confidence, this sudden disappearance of yours, to return in the equivocal position of tutelary famulus to the claimant of a neighboring estate, is open to some adverse comment."

"My dear Mr. Hillyard," said Fargus with great calm, "I am not so conceited as to think that any of my movements are likely to excite interest among people they cannot possibly concern; if they were to do so I would not care, nor, with greater reason, should you. I suppose, when you talk of what people think, you allude to your own feelings in the matter."

"You evade the question, and evasion is tantamount to admission. You admit, I say," said Charles, "that your erratic behavior, your very presence here, is suspicious?"

"I admire the rapidity of your deductive reasoning, but I do not indorse your conclusion. I admit nothing; I evade nothing. There is nothing in my coming here or going somewhere else, my shooting or not shooting, my making friends with a singularly pleasant and clever young man, and, in consequence, wishing to stand by him at a moment when he has need of a friend—nothing, I say that cannot be explained in the most obvious and simple manner in two words—individual taste."

The veins on Charles Hillyard's broad forehead swelled with a sudden flushing of his cold face.

"I certainly have not come to have a skirmish of empty words with you. Colonel Fargus, the last time we met you showed yourself my enemy."

"No, no, my dear sir," interposed Fargus; "enemy is the wrong word; indeed, I wish you well. Say adversary."

"Adversary be it; what does it matter? I have come to play an open game with you, sir——"

"That you will always find to your advantage," interrupted Fargus. "Had you not played in the dark so much heretofore you might not have lost the trick."

"Pray let me speak," cried Charles, angrily. "I am here, Colonel Fargus, in consequence of that covert hint of yours, to come to some agreement advantageous to us both."

"A covert hint of mine? Please explain."

"What an actor you are!" exclaimed the young man, with undisguised insolence. "You are right to be cautious on principle, but surely this is a rather unnecessary assumption of innocence. It forces me to be all the plainer with you. You, Colonel Fargus, have come down here on the chance of making a good thing out of a contested inheritance, aiding and abetting the unrightful claimant. Oh, I have followed you step by step since you swooped down into this part of the world; I have pieced the whole plot together. When you first arrived on the scene, it is true, you puzzled me considerably. Your appearance at the Lone Grange was very nicely timed, it must be owned. How you managed to collate so much beforehand of Lewis' history I cannot pretend to discover—but it little matters. Whether you are the real Fargus or not is likewise immaterial. It quite suffices that you did find out all you required concerning the supposed next heir during the time you spent here before the squire's death. After that event, which coincides neatly with Lewis' return from India, you start off to Homburg. Without loss of time you got round him completely, and one way or another have persuaded him to think and act exactly as it suits your purpose. By the same extraordinary luck which throughout has attended your clever schemes, the master key to the situation has actually been placed in your hands by one careless act of mine. Mark you, Colonel Fargus, I do not accuse Lewis of conspiring with you to this fraud. You are willing to wait; you keep these proofs of my rights and his inability from him; you bide your time, and back this pitiful dupe of yours with any amount of fair words now. But when once he has entered into possession, when he has married perhaps, on the strength of it, and spent money as fast as most young men do on such occasions, then will be your opportunity. Then, indeed, will your hold on the situation prove, if cleverly utilized, a very mine of wealth to you; then, you think, will Lewis be willing to barter conscience for the sake of position, and wife, and chidren perhaps; and then will those papers be as valuable an investment as can be imagined. Poor simpleton Lewis, he little knows what a fate it is I would try to save him from!"

"Upon my word," said Fargus, who had listened courteous and unruffled as ever, "you have made a very ingenious story of it all, and I am glad to hear you are at least willing to credit your cousin with common honesty at present, though you seem inclined to refuse it to him in the future you have sketched out for him. But you have more to say, no doubt?"

"Ah," muttered Charles, "I thought we should come to business! Yes, I have still to touch upon the point which alone interests you. Well, sir, in plain words, what are your hopes worth? What are you willing to sell your chance of future hush-money for?"

"Really," said Fargus, an undefinable smile on his face, "I hardly know which to admire most in you—your delightful frankness in communicating your thoughts or your skillful reticence in concealing them. You were flattering enough to say, when last we met, that I should have made a good advocate; let me return the compliment now, and regret, from the æsthetic point of view, that your talents should have been lost to diplomacy."

For a moment, blackly and in silence, he scanned his companion's face, then said:

"You think, Colonel Fargus, that this woman's treachery has left me powerless. You are wrong; I am determined to get my own. Although these documents would facilitate matters for me, they are not indispensable. Now listen again; give them up to me. I know you have got them—I even saw you put them in your desk just now, or I am much mistaken. Give them up to me, and I am willing in exchange to bind myself to pay you right well for them when I come into the estate. I will bind myself thereto by deed beforehand, if you like. The property will bear a strain, and I am prepared to make a sacrifice; anything in reason you ask shall be forthcoming."

"Is it not curious," said Fargus, "that if these papers are not necessary to your designs, you should be willing to go to such lengths to get them back?"

Charles now fairly gnashed his teeth.

"Yes or no?" he exclaimed, fiercely, coming up close to Fargus, and standing over him menacingly.

"No," cried the latter in a loud voice, rising in his turn and confronting his nephew with commanding eyes. "Mr. Hillyard, clever as you are, you have mistaken your man this time!"

There was a dead silence. Charles tried to fight his adversary's glance with defiant eyes, only to turn away at last and fall to perambulating the room, unable to remain still any longer under the pulse of his angry blood.

Fargus strolled to the window, and for a while looked out with rapidly recovering placidity, then came back to his writing-table, and, sitting on the edge of it in a careless attitude, fell to filling a pipe; and to give him the necessary opportunity to cool down, bestowing no more attention for the present on his nephew, who continued his walk to and fro behind him.

Presently the fitful footsteps on the brick floor ceased, and, with a sudden sense of caution, though he had no explicable reason for alarm, the American dropped his hand on the revolver, which still reposed on the table by his side. But his caution was too late; there was not the danger. Suddenly, with a rude slash, a bight of cord fell about his shoulders, and, with lightning speed, two feverish hands bore it down and tightened it mercilessly over his elbows.

"My last resort, Colonel," said a panting whisper in his ear, while Charles' white face bent over him, and the same ruthlessly determined hands wound the fall of the rope round his throat, and, directed by well thought-out premeditation, secured the end to the prisoner's wrists, which were now fiercely pulled together, careless of possible dislocation.

"Sorry for you," said Charles, rapidly securing the last knot. "But you must be still, or you will strangle yourself."

The whole onslaught was carried on with such nervous, savage vigor, and had taken him so completely unawares, that, despite superior physical strength, Fargus found himself overpowered, helplessly bound, and at his nephew's mercy, without having been able to make even a show of resistance.

"You cowardly dog!" he cried, indignantly. Struggling to his feet, he threw all of his power into one effort to release himself, the only result of which, however, was to produce an ominous foretaste of the strangulation he had just been warned against, and a conviction that the cord, far from yielding, would cut him to the bone.

"I don't know," said Charles, who had confidently watched the experiment, and now came round in front of his prisoner and examined him with a pale smile that had something almost fiendish in its calm satisfaction. "I don't know whether you are acquainted with the peculiarity of the slip, or hangman's knot; such a knot now secures your elbows, and you have an opportunity to recognize its absolute steadfastness."

Fargus sat down again without answering, and waited for his assailant's next move. Mr. Hillyard drew from his pocket a silk handkerchief, which he proceeded to fold with slow deliberation.

"I wish," he remarked, "to use as little violence as possible; but lest you should take it into your head to call for assistance, I shall have to gag you, and when I have got out the papers I want——"

"Pray don't do that," interrupted Fargus, who now once more compelled Charles' secret admiration by his control .

over emotion. "Since that wound to my face, I find it some-what difficult to breathe freely through the nostrils alone. I acknowledge myself vanquished. If I were to call, there is no one about who could help me; but I will give you my word not to do so. You are master of the situation."

Charles hesitated, but ultimately replaced the handkerchief in his pocket.

"It is true," said he, coolly; "your servant has gone to Norton. I saw him on the road. You might scream forever before any one could hear you from the kitchen. You see, Colonel, I did not expect to find you so difficult to convince. But I knew you had those papers—that they must be in the house, and that if I had to search it through and through I should find them in the end.

"I have," said Fargus, "given you my word. Now let me tell you that the documents you look for are not here, nor, in-deed, any longer in existence."

Charles gazed at the elder man as if uncertain whether such a plea could be made in sober earnest.

"The key of your desk is, I believe, on your watch-chain. Allow me to detach it."

The blood mounted to Fargus' face as the young man's fair head bent over his breast and the unscrupulous fingers neatly detached the small ring of keys. Yet anger was quickly merged in the consternation of realizing that disloyal eyes were going, from the very outset, to pry into that secret he was so earnest to keep from all except his son.

"You are disgracing your name," he said, as his nephew now quietly turned to the writing-table and inserted the key into the lock of the desk; "and what is, no doubt, more to you, you are playing the fool. You will find there none but private papers, which you have no right to lay a finger on."

Charles looked round, while he raised the lid of the desk with one hand.

"You seem strangely anxious to keep me from this desk, if it contains nothing of importance to me."

He stooped over the open box, searched for and drew out the long envelope. "Aha! what of this? This bold address," tak-ing a step toward the bound man, and looking down on him with mocking eyes, "I had seen already, as the letter lay on your table, and it struck me that you must be a very method-ical person to load your piece so long before you mean to fire it off. It was written too minutely for me to make out at such a distance, but what does it say? 'In the matter of the Estate of Gilham.' You appear somewhat upset. It would have been better, would it not now, to have closed with my offer at once? You did not know your man. Now I will tell you, just to show who is the fool this time, that I was ready to give you well-nigh a third of my coming fortune—it is now once more practically mine, you see," shaking the packet before the prisoner's eyes, "for my chances were uncommonly poor without this."

Fargus remained silent. Mr. Hillyard, with a smile of insolent triumph, placed the papers in his breast-pocket, closed the desk, and laid the key on the lid.

"Now, Colonel Fargus," he said, "I believe we are quits. I regret to have to tear myself away, but I think I had better cut across the moor, whence I can take train for London. I hope your servant may return to release you. As for me, no one has seen me here or hereabouts but you. Good-afternoon!"

"One moment!" cried Fargus. "A few minutes more or less can make little difference to you," pursued the latter in the same manner. "You have rendered me perfectly helpless, and you know my servant could not possibly be back from the town yet. Do you not think it might be advisable to examine that packet before you carry it away with you?"

A darkening shadow came over the visitor's triumphant face. Sitting down on the sill, he pulled out the parcel in question. As he did so the seal for the first time attracted his attention. He looked at it closely.

"The Kerrs' talbots! How on earth—— Oh, that nincompoop Lewis again, of course!" and tore open the envelope with impatient hand.

For the moment he seemed actually stunned.

"You see," put in Fargus, "that what I said was true; these matters do not concern you. You would do better to believe me when I tell you that I have too sincere a regard for Lewis, too deep a conviction of his rights, not to have destroyed all the circumstantial evidence you had collected, at once, when I had the chance."

Charles turned a murderous look upon the speaker, but resumed his examination without replying.

"And now," continued Fargus, "perhaps you will be good enough to restore these private writings of mine into the envelope and replace them in the desk.

"No, by ——!" answered the nephew, hoarsely. "I don't forget how obviously anxious you were to keep me from it. As, by your own handwriting, it concerns Gilham, it must concern me."

"Do so, then, but never presume again to call yourself gentleman," exclaimed Fargus. "The perusal of other people's letters is evidently a favorite practice of yours. God indeed was merciful in that he spared your mother the knowledge of you as you are!"

Coming over to the table, he once more spread the written sheets out before him, and began to glance through them with cynical deliberation.

Matters were past remedy, and Fargus waited for what should follow.

There was not long to wait. Charles Hillyard had barely turned over the first sheet when he gave vent to a prolonged whistle.

"Indeed! So that is your game, Colonel Fargus. No wonder my modest offer did not tempt you, when you aim at nothing less than the whole pile. So it is to be a venerable dodge of personation after all. And who is to oust you if your son—the heir but for you—chooses to acknowledge his parent resuscitated from over the seas, to share in his good luck? It is a clever scheme, Colonel, upon my word!"

During the course of this insulting summing-up of his behavior Fargus had grown quite calm again.

"I neither expect you to believe, nor care whether you do or not, that I am George Kerr. If, however, you read further in the papers that you have now violated, you will see that my sole object in disclosing the secret of my past to my son is to remove any lurking doubt he may have as to his birthright, and if I choose to give him what belongs to me, there is no law of God or man to forbid me.

"If you choose to go on with it now, you will see that I decline to touch a penny of my son's money, and charge Lewis most solemnly to keep the secret from every one."

"You are really exceedingly entertaining!" broke in Charles. "I daresay you think, too, that you will be able to carry through this gigantic fraud of yours without further opposition. I fancy I may have some disagreeable little surprise in store for you there. Let me see; I am quite anxious to find out first how you work your case out."

CHAPTER XXII.

THE CIRCLE NARROWS.

Once more there was silence, while Charles now methodically perused the close writing. Fargus rose from his chair, wearied by his strained position and galled by his bonds, and began to walk to and fro with heavy tread.

At length Charles slowly freed him, not to speak, but to favor him with another prolonged scrutiny. He had absently taken up the pistol that lay at his elbow on the table, and, as though unconscious of the act, was weighing and balancing it in his hand. The young man's handsome face bore again a different expression, and in it Fargus thought he discovered now a sullen, despairing consciousness of defeat.

But in reality the disappointed man was still too firmly persuaded that the hateful interloper was an adventurer of the worst description to assign any but the lowest motives to his conduct.

He was roused from his darkling speculations by his companion, who, installing himself as comfortably as his fetters would allow on a corner of the broad table, thus addressed him:

"You are beaten, my dear nephew. And now let me speak to the practical man, and suggest that it might be more advantageous to have me as a friend than as an enemy."

Here Charles' gathering rage broke loose, all the more virulent for being an unfamiliar emotion with him.

"Stop a moment, Colonel Fargus!" he exclaimed, with a furious gesture of the hand that toyed with the pistol; "all this paternal drivel may have hoodwinked that simpleton Lewis, but I am not allured so smoothly. I can tell you in two words what you are, and what, by ——! I mean to bring home to you; a swindler, a clever swindler, sir. Determined to sneak yourself into the property you somehow or other got wind of, and too clever—I misjudged you there—to openly blazon your insolent and ridiculous impersonation of the late George Kerr to the world at large, you thought you would at least supply the required paternity to the unrightful heir. Once established as his father, you would never think of dispossessing him—of course not; there would remain a charming mystery between you two, a romantic situation admirably suited to that dolt's sentimental mania; one which, properly farmed, would prove, however, a very pretty investment. But, mark me, Mr. Fargus, or Colonel Fargus, or whoever the devil you are, I will have none of it!"

"You impudent jackanapes!" interrupted Fargus, "you forget yourself!" A sharp wrench at his shoulder checked the indignant movement with which he would have beaten aside the menacing barrel, and reminded him forcibly of his helpless position.

"It is you who forget yourself, Colonel Fargus! For the moment, at least, I am master of the situation. Insolent, am I? What if I were to chastise you for your insolence, your cursed assumption of authority?" He stopped a moment and bent his head nearer, to peer into Fargus' face with eyes half closed, lowered brow and curling lip. "You forget we are here alone. What if I could not resist the temptation, which has just seized me, to make sure? Here is your pistol in my hand; there are your letters telling a circumstantial tale, and looking as though written for a testament. Its wild improbability would be more readily believed from the dead than from the living, Colonel Fargus, so it is likely I should have to make some judicious cuttings there, you know. . . . What, I say, if when your servant returns he should find you stretched there with a bullet in your head and your hand still clutching the weapon that sped it? You are a man of mysterious habits, whom no one here knows anything about; what more plausible than a suicide, eh, Colonel?"

Fargus, in his helplessness, felt his blood run cold. A vision of descending death smote his strong heart with terror.

"What if the suicide were to be consummated now?" Charles went on, once more taking aim with the revolver.

Fargus sprang up with a cry that rang loudly through the room.

"Madman! do you really mean murder?"

The burst of mocking laughter which escaped Charles' lips suddenly died upon them. A door swung violently open. A look of fearful astonishment, then of returning rage, passed over his pale face, as petrified into his menacing attitude, he stared at the apparition.

"Maude . . . ? Hilda, you again!" An uncontrollable spasm passed through his frame. He raised his hand and shook it angrily at the intruder. There was a flash, a loud explosion, a scream; Fargus felt the well-remembered puff of a bullet by his cheek, and turned round. With an exclamation of dismay he saw Hilda Wren, her arm still extended with a gesture at once forbidding and entreating, in the act of falling forward. The bullet had dashed through her open, deprecating palm, unflinchingly sped through the shoulder, to end its straight course in the oaken doorcase behind her.

Fargus could not stop her fall; he looked back fiercely at Charles, who stood as if petrified, still holding the smoking pistol in his outstretched hand.

"Merciful God! you have done murder, after all!"

But the young man seemed too completely dazed to understand the meaning of the words; he turned his head away. Fargus thought that he was meditating escape.

"Coward!" he thundered, "would you dare to run away?"

This time the accusation stung Charles. Answering only with a dark look of anger, he threw the pistol from him and crossed hastily over to where Hilda lay, her dark head pillowed on the uninjured arm, the other still rigidly outstretched. He dropped on one knee and stooped to raise her, but the sight of her impassive face, ashen white against the deep blood stains that spread with such suggestive rapidity under the thin fabric of the summer dress, seemed to strike him with a terrible apprehension.

"Good Lord, she looks like death!"

"It will be death if this bleeding be not stopped," exclaimed Fargus. "Take that clasp knife on the table and cut me out of these ingenious bonds of yours, unless you mean to murder the poor girl in deliberate earnest! Pull yourself together, man! Ah, at last! Now, in that room to the right you will find water, towels, sponges—bring me a sheet off the bed, too; I must have something to make bandages of. Hurry, man, hurry!"

Fargus, the moment he found himself unpinioned, had lifted the heavy, inert form onto the broad settee, slipped a big book from the table under the helpless head, and now, without a moment's hesitation, set to work with skillful touch to cut the sopping clothes from the bleeding arm and shoulder. As the white, firm-skinned flesh was laid bare before him, it was with a sense of relief he noticed that the direction the bullet had taken was one which rendered the hurt, if the hemorrhage was only got under, not otherwise serious.

An extemporized tampon to the shoulder and a tourniquet to the armpit, hastily fabricated from strips of torn sheets and a stout silver pencil-case, sufficed for the moment to meet the principal danger—the welling bursts of bright red blood which drained away, with each slow heart-beat, a portion of that unconscious life.

The two worked earnestly together, but, save for the few laconic directions of Fargus, in complete silence.

At the American's suggestion they carried the still inanimate woman into the adjoining room, and laid her on the bed, where, after some minutes, they succeeded in bringing back consciousness.

Fargus, who, on the first flush of returning life, had laid a gentle hand on her arm, lest some sudden movement should undo all his handiwork, now bent over her and spoke with soothing distinctness into her ear:

"Don't be afraid; it was an accident, but there is no danger."

But, without heeding him, her circled, purple-lidded eyes sought her lover's face with a gaze of wistful deprecation:

"Oh, my God!" murmured the quivering lips. "Charlie, I prevented you doing it. It was murder! Oh, Charlie!"

The young man's look in answer was inscrutable. He walked away, out of sight of the languid, blood-stained figure, and stood by the open window.

The momentary bright flush upon Hilda's face faded again into pallor; with a shiver and a sigh she closed her eyes.

"Mr. Hillyard," said Fargus in his low, even voice, "shut the window, please; Miss Wren is cold. Thank you. You know your way about the house, I believe? Will you be so kind as to go to the kitchen and tell the housekeeper to come here?"

Returning the suspicious glance his nephew cast upon him, before leaving the room, Fargus, when he had traced the retreating steps to a sufficient distance, turned once more to his patient.

"Try not to give way to agitation," said he. "You are now in no danger if you do nothing to bring on the bleeding again. You saved my life to-day, for though that foolish fellow did not mean murder, as you thought, that playing at it was a dangerous thing, and, had it not been for your opportune appearance, my child, your lover would now be in an awkward fix, I fancy. Hillyard will come to see things in their true light by-and-by. You may live to look upon this day's work as the best thing that could have happened both for you and for him. You guess my meaning, I see; and you may be sure I believe what I say. Short as has been our acquaintance, I think we can trust each other. Here, drink a little more of this brandy. Are you in great pain?"

"Yes," answered Hilda faintly. "My hand is so cold, and my shoulder burns like a coal."

"But you can bear it. You must pay the price of success, you know."

She smiled gratefully back at his kindly face; but he peremptorily interrupted the eager assurance that rose to her lips.

"Here is Mrs. Sutton, my housekeeper; she will sit with you till the doctor makes his appearance, and Charles shall go for him at once. I am convinced there is good to come out of this business."

After a few brief orders to the old housekeeper, who courtesied a trembling and bewildered acquiescence under the stern eye that admitted of neither question nor outcry, Fargus turned to leave the room in time to arrest Charlie on the threshold.

"You must not go in again; you will only disturb her. Come with me; there is something which it is necessary should be arranged between us now."

Charlie silently acquiesced, and the two men passed together into the sitting-room.

Pointing to the scattered fragments of his whilom bonds, he remarked dryly to his companion:

"Your scientific slip-knot might well have meant an equally artistic and secure noose for your own neck, Mr. Hillyard. You would have found the theory of suicide somewhat difficult to maintain, I fear, had that poor girl's interruption been.but one minute later—indeed, if that bullet had sped but one inch more to the right, you would have had quite as difficult a task to prove manslaughter only under such suspicious circumstances."

"Pray," asked Charles with a sneer, "is this the theme you would confer with me upon?"

Fargus turned to answer hotly enough, but as his eyes fell upon the young man a change came over his face.

"You are right," said he at length. "This is a time for deeds, not words; it is important that Miss Wren should have proper surgical treatment as soon as possible—you will have to go for the doctor at once."

Charles started with an expression of angry unwillingness. Fargus continued unperturbed:

"It is, I see, an unwelcome task. My presence here is absolutely indispensable, for were the bandages to get displaced, the girl would simply bleed to death in a few minutes. You cannot, therefore, in common humanity, refuse a service which you alone can undertake. Come to the stables with me, while I saddle a horse for you; we can there talk over that matter which must be settled before you start."

Charles bowed his head after another rapid self-consultation.

"Do you know of a reliable surgeon?" asked the latter, with his hand on the latch of the stable door.

"Only the doctor who usually attends at the court," answered his nephew. "I shall have to hunt up some other fellow. Dr. Smith is such an old gossip, and——" He stopped abruptly under the indignation which blazed upon him from the other man's eyes.

"You forget," he said, calmly enough, "that the case is one which admits of no delay. Miss Wren is in great suffering; her state is serious enough to demand the best care obtainable. You will, therefore, go to Dr. Smith. What explanation do you intend to give the doctor about this accident?"

"I?" cried Charles quickly. "What do you mean? I shall give none."

"Then, have you thought of what my explanation must be?"

The young man quailed under the steady gaze that never quitted his face. "What do you intend to say, may I ask?" he inquired.

"The truth."

Charles answered by a slight increase of pallor. Fargus left tho harness-room for the loose-box, where, amid the amber straw, a slender-limbed, sleek-coated mare turned to look at him with velvet eyes, pricking her dainty ears, and sniffing the air with scarlet nostrils.

"Come," he resumed in less severe tones, "I am anxious to save you as much as possible from the consequences of your reckless proceedings to-day. Some scandal must inevitably arise; I shall not be the one to spread it—it lies with you to reduce it to a minimum."

"Explain yourself," said Charles, shortly.

"If it be published to the world at large," Fargus went on quietly, as he fitted the snaffle, "that Mr. Hillyard, the rising economist, the university don, the bearer of a hitherto so honorable name, feloniously broke into one Mr. Fargus' house, in order to steal some papers which he believed to be in Mr. Fargus' custody—papers which the said Mr. Hillyard himself has no right to claim, but with the aid of which he hoped to dispossess his cousin, his friend, of an inheritance—if it were published to the world that, to this end, he first assaulted treacherously, then bound, and threatened to murder Mr. Fargus in cold blood—a consummation only prevented by the timely interference of a young lady, Mr. Hillyard's mistress, who, in despair at his desertion of her, had come to the Lone Grange to seek news of him, and who, interrupting him at this interesting juncture, was herself grievously wounded by him—all this, methinks, would not redound much to Mr. Hillyard's reputation. Hush! Allow me to finish, pray! That is what I should have to say, did you oblige me to it. I should owe it to my own honor to clear my house from the smirch of the scandal you have cast upon it; and Miss Wren, who, no doubt, overheard all that passed between us, would have to bear witness to my veracity. But another course is open to you. Let the world hear only that Mr. Hillyard, while paying a visit to this Mr. Fargus, with his wife, had the misfortune to shoot the latter through the incautious handling of a revolver. Amazement at your secret and unequal marriage, gossip about it, there may be, but your good name will be safe, and any one who has the good fortune to make acquaintance with your wife will readily understand the weakness."

"Still trying on the game of benevolent relation, Colonel, I see. What a simple way of getting rid of the awkward consequences attending the strange discovery of a fine young woman, to all appearance comfortably established at the Lone Grange on the most intimate terms with that grave and reserved person, Colonel Fargus! I grant you have concocted a pretty likely plot; but, after all, I am not quite so absolutely in your power as you are pleased to suppose."

Fargus, one hand on the mare's bridle, had listened with immovable intentness to this speech; and Charles, gaining fresh confidence in himself from his silence, proceeded:

"What if the world at large should be told how a certain Miss Wren—a young lady whose antecedents will not bear close investigation—when discovered by Mr. Hillyard installed at the Lone Grange, with the most admirable self-sacrifice rushed in between her quondam lover and her elderly entertainer, to preserve the latter from the possibly unpleasant results of the former's not unnatural jealousy, and is thereupon most accidentally hurt in the scuffle; how Colonel Fargus, in this dilemna, endeavors by threats to palm off the aforesaid compromising young woman as the wife of a man who had once been an admirer of hers, and who, in an attempt to unravel a swindle, has still more foolishly given that adventurer a hold upon him? Would that redound much to Colonel Fargus' credit?"

The elder man flung the bridle away from him with so sharp a gesture that, with a snort, the startled animal plunged backward. Then slowly he advanced toward Charles, his figure seeming to dilate, as he came; his eyes, stern and piercing, fixed upon his nephew as if they would search down into the depths of his soul for his most secret thought; his face crimson with a generous flow of anger. He laid one hand upon the young man's shoulder. The latter almost staggered under it, as if he felt it crush him toward the earth.

"Look at me," he said, "and dare to repeat that infamy—infamy to her whose only fault has been love for you! to me for your own consciousness of its falseness!"

Then, as Charles could find no word to answer, Fargus went on in a voice that, despite himself, thrilled his hearer:

"Not by one word will I answer what you know to be a lie. Charles Hillyard, go your way; I have done with you. You can do me no harm nor all the evil tongues of the world. Here, sir; the horse is ready; and remember—if the warning carry any weight to such as you—that a life endangered by you hangs on your promptitude."

Still speechless, Charles, mechanically obedient to the strong will, mounted as he was told and gathered the reins into his hand.

Then Fargus, leading the mare through the gate, turned her head in the direction of the town, and released her with a stern "Go!"

Instinctively Charles pressed his heels to the sides of his

mount; lifting her graceful head to the breeze, she broke into a frolicsome canter.

Bareheaded stood David Fargus looking after them.

Slowly he retraced his steps, pausing a moment to gaze at the desolate old house. Of all the scenes ever acted under its low roof, none stranger, surely, than what had taken place this day!

CHAPTER XXIII.

. . . TO A WEDDING RING.

Over the purple moor, blind to the beauty of sky and earth, Charles, shut up for the moment within the small world of his own mind, was conscious of but one clear conception; the necessity of speedily fulfilling his obnoxious errand.

Never pausing, never even questioning with himself, it was only when he drew rein before the doctor's pretentious granite-built house and dismounted to ring the bell that he felt, with some surprise, the exhaustion of the unwonted exercise and noticed the steaming distress of his horse. He passed his hand over his wet brow, as if awakening from a dream.

Approaching footsteps resounding along the flagged hall inside warned him that he must come to some settlement in the present curious dilemma. Hurriedly determining to commit himself to nothing, he was somewhat relieved to hear that Dr. Smith was out, but was expected home every minute.

The proposal to wait hastily declined, Charles wrote a brief message that a visitor of Colonel Fargus', at the Lone Grange, had been accidentally shot by a revolver, and that Colonel Fargus begged Dr. Smith to attend to the case as soon as possible.

"It is urgent," added he to the servant, "do not forget." And satisfied that he had conscientiously fulfilled his undertaken duty, he turned the little mare's head homeward.

He went but slowly, avoiding the high-road, to minimize the risk of an encounter with the doctor before he had resolved how to act.

He had reached the outskirts of the town, the sun had just dipped below the horizon; Charles shivered; he was cold and weary, angry and sore perplexed. The scale seemed irrevocably turned against him. The long-craved-for dream of love; the riches which to him meant so much, the deprivation of which had galled him in secret all his life; position, power, more open fields for his great talents, for his widespreading ambition—all this had been almost within his grasp, and inch

by inch it was slipping from him by the unexpected interference of a stranger, without whose help his only opponent
would been as wax in his hands.

Involuntarily he reined in his horse and struck his forehead
in passionate irritation at his own impotence and aridity of
device.

As he paused in the solitary lane and glanced hopelessly
over the darkening vista there came upon his inattentive ear
the brisk trot of a horse over the side turf of the road, already at close quarters, and, looking round, he saw with a
contraction of the heart that Maude Woldham was beside
him.

The recognition was mutual. Miss Woldham reined in her
bright bay cob with a cry of frank amazement.

"Charlie! how extraordinary you should be here! I have
just this instant come from your sisters, and they said you
were installed at Cambridge until Christmas. Why, you are
riding Mr. Fargus' mare. Are you stoppng with him, then?
How unkind the girls will think it of you not to have gone to
see them!"

There was a heightened glow upon her cheeks, a sparkling
joyousness in her eyes.

Without a word he extended his hand, but before it could
close round the slim fingers, she had drawn them back from
his touch with a slight scream.

"Oh! what is it? Your cuff is steeped in blood! Are you
hurt?"

Charles flushed a sullen crimson.

"I have had to go to Colonel Fargus, on business," he
answered haltingly. "There was an accident . . . to one
of his dogs; caught its leg in a trap, or something. I never
noticed the disgusting mess the brute had made of me till this
minute." Tighter and tighter the meshes of the net seemed
to be closing round him.

The girl glanced at him wonderingly; something in his
tone struck her as strange, while his evident want of feeling
for the dumb sufferer impressed her animal-loving mind disagreeably.

"Mr. Fargus has only one dog. Poor Dinah! I am so sorry
she is hurt," she cried, reproachfully.

There was a pause; Miss Woldham observed briskly that
night was coming on.

"Papa would be really angry if he knew I was on the road
so late, but luckily he has gone to York for the night."

"Our ways lie together, I think," said Charles, rousing
himself. "I trust you have no objection to my company?"

"I shall be very glad," answered Maude, lightly; "and as

it happens I could not have gone over the moor by myself at this hour, your escort will be doubly acceptable. I am sorry we cannot indulge in a good canter, but I think it would be rather hard on poor Lady Jane; you must have been taking her at an awful pace." The scrutinizing gaze that swept his reeking steed here ended on the rider's face. "And you, too, look dreadfully tired; are you ill? Is anything the matter with you, Charlie?"

They had reached the turning-point of the road, from which the path across the heath branched off. To the right rose Gilham, with its sky-defying pride of turret, pinnacle and vane. And between him and that vision came the swaying litheness of his companion's form, her sweet, inquiring glance, the tantalizing beauty of her face. . . . Maude and Gilham—the exquisite woman, the goodly inheritance! By heaven, he would not give them up without another effort!

Drawing his horse closer to hers, as they turned away from the road on to the springy turf, he bent forward and fixed his eyes upon her with passionate intensity:

"Maude," he said, in a low voice, "I am in great trouble of mind." In the waning light he saw the spreading iris of her blue eyes look fear'essly and pityingly back upon him. "Listen to me, Maude," he went on, in quick, whispered tones that quivered to the wild beating of his heart; "you alone can help me—but you must have patience and let me tell you all first, before I can show you how. A month ago, as I watched beside my uncle's death-bed, he most urgently implored me to take into my possession and make proper use of some papers addressed to Lewis, which I was to find in his desk. Now, it seems that just before he died, my father, who was, as you know, Lewis' guardian, had gathered certain documents together for Lewis, who was then in India; but his death coming comparatively suddenly in the end, they were discovered by the squire, his executor, unsealed."

A look of astonishment came over Maude's face, but she said nothing, and Charles went on with fresh impetus:

"Forgive this long preamble. My uncle then gave these papers to me, and made me understand that the use he wished me to make of them was to keep an interloper from inheriting Gilham. I carried out his instructions, examined the parcel and found proofs that Lewis has no right to the name he bears; in fact, that Gilham is mine, if I only assert my claim."

Maude, her brow slightly contracted with the effort of comprehension, here broke out with an abrupt exclamation of incredulity.

"Lewis! How can it be possible? I don't understand."

"Have you never heard of the suicide of my uncle, George Kerr, the man supposed to be Lewis' father? Never heard of that strange scandal that the family tried so hard, and in vain, to hush up? Maude, did it never strike you as strange that the squire all but publicly disowned his supposed nephew? Lewis is the son of George Kerr's wife, but not of George Kerr; it was the knowledge of his dishonor that drove my mother's brother to his death. I had the proofs of it in my hand, I tell you, Maude, only a week ago. Lewis would have instantly withdrawn his claim, could I once have convinced him that there was even room for the shadow of a doubt. The papers were treacherously stolen from me before I could show them to him myself. He has fallen into the hands of a sort of adventurer, and now acts altogether under his advice, and looks upon me as the basest of individuals for even attempting to establish my rights."

"I would like to understand a little better," interrupted Maude. A curious stillness seemed to have come over her, and she had bent her head as if in profound thought. "This —this discovery of yours was known to Mr. Hillyard and to Susie, and yet both treated Lewis as if he were one of the family. Susie often told me that she loved him like a son, and loved him chiefly because of his resemblance to his father."

"Oh! my poor mother could never believe ill of any one; not even of the woman who drove her brother to suicide—and my father, he was slow to pronounce judgment, unless judgment was imperatively required. To me, however, the proofs, that were so providentially placed in my hands, are as convincing as they are to the lawyer to whom they were shown."

Charles, emboldened by her pensive attitude and silence, began again in louder and more assured tones than he had yet been master of:

"You can see why the loss of these documents should be such a misfortune for me? Have you not seen how I love you? how I have loved you for years? I valued this unexpected inheritance only because it would set me free to tell you of my love. Whatever you may have heard of me during that long time—whatever doubts you may have about me—do not doubt the singleness of my passion. Maude, I have sometimes thought that, in secret, your heart was not averse to me. My beautiful Maude, tell me that you will not refuse me, if, as master of Gilham, I come to lay all its wealth and pride at your feet. Give me your promise, and I will have strength to fight the fight to the end, and gain it, too. Just now you appeared upon me as a messenger of comfort. I must win, even against greater odds. May I accept the good omen?"

Charlie's voice had risen once more, clear and sonorous in the silence of the desolate heath. Yet she said not a word.

That silence which had at first encouraged him now struck the woer with misgivings.

"Do you think that I am pressing my love on the strength of a hopeless cause? Believe me, it is not so. Lewis himself is, unconsciously, my strongest ally; for if he can but once be brought to see the truth of my statement—be made to understand the whole case as it really is—he will be the first to withdraw from the contest in my favor. But to do so, it is necessary to unmask the unblushing swindler who has got the lad in his clutches, and to unravel a pretty well-concocted conspiracy. But with you as an ally, with the sympathy of your father, whose opinion has such weight with every one, I cannot doubt of ultimate success. Maude, darling love, will you help me and give me courage?"

"Mr. Hillyard," cried the girl at last, in accents of such concentrated indignation that her voice was almost unrecognizable, "that is enough." Then, slowly, so that each word fell by itself, as it were, with the deliberation of a blow, "And this is Susie's son! this cowardly, treacherous thief! Oh, let me speak!" passionately overbearing his inarticulate cry of protestation. "I have listened to your insults patiently enough, heaven knows! I must answer now, or I shall choke. You ask me, sir—me!—to help you in your infamous plot!—to be your ally in striving to ruin the life of your young cousin—to blast his good name! you hold out your chance of success in such a scheme as an inducement for me to marry you. Truly, I believe you deem me a fit mate for such as you, to dare to come to me with your vile proposal!"

"Before Heaven, Maude, I have not deserved this at your hands! In all openness and honesty, all confidence in you, deepest love—yes, Maude, love—I told you how I was placed; I offered you all a man can offer."

"All openness and honesty!" echoed Maude, in scathing bitterness. "Yes. I will grant you were open enough, in all conscience, but honesty—save the mark! Honesty in one who, of his own mouth, confesses to having read and appropriated papers addressed to another! Then you find in these papers proofs, forsooth!—proofs that are convincing to your greedy, envious eyes, which some lawyer tells you would make what you call a 'good case,' and show that your cousin is no Kerr—rob him of his land, his name that he holds so dear. Of the blast, the stigma, on him, your own kin; you rake up some miserable old story. I know it all; Susie often told me about her brother's death—and you come to me to get my father to lend weight of his countenance to such a conspiracy —my father, the soul of honor and chivalry, who loves Lewis almost like a son—— I ought to be flattered, truly, by your confidence, your love. I don't care what sort of evidence you have. Lewis is a Kerr, every inch of him; every one has always said so. One has only to compare him with some of the family portraits to be convinced of it. If all you say were true—you whom Lewis loved—you his friend of years— if you had one generous impulse in your soul, you would have thrust these proofs into the fire, and buried their secrets in your heart."

"I see," said Charlie, bitterly, "I see I have made a great mistake. The boy and girl attachment is reviving."

"You are wrong as well as insolent, Mr. Hillyard," said Maude, her hot blood tingling in every vein at the insinuation. "Lewis is not my lover. But, of course, faithfulness to a friend is a matter I could not expect you to understand." She paused, and her thoughts wandered back to a scene under a silver-leaf aspen which trembled under the morning sun— and there rose in her generous heart a tide of affectionate pity for the brave, loyal fellow who had looked at her with such true, sad eyes as she had given the death-blow to his hopes that sunny morning. "But I will tell you this," she added, with renewed indignation, "that were you as rich and great as you would make yourself—were you the head of Gilham and master of all the country besides, and were Lewis as poor as you wish him to be, as nameless, as humiliated, I would marry him, cheerfully and gladly, rather than become your wife! I liked you for the sake of my dear Susie; I used to enjoy hearing Lewis sing the litany of your praise; but now," gathering up her reins and turning back, as her horse made a spring forward, to cast a Parthian shaft at the scowling, gloom-enveloped figure behind her—"now that I know you, as no one evidently has known you yet, I have no words to tell you how I hate and despise you!"

Her whip whistled into the dark air with a sound that struck him as though she had aimed the cut at his face, there was a dull thud of hoofs striking on the turf, then the retreating, precipitate cadence of a wild gallop.

He shook his reins and started off on his way. His mind was made up; the habit of stern practicality was too deeply ingrained to permit him to contemplate, after the first heat of passion had dissipated. The battle was lost and won; he was beaten; the feverish dream was over. He would throw up the sponge—let Lewis step in, while Charles Hillyard retired gracefully from the scene. His position in his own world could be no worse than before; he would have the enviable position of lecturer and coach to youthful undergraduates, and of husband to—Hilda. . . .

Down deep in his heart somewhere had blossomed shyly, and all unknown, a curious attachment to the handsome, faithful girl, and now, no longer overshadowed by more ambitious passions, he found that it had struck deeper root than he could have believed.

She had played him a scurvy trick, it was true, but it was in fear of losing him—him, whom Maude had just now covered with contempt. What if she, too, were to fail him? He had never doubted. But she was badly wounded, and by his hand. What if she should die? What would become of him now without Hilda?

By a happy coincidence, as Charles staggered into the lighted sitting-room at the Grange, to read reassurance of his deadly fear in Fargus' placid look, the bustling little doctor entered by the opposite door.

Fargus rose and greeted him in a few words, then markedly gave place to his nephew.

There was a moment's pause; resting his hands on the table, as if to support himself, but speaking with all his old deliberateness, "Doctor," said the young man, "the person who has been so unfortunately wounded is my wife. I need not say how anxious I feel to hear your opinion of her case."

As soon as he had spoken he shot at Fargus a look full of such implacable defiance that it told of an undying enmity more explicitly than whole volumes of words. But even his keen eyes, sharpened as they were by hatred, could read neither triumph nor pleasure on the elder man's calm face.

"Mrs. Hillyard is in this room," Fargus was saying; "will you be so good as to go in to her?"

Hilda's wounds had been examined and dressed again. The doctor, after many compliments to Charles on his wife's great fortitude and her splendid physique, to Fargus on his success and promptitude in arresting the blood-flow, had assured them that she was in no danger, and taken his leave.

In the dimly-lit room Charles was sitting alone by her bedside. The patient's eyes were closed; she seemed satisfied with Charles' presence and the mute assurance she had read in his face that his anger against her was over. Prepared by Fargus' few words of comfort, she was happy enough in the present, and, in her woman's shrewdness, had accepted the title bestowed on her by the doctor in the most natural manner.

Charles looked at her for a while in silence. Presently he

stooped and kissed her left hand—then the large, taper third finger, on which sat that plain gold ring with its tacit lie.

Startled by the action she turned her pallid face languidly toward him, and saw that in her lover's eyes which she had never seen before—something like real tenderness.

And in answer to the mute, astonished inquiry:

"My girl," he said, still trying to speak in the careless, patronizing manner he generally assumed toward her, "I wonder whether you would like me to put that ring on your finger before the altar, the registrar, and all the rest of it?"

After the doings of the day, Hilda's nerves were scarcely as strong as was their wont. The tears again welled to the heavy lids as she pulled his hand feely up to her hot lips.

"Oh, Charlie! Charlie! are you really going to raise me to you at last? How can I thank you?—how can I tell you how I love you? Oh, Charlie! and after what I did!"

"There, don't cry, child. There, my girl, we shall let bygones be bygones, and start afresh."

CHAPTER XXIV.

MAN PROPOSES.

Along a northward-bound line, weighted with living freight, a noble engine dashed its panting way. In the window-corner of his well-cushioned carriage sat Lewis Kerr, watching, as they flew past him, the tinted hedgerows, the beautiful homesteads, the wide stretches of pasture, the busy towns.

Once he drew from his pocketbook the charm that had removed the evil spell—a letter, the cover of which was addressed in goodly round style to Lewis Kerr of Gilham, Esquire, and the contents of which he had already so studied as to know them almost by heart.

The letter was dated some five days back at midnight, and thus had Fargus written to his son at the close of that eventful day which had seen the final crumbling of Charles Hillyard's scheme and the rise of Hilda Wren's new hopes:

"My DEAR LEWIS: Your letter would have been a very grievous trouble to me, were I not happily able (owing to a concatenation of circumstances which will seem to you the most extraordinary, the most unforseeable) to give you that very proof without which you now propose to abandon fortune and happiness. I can prove to you, and beyond all doubt, that you are George Kerr's son, and that as such you have the most indisputable right to his name and the property that would have been his.

"Something very inopportune has occurred which must retard your arrival. Miss Wren, poor girl! in great and natural anxiety concerning her lover, landed here to-day, to seek some information concerning his movements. She was still here when, as fate would have it, Mr. Hillyard himself made his appearance—on what errand I imagine you can guess; then he had the misfortune to wound her seriously while incautiously playing with one of my revolvers. It was purely accidental, and he has shown more feeling for her than I could have believed possible. Meanwhile, however, she will not be fit to move for a day or two, and as he is constantly with her you will understand why I think it better to postpone your visit. These are strange things to happen in my quiet house, are they not? One thing is certain, namely, that your cousin has finally abandoned all idea of contesting your rights any further, though I should be conveying a false impression were I to allow you to believe that he is anything but furious at the turn affairs have taken. Now, my dear boy, it is very late and I am very tired after an exciting day. Keep a good heart till we meet. I shall telegraph as soon as the coast is clear, and then you will come at once, will you not? I have satisfactory news for you on other scores besides that one vital question.

"General Woldham and I have had long gossips about you. He really loves you like a son. Charles Hillyard seems to have kept his evil counsel to himself very closely, after all. So much the better for all parties; more I cannot say now,

"Ever yours,

"DAVID FARGUS."

When Lewis reached the end, he replaced the letter in the case and musingly drew out the telegram that had reached him the previous night up in his attic rooms. It contained but the most laconic message: "From David Fargus, Widley Grange, to Lewis Kerr, Staple Inn, London. Come." Nothing more, but the four letters of that little word seemed to flash out of the pink paper. It seemed to mean so much. Ah! the world was a glad and good place; it was well to be alive and young.

Lewis greeted them all as old friends. He was not recognized at first; it was so many years since he had been there; but the porter, having put his single eye to good purpose, soon discovered the identity of the only passenger the train had left to them from the label on his portmanteau. An excited whisper went round the little station: "'Tis young squire himself!"

"We did not think you'd take us unawares like that, sir," said the station-master, coming up and touching his cap with a new deference. "Folks have been talking of getting up a welcome for you. But we're right glad to see you here at last, sir, all the same."

Lewis laughed as he responded suitably. But, in his heart, the little tribute to his position, and especially the unquestioning way it seemed to have been accepted, was pleasant to him.

It was now only three of the afternoon, on a mellow, sunny, brisk-breathing day, and the thought of a walk along the country roads was inviting after an eight hours' railway journey, and so Mr. Kerr of Gilham, announcing his determination to make use of his legs, engaged the flyman with his ramshackle vehicle to convey his luggage to the Lone Grange, and set off at a swinging pace.

And now a turn of the road brought him upon one of the avenues leading to Gilham itself, and in the undulations of the park he saw the herded deer; saw the noble, ancient house between the trees. He stood and gazed, and his heart swelled with a feeling he had never before experienced—the pride of possession. "Mine—mine—mine!" he could say of each rich acre that he had been traversing, each living thing that met his glance, each stone of the home his forefathers' hands had raised.

A quaint idea crossed his brain. "I feel," he thought, "like the Marquis of Carabas—the ogre is dead, and his lands are mine. And presently I shall lead the princess home; and the good friend through whom all these good things have come to pass"—here he laughed in the lightness of his heart at the comparison of grave Fargus to Puss in the fairy tale— "the dear friend shall come and share them, and be honored by us and our children."

Presently, as he walked on, the sound of voices struck upon his ear, then the impetuous barking of several dogs, and upon this a dachshund and two brown spaniels tore out of the underwoods toward him with a great appearance of ferocious resentment, which, however, soon subsided into abject amiability of recognition when they came close enough. Next, well-known tones were heard, freely damning the noisy rovers with the same well-known emphasis, and the spare figure of the general himself emerged upon the path a little higher up. He stood with a sedate black retriever beside him. The keeper, a picturesque figure in far better clothes than the master, remaining respectfully distant among the brush-wood.

Lewis sprang forward, and the next minute the old man had seized him by both hands with a cry of delighted recognition.

"Lewis, my boy, glad to see you again! Hang you, where have you been all this while?"

There was a hurried interchange of greeting and explanation, and presently, the first emotion having subsided, the general linked his arm affectionately through that of the young man, dismissed the attendant keeper with a pleasant nod over his shoulder, and carried his visitor onward along the path.

"Gad! I knew you at once, in spite of that scar on your face. And, by the way, tell us about it. How was it we never heard you were wounded?"

Then, wheeling his companion round again, and halting, the old man looked into his embarrassed countenance with a suppressed enjoyment of his own great joke. In another instant he had exploded, and was slapping Lewis on the shoulder.

"Why, I know all about it. Confound you, sir! so you've killed your man already, and pocketed this pretty little token to improve your beauty, have you? And what do you think the ladies will say to that face of yours, sir?"—this with an elaborate wink. "I believe some will like you all the better for it. When did you come? You are stopping at Fargus', are you not? Capital fellow that! And you were on your way to pay us a dutiful visit, I assume?"

"Why, no, General. I have only just arrived from town, and was finding my way to the Grange by the short cut. I thought you would condone the trespass."

"Why, I suppose I shall have to condone it," quoth the veteran. "You are a great man in these parts, and you will soon grow accustomed to lording it about here." This idea tickled the general afresh. "So you have only just arrived. There will be news here for you. Fine goings on there have been at the Lone Grange with that scamp of a cousin of yours. You must have heard something of it, I expect."

"I heard of the accident, sir, if that is what you mean," answered Lewis, whose heart began to beat faster.

"Aha! the accident? You do know then. Well, what do you think of your precious cousin, my boy? You used to look upon him as a sort of little God Almighty. What do you think of him now, eh? Scamp! With his air of wise superiority, taking us all in; coming among us to lay down the law, knowing better than anybody. Gad! A humbug, that is what he is—married in secret to some poor disreputable creature and leaving her to starve—starve, people tell me—while he comes here among us with his wisdom. It makes me sick!"

There was no mistaking the genuineness of the amazement depicted on Lewis' countenance as he stopped during this tirade, and ejaculated under his voice:

"Charles married!—are you sure, General? Married?"

"Yes, my boy, married. No mistake about it, Lewis. Old Smith told me in detail. Old story, you know—low marriage; gets tired of her; wants to drop her. The poor woman is miserable; comes after him here; finds out he's at the Grange, and follows him there. Frightful scene between them; and the upshot of it all is she is shot. An 'accident,' they give out; but, Lord! I dare say he was in such a rage at being found out he did not know what he was doing. It is hard to get at the truth. Anyhow, he went to fetch Smith for her himself, and seemed quite in a way about her, Smith says. If it had not been for Fargus, as Smith told me, she would have bled to death in ten minutes. That is a pretty thing to happen in a fellow's house, is it not? Lucky for Hillyard he had to do with such a man as Fargus! The colonel would not tell even me anything about the occurrence. 'Whole affair accidental,' says he, when I rode over to see him and asked him for the rights of the story. But I honor him for it, Lewis. What was it you heard, may I ask, since you knew there had been an accident?"

Lewis roused himself to answer with great caution:

"I know no more than you do, sir. My only informant was Colonel Fargus, who wrote to beg me to put off my visit on account of an accident which had occurred to a visitor of his."

"Well, Smith told me a good deal," said General Woldham. "There is no mistake about the marriage, for Hillyard himself informed me he was married. Ay, for I met him and asked him. And there is no mistake about her status either, for, according to Smith, she spoke broad Cockney, and scattered her h's and all that kind of thing. Fine, handsome woman, Smith says; and then what do you think he added—'most extraordinary resemblance to Miss Woldham,' he said. But he stuck to his point, damned little pill-box!"

Lewis made no answer, and for a while they meditatively progressed together.

"Here I must leave you for the present, I fear, sir," said he; but the general's thin old hand held him tightly by the arm.

"No, no, my boy! Come and pay your respects to Maude first, and take a cup of tea. She will be delighted to see you."

Lewis threw an anxious glance at the kind, wrinkled face, with its meaning smile.

"I wish I could think it would be a pleasant surprise for her," he said at last, almost bitterly.

"Hullo, hullo!" cried the general. "Why, you used not to think so humbly of yourself, or be so shy of your old——"

On the point of saying "sweetheart," the old man checked himself to substitute "playfellow."

With head half turned away, Lewis fell to decapitating undergrowth twigs with flips from his stick. The general went on in puzzled and slightly exasperated tones:

"Of course, you know your own business best; but I must say, Lewis, if it comes to a question of being pleased to see you, you have not seemed over-anxious to give us a chance. Why, I made up my mind you would run down here first of all. But instead of coming to us, or coming to show yourself on your property, you fly off to Germany, and never even seem to think of taking train to pay a visit to Maude, who is within a few hours of you. And then you tell me you think she may not want to see you. It is all a blanked riddle to me."

Lewis wheeled round and confronted the speaker.

"Didn't Maude tell you then?" he asked, in a low voice. "I did go to Homburg. I did see her, sir. And I made a fool of myself."

The General's eyes grew round and his face grew red.

"You saw Maude! You went after her to Homburg—I was right, then. And she sent you about your business? Why the dickens did she do that?"

"I cannot say, sir," said Lewis, with extreme simplicity. "It has come pretty hard on me, I assure you."

The old man marked how Lewis' lip trembled as he spoke.

"Oh, tut, tut, tut! She did not mean it. Why, I proposed to her mother four times before she would have me, and, what is more, I would have gone on till I had got her. And Maude is just such another as she was. They never know their own minds. They like you, but they don't like the thought of harness. They are coy. Why, the sly puss, she never told her old dad a word about it, though she did hang her head a bit, now I come to think of it. I fancied she was not quite herself. I thought it was because you had not come near us. I gave her a hint or two, the other day, that we might be expecting a new neighbor to visit us—about a fellow who had been in the wars, and was going to settle hereabouts, and she has brightened up uncommonly ever since."

Lewis grew crimson and white again in rapid succession.

"My God!" he murmured, "if I could only believe it!"

The general watched him from the corner of his eye, and fell to chuckling, in a delighted state of excitement.

"Believe it? Come and see for yourself, my boy. Come and see for yourself!"

The father's confidence was infectious. A fire of joy coursed through his frame. With transfigured countenance he turned toward his companion, and seized his hand.

"Then I have your permission, sir; you yourself encourage my hope."

"I don't say I think any man alive equal to my girl; but there is no one I would trust her to sooner than you, Lewis. You will settle down on your place, as you ought to. I am afraid," said the general, smiling, "I should not be quite so ready to hand her over to you if I thought you meant to carry her off. I care little for the mere fact of your being so rich. I want a good fellow, of good blood, that will make my girl a good husband. I am none the less pleased she should make the match of the county—eh, my boy?"

A flickering shadow had descended upon the ecstasy of Lewis' face as he listened.

"Before we go any further," he said, quickly, "there is something I must tell you which I had well-nigh forgotten. Something which may be the explanation of Maude's rejection of me at Homburg."

"Well, out with it," said the old man, looking keenly at Lewis.

"The fact is, my cousin Hillyard has been getting up a scheme against me—a scheme to dispossess me of my uncle's property, on the score of alleged illegitimacy on my side."

Lewis spoke with determined clearness; the trouble had gone too deep not to leave him very sore still.

"The devil he did!" cried General Woldham. "Wanted to make out you were not a Kerr, did he? Scamp! Why, my lad, I'd know you for one of the family in a thousand. You are as like the squire—your grandfather, that is—as two peas. And I knew him well. You not a Kerr!" snorted the general, working himself up. "No, your worthy cousin did not tell me that—he knew better than to tell me that. What did he go on to support such a suggestion?"

"Thank God," said Lewis very low, "the dastardly scheme has collapsed from the very outset. And yet it was well worked out—some old letters of my father's and my Spanish mother's, coupled with the sad story of my father's death, the fact of my having been born abroad, and the squire's refusal to have anything to do with me, were pieced together into such a damning array of circumstantial evidence against me that, at one time, only a few days ago, I was almost ready to believe myself an interloper, and to go back to India, never to show my face again in the old country. Thank God, it was not true, and the scheme has fallen through! Colonel Fargus—oh, sir, if it had not been for him I hardly know what I should have done these times! has written to me to say that he has secured the actual proof of the slander; that he has seen Charles, who is completely convinced himself, and who has abandoned his claim. I do not know what the proofs are yet. The colonel has done everything for me. I believe it was the late squire, on his death-bed, who set all this mischief working."

"Just like the cantakerous old numskull," muttered the general. "He hated your father—quarreled with him, turned him out of the house. I well remember hearing about it all from my poor old aunt, who had this place at the time. And he hated you simply because you are his son. But that your own cousin, a man who was your friend, should lend himself to such a thing! And so you thought Maude had heard something, did you? No, my lad; you may think yourself very much in love, but you don't know my girl if you fancy she would lend an ear to such a thing as that. Bless me! I don't pretend to know why she would not say 'yes' then, but I lay my oath that was not the reason. And now come and find out for yourself, as I said before."

Lewis' pulses beat thickly at the prospect which seemed to grow nearer and more assured every instant.

"Perhaps I had better see those proofs Colonel Fargus has for me first, sir," he said, as quietly as he could.

"Damn the boy!" cried the general. "I was not such a hang-off, punctilious sort of lover as all that. Your nose alone, sir, is proof sufficient for me. Come along; give me your arm again. Maudy will be on the look-out for her dad. Begad! she little guesses the visitor I am bringing by the ear to see her!"

CHAPTER XXV.

GOD DISPOSES.

"So Fargus has helped you along, has he? Thorough good fellow that—never was a man I liked more; couldn't have a better friend, Lewis! But why did you never come to me, my boy? I would have settled that Hillyard chap in ten minutes. 'Confound your letters and your trumpery evidence, sir!' I would have said to him. 'You tell me Lewis is from the wrong side, do you? Very well; stand him before his grandfather's picture, the Peninsular man; then come and repeat that to me, sir.' I should have liked to see him then, my boy. Whole thing would have burst like an air-bubble.

"So Mr. Hillyard wanted to oust you, did he, and set up that low wife of his as mistress of Gilham, I suppose? Upon my word, he has turned out well! I met him the day before yesterday, just as I was coming away from Fargus. Very down he looked, too, and not over-pleased to see me. 'Funny stories these are about you, Charlie,' said I. 'We hear you have married a wife.' He made no answer, but gave a queer kind of smile. But I was not to be put off in that way. So I asked him point-blank if it was true it was his wife that was hurt. 'Was that what you heard?' he answered me; 'that is true, anyhow.' So then I whipped up my horse and rode off, giving him the 'Good-afternoon' pretty shortly. He called after me, 'Good-by, general; it will be a long time before you see me in this part of the world again.' And yesterday, I hear, he and his wife went off together to London. As for the Hall, he certainly shall never cross my doors again. But you are not listening to me, man. Oh, bless you, you need not apologize! I have been young myself once; and in love, too, more than once. I know all about it. And here we are. We shall find her ladyship in the library, I dare say."

As they approached the open door of the old house, Lewis found it indeed increasingly difficult to follow any thought but the central one of Maude. It was too late now to pause and examine the wisdom of this hurried visit, nor could he collect his tumultuous senses to settle with himself what he would say to her. He was carried away, unable to resist the current of his companion's slapdash geniality; the past was all a mistake; he was going to see her again—Maude, his own Maude, at last!

He was stumbling across the threshold, when the general checked him sharply by the arm.

"One moment, Lewis," he whispered. "Don't you mention that fellow Charlie's name to Maudy. You are hardly likely to. She was terribly fond of his mother, and I think she liked him, too, in a way. And when she heard of the scamp having made a match like that, it quite upset her. She would not believe it at first; and then I never saw a girl look so angry. She turned quite white, and could hardly speak for a bit. I suppose Smith could not keep quiet about his story of the woman's likeness."

"Of course—I know," he answered mechanically, while his eyes wandered around the great, dark hall with eager yet almost fearful seeking.

"She must be out," said the good man, with a cheerful philosophy. "Come and have a pipe in the smoking-room. She is sure to come in to give me my tea in a little while."

As he spoke he marshaled his visitor through the stately library, where the tea paraphernalia were already arrayed, to his particular and beloved sanctum at the end of it. Here he provided himself with a pipe, and scoffed good-humoredly at the absent fashion in which Lewis took the implement proffered him, only to lay it down unfilled on the table. In unconscious, silent reverie, the young man was gazing around the comfortable, untidy room that was so full of memories for him, when Maude used to come and listen to their talk, between the smile of her father and the silent adoration of his guest.

"Well, you are a sociable fellow!" he was beginning in a bantering tone, turning once more to Lewis, when a change on the latter's absent face, as he intently gazed out of the window, hushed the speaker to silence. Maude was passing slowly across the terrace toward the house, her special canine attendant following her with solemn step. She glided noiselessly on the soft turf past the window, with beautiful bent head, unconscious of observation, and apparently mindful only of the world of her own thoughts.

While she approached and until she disappeared, there was silence in the room. The old man looked alternately at the graceful figure that seemed as if floating by in the sunlight—a vision of youthful perfection—to the watchful, almost ecstatic face of his companion, who had risen to his feet and stood gazing at it, with all his soul in his eyes, as if completely forgetful of his surroundings.

When she had passed out of sight the two men looked at each other.

"Oh, sir," said Lewis, almost in a whisper, "if these should be false hopes after all!"

"Not a bit of it!" ejaculated the other. "Lewis, I know what I am talking about; I am not a child or a fool. Hush!" putting his finger to his lips as a light footfall sounded from without. "Tell you what, by boy," struck by a brilliant idea, and burning to assist in the bringing together of the young couple he held in such affection, a delicate task he considered especially suited to his great diplomatic capacity; "tell you what, man, I'll go and prepare the way for you a bit, eh?" chuckling and winking in irrepressible glee. "You stop here, you know, eh?"

The further door of the library creaked on its hinges, and the slow rustle of Maude's gown came in upon them through the parted curtains; then the sound of her voice calling:

"Dad—tea!"

"Coming," grunted the general, pushing the bewildered Lewis aside, after further bestowing upon him sundry highly-expressive winks and admonition, and trotting briskly off in a convulsion of subdued chuckles.

"Well, dad, have you been in long?" came the dear, tender voice; then the general's reply, in laboriously natural tones; then the rattle of teacups, and a silence.

Like one in a dream who can comprehend, enjoy and suffer, but is powerless either to suggest or control, Lewis stood motionless, where he had been placed, all his faculties wrapped in what was now almost an agony of listening. With all the glowing reality of second-sight the scene on the other side of the wall rose before his mind.

"Why, papa, what on earth is the matter?"

A ripple of laughter tripped up and shook the witching voice as it again broke the silence. Lewis remembered how she used to look when she laughed.

"What makes you think there is anything the matter with me, eh, you puss?"

Interval of snorts and renewal of laughter.

"Dad, there is no use in trying to deceive me. You have been up to something, I know. There is the stamp of guilt on your face. Confess, dad, confess! You will be happier, and be able to enjoy your tea when it is off your mind."

"Pooh, pooh! nonsense, child!" with a suspicion of tartness. "Don't know what you mean," with some solemnity.

"Yes, dad."

A sudden cessation of laughter.

"I met a friend of ours to-day, my pet—an old friend, I think I may call him, though he is a new neighbor."

"Yes, dad."

A change, a slightly tremulous tone in the voice, now suddenly become grave.

"We had a long walk, child. I met him in the pine-woods, the short cut to the Grange, you know. Tell you the truth, I have been expecting him this last week, but all this row— Charlie Hillyard's business, and all the rest—kept him away."

"Yes, dad; I, too, wondered why he did not come."

The last words were spoken with a slight hesitation, and in a perceptibly lower key.

"Oh, you were expecting him, were you, eh? The old man is to be kept in the dark, eh? Never to know what is going on under his nose, eh? There, there, never look so scared, my pet; I am only joking. Fact is, this new neighbor of ours has been confiding in your old dad. Queer, outlandish sort of thing to do; but the fellow, as you know, is full of old-fashioned notions of honor and loyalty and the like. Can't say I think the worse of him for that. I must let him speak for himself, must not I? The young birds must fly out of the nest some day, and in this case it will not be very far."

The old voice quavered a little. There was a smothered exclamation. Lewis knew the warm young arms were round the father's neck, and that the beautiful head was lying on his shoulder. And the young man's heart beat so quickly, so loudly, that he feared, clenching his hands, it might drown the soft tones he was straining every nerve to catch.

"Well, well," said the general, "as I told him, I do not so much disapprove. There you come back from your foreign trip as demure and close as a nun, and know your poor old father is racking his brains over the fellow's extraordinary proceedings. Oh, oh! that is a tell-tale blush! Yes, I have heard all about it; he went after you, but there was some little mistake, eh? He is a good fellow, Maude. He has promised to remain down here, and not carry you away from me. And as for that ugly scar—though we cannot say he got it in regular warfare; though I cannot pretend it is becoming—I am sure you would not have him without it for the world now, eh? . . . What! won't you speak, my child? Ah, well, if your mother had been alive you would have told her all, I'll be bound."

"Oh, darling!" said Maude, in low, caressing tones, "do not say that—I will tell you all. Indeed, I am not ashamed of my love for him, now that I know he loves me, too; I am proud of it—more proud, more blessed than ever woman was! Darling, forgive me; I could not tell you before. You see, I did not know; I only thought—feared—hoped. He never spoke a word of love to me—I thought he always treated me like a child—but from the first moment I saw him I knew I should never care for another man. Don't look so surprised, dad. From the first you said he was a man after your own heart. But I never dared to think he loved me, though at times there was a look in his eyes, when he turned them on me, that would set me fancying and wondering. And then, about Homburg. Yes, I will tell you the truth; a thought did flash through my mind when I saw him there—'Has he come for me?' But then—then—then I only saw him once, for a second, the night he came; the day after he was gone. Dear dad, do you wonder I did not speak of it? But now I think I know what it meant. There was a mistake, as you said. He must have seen me next morning with some one else—early in the morning, among the trees. It was Lewis; he had followed me from the hotel. Poor Lewis! it seems he had come all the way after me, too. I could not tell you that, either; it was not my secret, you see. But now that he has spoken to you, that you have assured him there was nothing in that silly boy and girl affair——"

"Why—what the dickens!" interrupted the general. "He —him! Who's he? Told you what? What boy and girl affair? What are you talking about?"

"Father, how strange you are! Did you not tell Colonel Fargus?"

"Fargus!" with a shout of astonishment and despair; "what the devil should I tell Fargus anything about it for?"

A moment's dead silence. Then—could that unknown, hard, fierce voice be Maude's?

"Who, then, have you been talking about all this time?"

"Why, who should I have been talking about? Lewis, of course. What! you don't mean to say you thought it was Fargus? Oh, damn it all!" in a sudden frightened whisper. Then Maude, speaking again in the same strange accents:

"So Lewis is not content with what I told him. I told him plainly enough I never could love him now."

"Hush! hush!" in the father's tremulous undertone. "It is my mistake. Maude, come to me—don't look like that, child. Oh, Lord! what have I done? There, my darling! there, my darling! It will come all right. Eh! what, child —are you angry with me? What is it? Oh, Lord!"

"Don't try your hand at match-making any more, dad," with a quivering attempt at lightness. Then there was a sharp sound, as if she smote her hands together, and a sudden, low cry, as if of pain. "Oh, father! father! father!"

"Maude—my poor girl!"

A low sob, strangled, and the old man's voice raised in incoherent, soothing terms, and muffled as if his head were enveloped in something soft and close.

"My dream is gone. I don't want to leave you ever."

*   *   *   *   *   *   *   *   *

When the general—limp, tottering, the very shadow of the cheerful, vigorous, self-sufficient general of an hour before—crept at length around the smoking-room curtain once more, it was to find that Lewis was gone.

CHAPTER XXVI.

DEADLOCK.

The window of the guest-chamber at Widley Grange was open to the fragrant breeze of the moor, and through it the wild hollyhocks peeped in upon a picture of more than usual order and comfort.

Lewis's room! The master of the house had been unwontedly particular as to the perfection therein of the smallest detail, and now it was ready and awaiting the long-expected visitor.

And, as he looked, a dreamy smile crept under Fargus's mustache. Before a certain dear, tired brown head pressed yonder pillow to-night the father would have confessed and been judged. Despite the coming ordeal, despite the unsparing clearness of vision with which he looked forward to its possible results, there had come to him, once familiarized with the idea of self-disclosure, a secret foolish and unacknowledged sweetness in the thought that the barrier he had himself erected would at last be broken between him and his son. And besides, there was the keen satisfaction arising from the certitude of being able thereby to assure this son a fair future and mental peace, of being able to expiate to the full, and repair the old wrong, no matter at what cost to himself.

And thus it came to pass, David Fargus, confident in his power of benefiting him, awaited his visitor with almost joyful anticipation.

He glanced at the clock, which marked close upon four, and thought with impatience of the three long hours that had yet to elapse before he could clasp the brave young hand; then, pausing in his pensive walk, he suddenly stood gazing at his own reflection in the looking-glass, struck by a curious thought.

No doubt that face of his, however battered, burned and worn, was like his son's, but the most salient features—the mouth and chin—were hidden by the close, thick beard. Why not remove this mask, originally adopted to disguise the very identity he was now anxious to vindicate? Once more shaven, but for his heavy mustache, the resemblance between them would be something striking, or else he was much mistaken. Moreover, David Fargus' connection with the youthful portrait, now in the Staple Inn chambers, would then perchance be apparent—that portrait which Lewis did resemble.

Delighted with the idea, Fargus returned to his own room, rang for his man, ordered some shaving water, and forthwith began clipping the silken, brown, silver-streaked hair from cheek and chin as close as scissors could reach.

But as Turner was hastening to him with the steaming jug, the unwonted sound of wheels broke upon the outer silence.

Lewis already? Impossible! He drew near the window and looked out over the hedge to see and recognize the well-known portmanteau and traveling-bag on the box of the station fly, and the next minute to discover further, not without an inexplicable misgiving, that the ramshackle vehicle was empty.

While he stood staring somewhat blankly at the again departing carriage, Turner, who had gone out to attend the bell, re-entered the room.

"Mr. Kerr's luggage just arrived from the station, sir. Mr. Kerr sent word that he was walking up."

Fargus drew a smiling breath of relief. The probable delay was not unwelcome, after all. But the business must be hurried with; it could not be very long now before the visitor made his appearance.

"Turner," he said, stopping the servant as he noiselessly retired, "judging from your appearance, you must have good razors."

"Yes, sir."

"Please lend me one—and, by the way, I have not shaved myself for more than twenty years. Among your numerous qualifications would you reckon a competence to shave me?"

"Certainly, sir."

Ten minutes later Fargus emerged from the careful hands of his attendant a curiously altered being. Though the peaked beard had been a not unpleasing adjunct to his grave, rather melancholy countenance, its removal disclosed to advantage the handsome lines of mouth and chin, and reduced his age to all appearance some ten years. He paused to contemplate himself with a satisfied smile; the likeness to Lewis was wonderful.

The task completed, Fargus strolled into his wild garden— to look forth, across the privet bushes, toward the Woldham pine-woods.

Five o'clock by his infallible watch. What was the boy about? Then a sudden light gleamed through the growing anxiety. Of course, of course, he had gone to Woldham! Having placed himself so near the magic circle by taking the short cut through the woods, the lover had been unable to resist the attraction.

As the afternoon dragged on, however, and still there came no sign of his son, he began to grow warm with a new hope.

The wind ran with little shivers through the hollyhocks. There were great cloud banks to the west. "We shall have rain to-morrow," thought Fargus. "I am glad it is fair at least to-day, for my boy's home-coming."

And then, as he reached the end of the narrow path once more, it was to see a dark figure rapidly emerging from the borderland of pines into the slanting sunlight of the heath. Could it be Lewis? This man's shoulders were rounded, he stumbled occasionally, and dragged his feet, although he came so quickly, in a way as unlike as possible from the young soldier's upright carriage and clear, swinging gait. Perhaps there had been an accident. For a moment the watcher's heart grew cold, and the bright view became black to his eyes; but the next minute all was clear again; it was Lewis, and he was only within a few yards of him now.

In the revulsion of his hurrying joy, Fargus waved his hand and ran back to the little gate to welcome him. Lewis was rounding the hedge, swaying and tripping over the rough ground, as Fargus emerged from the garden gate and met him face to face. But all the father's warm delight was swept away by a chilling doubt, and the words of welcome died unspoken on his lips when he encountered the haggard, unrecognizing stare of two blood-shot eyes, which were fixed on him till their owner moved quickly out of his path and started again on his headlong way. Fargus hied after his son.

"Lewis, what is it? For God's sake, what has happened? Is it possible you don't know me? Pshaw! I had forgotten about that beard of mine!"

At the sound of the voice, the bent, hurrying figure started, halted and wheeled slowly around upon the pursuer.

The young man's face was hard-set; there was inexpressible bitterness, unmistakable enmity, in his eyes as he measured Fargus from head to foot, and smiled in a way which made the latter's blood run cold.

"Is this indeed you, Colonel Fargus? You must forgive me for my stupidity in not recognizing you under your altered aspect!"

The voice was as much changed as the rest of the man. For a while the father could only stare; then, when he tried to speak, he found that, under the angry antagonism, which it was so hard to meet from those eyes, ideas and words seemed to fail him alike. He could only stammer again:

"Lewis, what has happened? Has Charles Hillyard dared——"

"I have heard something that was news to me," answered Lewis, incisively. "I have been at Woldham; I should not have been surprised to find you thus beautified and young after what I heard there, should I? It is a great improvement, Colonel Fargus; I congratulate you in every way."

"Lewis, are you mad?" with an outburst of indignant affection. "My boy, things have gone wrong with you again; but what can have come between you and me? Tell me what has happened at Woldham. I thought you must have gone there, and my instinct about it was right. Oh, why did you not come straight to me first?"

"You would have prepared me, I suppose?"

"Prepared you for what? Is it Hillyard again—has he come between you and your happiness here, too?"

He was interrupted by a fierce grasp on his arm as Lewis stepped closely up to him and looked into his face.

"Is it possible, Colonel Fargus, that you are speaking in good faith? Is it possible that you do not know—that you have been true, after all? Bah!" flinging himself away with violence; "what a fool you must think me, to imagine I can be taken in by this! No, by God! you shall not feel my pulse! I am sick of this pretense!"

"Come into the house," said Fargus, gravely. "There is a terrible misunderstanding here, or else you are, indeed, delirious. Lewis, you owe me an explanation; you must tell me what is the meaning of this."

Again giving him a mistrustful yet wavering look, the young man sullenly complied. When they came into the old, pleasant room Fargus had left so full of hope, the latter said, in accents almost of entreaty:

"Now, Lewis, speak."

"Colonel Fargus, I—I may be wronging you; pray God I am. And yet why should I wish it, after all? It means happiness to her; why should I grudge her her happiness?"

"My dear, dear boy! Do try and tell me what it is."

"Are you sure you are alone—that no one is within hearing?"

More and more convinced that Lewis' senses were wandering, the father, in great distress, rose to humor him, opened the heavy doors of the adjacent rooms, to close them again and assure him of the impossibility of being overheard. When he came back, however, and sat down opposite his son, the look that the latter fixed upon him was once more keen and reasoning as his own.

"Do you really wish to hear my news, Colonel Fargus?

Do you really need to be told that Maude Woldham never loved Charles Hillyard; that, although she may once have loved Lewis Kerr, the man who has won her heart—who holds it now—is no other than Colonel Fargus himself?"

For a second the father again thought the speaker mad; but the next moment, with dire, irresistible conviction, the truth of these evil tidings was borne in upon him. Maude loved him—him, Fargus! It was he who had killed his son's happiness. How terrible it was! A spasm passed over his face, and beads of cold sweat broke upon his forehead; his parched tongue cleaved to his palate.

The cruel scrutiny of Lewis' eyes relaxed. He flung himself on a chair, and buried his face in his hands.

"Forgive me, Fargus," he cried. "I see I have been wrong. Everything is wrong, is it not? I ask your pardon; I must have been mad indeed to doubt you."

"My God!" The words burst from Fargus' lips at length, with a sort of groan. "It is incredible, impossible!—an old man like me! Lewis, it cannot be true!"

Lewis looked up again—read consternation written on every drawn feature; met distressful eyes that eagerly sought his face, only to be averted again as if in shame; and, seeing thus broken down, thus struck with innocent anguish of guilt, the man he had learned to honor as single in strength and dignity among men, was smitten with remorse in his turn.

He rose and went over to his host. Their eyes met in a long, deep look.

"Do you account yourself an old man?" said Lewis, sadly. "What do years signify if years bring no waste? What have they brought to you but greater wealth of mental and bodily strength? A man is aged as he feels—do you feel old? I take it, there is not a man of thirty within this wide horizon you could not dispose of out of hand; and in point of influence—— What is there strange in her, too, having felt what I, careless fellow that I am, who have knocked about the world so much already, succumbed to at our very first meeting? You went often to Woldham; she saw you often. No, there is nothing incredible, nothing impossible, in the matter. It was natural she should love you, when she thought that you loved her; it was natural she should love you, even without thought of return. But it is the end of my hopes—yes, the end!" raising his voice to drown the attempted protest. "I heard it from her own lips, I tell you; she did not know I was near. The poor old general had set me there to listen, while he prepared the way for me, as he said. But she thought he was speaking of you. I cannot tell you how it came; but I know the truth at last—the truth! She will never care for man again. Her whole heart is yours—she is all yours! Oh, if you could have been there in my stead! She loves you as wholly as I love her. Can I say more?"

Stricken by the magnitude of the unforeseen disaster, Fargus sat in hopeless silence. As a flash of lightning darts its far-reaching glare across mighty space, to die next instant in utter blackness, so a brief apprehension of the endless import of this revelation, in all its manifold phases, had broken upon the darkness of his thoughts, only to leave them again in fathomless misery.

"You never suspected this," pursued Lewis, halting in front of him once more, and now speaking in milder accents. "Your surprise is as genuine as your distress. But can you wonder at my suspicions? Was it conceivable that woman could be so deceived? And then to find you so altered, looking so changed, so handsome, so young again! Oh, why have you cut off your beard, Colonel Fargus?"

A smile of exceeding pain quivered on the elder man's mouth.

"That I shall tell you by-and-by. It had nothing to do with Maude Woldham."

This simple statement laid at last the ever-recurring doubt.

"I might have known," said Lewis, "that you could play no one false, let alone me—you who, when I was despondent, urged me not to yield; who have secured me my rights—my rights! What do I care for them? What is their value now? Charlie might as well have had them all. What a mockery it all is! And yet I am blackly ungrateful to you! Could you but know what this is to me!"

"Who could have foreseen," interrupted Fargus, hoarsely—"I, who have had no thought of woman's love for more than half a lifetime—that this should come upon me?"

"I could, I suppose, had I been here to see," cried Lewis. "Colonel Fargus, what comes to you as a trouble would have meant to me happiness beyond dreams. And out of this miserable waste and discord nothing is to come but more waste and discord; misery for me, sorrow for her—poor Maude! She cast me off with contempt. She called my love persecution. Can a man ever forget that? It has seared me to the soul! I, whose whole being was encompassed by but one thought, that—Heaven forgive me!—I would gladly damn my eternal soul for her love!"

Lewis stood still, and again lifted his hands to his head with a gesture of passionate bewilderment.

"Colonel Fargus, you do not speak; but you must forgive

me. Colonel Fargus, I do believe you when you say you knew nothing of this. I believe you are all I thought you were; but, now that you do know, is it possible that you can throw away the prize within your grasp? Think of it, colonel—she loves you. You cannot be in earnest when you say you do not mean to take advantage of this."

Fargus rose from his chair with a stiff, slow movement. In a moment he had decided upon his course of action. He would speak now, tell his heavy and precious secret, though the moment was inauspicious indeed.

"You do not answer," said Lewis, impatiently.

"I do not answer, my boy, because to me the question is painful in its absurdity. Not more surely than if I were stretched on my deathbed are such things over for me. And now—would to God it could prove anything but further grief to you!—I will tell you how it is that the news you have brought to me to-day is indeed a calamity to me. These proofs, Lewis, that I wrote to you about——"

Lewis, who had looked up, impressed by the strange solemnity of his companion's manner, here again broke forth impetuously:

"The proofs! the proofs! In God's name, Colonel Fargus, do not talk about that now! What can it be to me without her?"

"But you must listen to me, Lewis. It is absolutely necessary—if not for your own sake, for mine."

"For yours—what do you mean?"

"This question concerns me as nearly as you; my fate is bound up with yours; in your misfortune vanish all my hopes. It is the death-blow to my happiness. I speak in riddles, I know; but all will soon be clear to you. You have wondered often at the strange interest I seemed to take in you. You wondered, yet you were grateful to me for what you called my kindness, and you were as willing as I, in the openness of your heart, to take advantage of those incidents which ripened into affectionate intimacy the acquaintance begun in a seemingly casual meeting."

"Seemingly?" echoed Lewis, with a frown.

"Yes, seemingly. When the stranger, David Fargus, crossed your path for the first time, one night, in an out-of-the-way, empty tavern-room, it was of set and deliberate purpose. He had gone over there to seek you."

The frown deepened on Lewis' face. He bent his head to listen with a quickening breath.

"Fortune favored the scheme. Acquaintance soon ripened into intimacy, intimacy to affection. You could not suspect that this American's very presence in Europe was connected with you. Far less could you imagine, when we listened together to the history recounted, with such unwarrantable conclusions from insufficient facts, by Charles Hillyard—the story of your father you never knew—that I, your informal adviser, not only knew already every detail thereof, but much more besides than any one else in the room."

Lewis had started violently at the mention of his father, but he said nothing, and continued to look keenly into the speaker's eyes.

"What this knowledge is," pursued Fargus, "I will now tell you in a few words. It never could occur to you, since it never occurred to George Kerr's contemporaries, that no man should really be accounted dead on the ground of mere disappearance. For God's sake, Lewis, be calm! Your father was not drowned, as you and every one else were led to believe. And with this indubitable fact are connected the coming over of David Fargus and his present relations with you."

"My father—alive! You have seen him?" cried Lewis, jumping up and staring wildly at the speaker. "He is alive now?"

A look from Fargus was sufficient assent.

"You come from him! Where is he, Colonel Fargus?" Then the ringing excitement of the voice suddenly dropped. "Why this mystery? Why have I been so long disowned? It is incredible! I have cherished and hugged the pride of my dead father all my life. What can I now feel if it be true that he is living, and that for five-and-twenty years he has ignored me, cast me away? What am I to think of this sudden interest taken in me by the man who now claims to be my father?"

Fargus had grown whiter than ever under this cruel arraignment, but he made no attempt to check it, and Lewis, carried away by the current of his bitterness, went on:

"Pah! what a day's work this has been! Am I also to find that even that supposed friendship was also but an element in this disinterested scheme? That the man to whom I confided not only my private affairs, but my most cherished hopes, was after all but an emissary cleverly preparing the way to place me in the position it was requisite I should occupy? But I interrupted your exposition of the case, Colonel Fargus. Let me hear the message."

"Lewis," he answered, deliberately—there was an immense sadness beneath his calm—"Lewis, your impatient, hasty conclusions at the very outset of a difficult explanation are unjust to your father; unjust to me, with whom none of your

previous relations have given you a right to assume a
sneering tone."

Lewis waved his hand impatiently. "Go on, in Heaven's
name! This is a cruel blow to me."

After a short pause of painful consideration, Fargus went
over to his desk and brought out the manuscript.

"In this," he said, "you will find all. I wrote it for you,
as soon as I received your last letter—wrote it with the sole
intention of giving you back your peace of mind. One
moment more," he added, as Lewis hastily extended his
hand. "Every word you will read here is true in fact and
in spirit. As a legal document in your favor—as a document,
I say, to prove your position as the legitimate son of George
Kerr, and in his absence as the heir-in-law—I know its value
is nil. Happily, no such thing is required now. What
was, however, required, what was due to you, was a statement of such evidences as would disburden your mind of that
gnawing doubt, that uneasiness, which has of late helped
to poison it."

Lewis spread the papers on the table without a word, and
almost threw himself upon them in a vain endeavor to
decipher them in the darkness, while, with a heavy sigh,
Fargus rose and left the room.

CHAPTER XXVII.

FATHER AND SON.

Oppressed by the accumulated disappointments, Fargus instinctively sought the cool twilight spaces out of doors.

He was standing beneath the room he had just left; the
servant had even then brought in the lamp, and Lewis,
once more alone, was at last about to read for himself the
story of his father's life.

Fargus stopped and watched the silent scene within. The
light fell full upon the young man's troubled forehead; notwithstanding the distance, every shade upon it was visible
to the watcher, as, seated facing him, his elbows upon the
table, Lewis closely scanned the written sheets. From his
post in the outer darkness Fargus could follow his progress
almost line by line; in his mind was looking over the broad,
bent shoulder, seeing the words as they passed beneath the
downcast eyes; he could have told well-nigh the very thoughts,
the impatience, suspicion, anxiety, that were struggling behind the drawn brows over these first pages of careful prep-

aration, and necessarily somewhat lengthy preamble. Presently the reader made a startled movement, bent over the writing with staring intentness for a moment, then looked up and dropped his hands, and, as under the light his face was blasted with a white, stony astonishment, Fargus knew that the name adopted by the George Kerr of old, on the day of his civil death, had now, for the first time, appeared on the pages of his biography.

After a long interval Lewis brushed his forehead with the familiar gesture, and once again resumed his task. And the father knew that under the son's gaze was now spread forth the strange history of George Kerr's transmigration of soul, of his varied life under the new personality, his sudden return to things of old, and the novel relations which had existed between him and his new-found kinsfolk until the present hour; and he earnestly watched for any indication of the mood in which these revelations were received.

During the perusal of this last part Lewis paused several times. When he came to the end he slowly gathered the papers together, replaced them in their envelope. Then, with his profile blackly defined against the inner light, he became wrapped in stillness, as though plunged in profoundest converse with himself. Fargus re-entered the room.

His son turned upon him a hard, scrutinizing glance; his face was as a sealed book to the father's eager eyes. The latter's heart sank.

"Great God! he does not believe me! Oh, Lewis, my own boy!" The last words forced themselves audibly from his lips.

The young man seemed moved by this cry of anguish, so unlike the usual deliberate speech of the man. Rising to his feet, he advanced and faltered out:

"What can I say? Colonel Fargus, I am utterly bewildered."

"Colonel Fargus!" repeated the other. "It is so, then. I am only David Fargus! Of course, how could Fargus claim George Kerr's son? And yet," with savage earnestness, "you are my boy, and I do claim you—and all I have tried to do for you shall not have been done in vain! You must believe that I am your father, that I am the George Kerr whom the world has forgotten and will never know again!"

Without taking his eye off Lewis' now wondering countenance, he seized the lamp with one hand and with the other grasped the young man's arm.

"Come and see for yourself!" he cried, and drew him into the adjacent bedroom, halting with him in front of the mirror. There, clasping him round the neck, he drew the youthful face near his own and, stooping forward, held the steady light aloft.

Their eyes met in the glass. Brown eyes in both faces (set wide apart and well covered under an energetic brow), with the same double furrow between, fostered by habitually reflective mood, less deep-set, perhaps, in the younger face, but not brighter. Now, with pupils widened in the insufficient light, and under the strain of growing emotion, they were strangely alike, for all the five-and-twenty years of life which separated them.

As the first recognition of this unthought-of resemblance flashed upon Lewis, he made a movement as if to disengage himself and turn around upon his companion. But he checked himself and peered into the glass, to become finally quite absorbed in contemplation.

Never before had Lewis subjected human physiognomy to such unsparing scrutiny. Feature by feature, line by line, he compared the two faces reflected before him with intent, eager, yet deliberate criticism. In some details they were unlike. His own straight nose, somewhat short and wide, in no way recalled that of Fargus—high-bridged, aquiline of bend and narrow of nostril. The ears, too, were dissimilar, in his case smaller and less masculine, inherited, in fact, from the delicate beauty of his Spanish mother. But in all the other features which gave character to a face the reproduction was unmistakable, and shone forth assertingly, since Fargus's masking beard had been discarded.

The strong, square chin with the cleft dent—a well-known Kerr characteristic; the straight mouth, larger and less thin-lipped in Lewis, but unmistakably cut on the same lines, set with the same firm yet kindly decisiveness; the square brow, solid and smooth, with low-growing hair of the same brown, now touched with gray upon the elder man—all tallied unmistakably, unusually, even down to the curious coincidence of the deep scar, still red and angry upon the son's pale face, while showing markedly upon the father's cheek, white even as the recent invalid's where the razor had passed that day.

And presently, as Lewis gazed, a sudden discomposure spread over his countenance.

Fargus put down the lamp on the table, and with a twist of his fingers turned up the ends of his mustache after the Velasquez-like manner which Lewis cultivated. This last touch was almost magical, qualifying as it did the habitual gravity of his mien.

"Now, my son," said he, speaking to him for the first time

in the Spanish tongue, "thou no doubt seest my reason for attempting to regenerate myself a little. Dost thou want further proof, Lewis, my son? Give me thy hand."

There was music for Lewis' ears in that language, the sound of which was associated with the only "home" he had ever known. He was, however, too bewildered by the torrent of new conceptions that during the last hour had swept through his mind to feel fresh surprise.

Noting the increased intentness in his son's looks, Fargus again approached the light, took the young man's hand, and turned it palm upward.

"Lewis, all I want is to show thee another sign of thy heredity. See that straight line, cutting thy hand from side to side with such curiously marked definition."

Without answering, Lewis looked obediently down upon a palm of a description to have indeed puzzled a chiromancist.

"No doubt you never even noticed this peculiarity; and yet it is quite singular, quite unlike the irregular and broken lines, with ends overlapping, which you would find, more or less diversfied, but always essentially the same, on other people's hands. Now, there is the mark on your hand. I looked for it and found it when you lay ill and unconscious in Brussels; and here it is on mine!"

Fargus turned his own hand supine, and placed it beside his son's; they were identical in their unusual characteristic. After a moment's pause he closed it again, and silently pointed to the signet-ring, on which Lewis at one glance recognized the ancient crest, and a moment later the same heraldic device upon the inner case of the watch, which was next proffered for his inspection.

"But why have recourse to such by-evidence? Lewis, bring before your mind the portrait of your father, taken when he was no older than you are now. Through the mask of these many years can you not see the same man again before you?"

In that almost spiritualized state, born of great mental excitement, which in singleness of thought is akin to dreaming, Lewis found his gaze riveted on the bright eyes which looked with masterful glow so straight into his. A vision of the portrait arose before him and overlapped the living image, to fade away again and leave him gazing at the reality, uncertain for a moment which was which. Those were in truth the same eyes that had watched him in pained faithfulness in his cradle at Seville, in his lonely Edinburgh lodgings, in his College rooms, in Staple Inn!

They stood face to face one moment, with eyes searching

each other's thoughts; then their hands joined by one warm impulse, and the younger, in a low, humble voice murmured:

"I do believe—forgive me."

At this, Fargus, the stern and self-possessed, broke down; tears started to his eyes.

"Forgive you, my son!" he cried, in halting accents; "is it not I who should ask to be forgiven for the past, and still more for the harm I have unwittingly caused you now?—I, who never deserted a son like you, my big, brave, clever boy!"

He paused, and for a while silently contemplated the young man from head to foot, with pride burning through his wet lashes.

"And yet it has been my fate to bring nothing to you, after all, but misery. My first step across your path all but cost you your life . . . my very efforts to help you on toward happiness have destroyed your hopes."

Letting the young man's hand fall, Fargus stopped, his face stamped with such depth of sadness that Lewis' heart was filled with compassion.

Filial respect is innate in all refined natures, but filial love can only spring from prolonged association. It was this sense of respect, however, which stirred Lewis' brave, warm heart into protest at last.

"For God's sake, sir, do not so misunderstand me! Do not believe that I would now take upon myself to pass judgment on—on my father's actions. I am—we are both victims of circumstances. The past is beyond recall."

"One thing, at least, sir, you have done for me to-day, for which I owe you gratitude—you have roused me from my foolish weakness; the time has come to be a man once more, and resume self-control. Before I again leave England you must be restored to your rightful position as the master of Gilham——"

"Lewis!" cried Fargus. "Is it possible you can so misconceive the position? Never, never speak so again. I know you did not mean this affront. George Kerr is dead—dead to all but you. The money is yours, the place is yours; do with them what you will, but for God's sake never insult me again by offering them to me!"

*   *   *   *   *   *   *   *   *

Dinner was over at last; host and guest sat on either side of the hearth with unenjoyed pipe in hand, absently watching the metamorphosis from yellow flame to red and gray ash of the piled-up wood fire. The meal had been an unpleasant ordeal.

Before the end of dinner many had been the spells of

meditative silence between father and son as they sat opposite each other, and when they at last adjourned to the study both by tacit consent yielded to the impression of the hour, and fell into silence, to follow undisturbedly the drift of their own thoughts.

And then to Fargus slowly but fatally there once more unrolled itself to view a picture of the consequences he had brought upon himself and others by his own acts. Lewis was indeed now master of his inheritance, but at what cost— only through the incongruous interference of an angry woman! From the father nothing had come but failure, irremediable miscarriage of purpose; worse than all, his was the black shadow now cast upon his son's life—upon two young lives; for bitter, no doubt, were the thoughts evolved at that very moment within the lovely head yonder among the pines on the hill. What would he not give to be able to recall, if it could be done without jeopardy to Lewis' prospects, their former easy relations of friend to friend, instead of this ghastly constraint, this terrible playing at father and son?

Such were the thoughts which for Fargus, on that long-looked-for evening, filled the silence of the chamber at the Lone Grange.

In equally absorbed mood sat Lewis, absently smoking, now gazing with unsettled speculation at the figure opposite him, at once so familiar and so strange in its new character, now dreamily peering into the dance of flame on the hearth. He had said he would be a man again, would cut off the past with its clinging and disabling sorrow, its sapping longings and unmanly weakess of despair, and begin a new life; ay, but how? His heart grew faint at the thought of existence at Gilham Court in deadly monotony and tantalizing proximity to his lost ideal.

Could he leave that pale, sad man who was his father? could he refuse the duty he had cast upon him, and abandon the headship of his house? And with a weary sigh he would see all his plans crumble again into blank uncertainty, and chide himself in vain for the mental palsy which seemed to make him so absolutely indifferent to the great fact that he had found a father.

The clock-hand went its dreary round twice over the hours, the fire fell and sank low, the pipes had long been cold, when the eyes of both men met again at last. In one look each saw how devious paths of thought had brought them to the same point—a dull and blank wall of utter hopelessness. There was no need for words.

Fargus rose with a sigh of weariness.

"When I think, my dear boy, that you, on whom I have brought all this—you spoke about my forgiveness——" He paused in eloquent speechlessness; then, as one who gives up the search after an impossible solution, continued: "To-morrow, perhaps, we may come to a decision as to what is best to do; now my head is spent. Good-night. Do not brood too much; to-morrow we shall talk. God bless you, Lewis!"

He lit a candle for his guest, then one for himself. The light flickered upon his face, and Lewis, with a sudden sharp pang, saw how lined and worn and drawn it was. Only a few hours ago the young man had bitterly reproached him for his youthful appearance; now, as he stood, and in silence pressed his hand, his father looked indeed an old man.

With the relief-bringing hour of dawn, sleep came upon Lewis' tired brain. He had passed most of the night in ceaseless walking up and down the room, fighting with the problem he was unable to conquer, and at last, worn out with fatigue, both mental and physical, he had flung himself, without undressing, on his bed. And now sleep had come to him; but it was the unrestful, dream-tossed sleep of a mind swinging on the hinge of indecision, from recurring worry of bootless search to recurring failure.

It was dark around him, and yet there was light somewhere. Chilled to the marrow, still under the spell of his nightmare, he sprang from the bed and pushed open the door, dimly wondering to find it ajar, for he remembered to have closed it over night. In the inner room a candle was fitfully burning itself out in its socket. Seized with a childish terror, he rushed to Fargus' room and knocked loudly. There was no answer. He took up the flickering light and went in. The room was cold and empty. The bed was undisturbed. Hardly knowing what he was doing, with dread apprehensions upon him, he came back again, and began to search the house. With the draught in the cold passage the dying flame went out, but the cold light of breaking day was already spreading through the curtainless windows, and showed him each room as he entered it as forlorn and abandoned as the last. Up and down numberless stairs and passages, into chamber after chamber, he hurried in frenzied seeking, ever and anon calling Fargus' name in fearsome voice, to receive no answer save the dismal, ghostly echo of the empty house, to find everywhere the same silence and void—all empty and solitary as in his dream.

With that last vision of his father's face, grown so old and sorrow-stricken in his eyes, he returned at length to the study, too much troubled even to feel shame of the terror which encompassed him. There, in the shuttered darkness, he had to procure another candle, and, as the light shot up, his eyes fell upon the white glimmer of an envelope prominent upon the green cloth of the center table. He lifted it with a shaking hand, to find his name upon it—his name in his father's writing—and tore it open.

"DEAR SON (it read): "I must go. The whole of the night I have spent in trying to think what is best to do. There is only one way; I must leave you. Better, perhaps, for you had I never sought you at all; and if now by going from you in this hurried manner, and seeming to desert you again, I cause you fresh trouble, you will forgive me, thinking how terrible it is for me. I must leave you, dear son. This is to be my punishment for a selfish past, and as such I accept it, and hope that it may remove one cause of distress in your life. Do not henceforth think of the father, but only of the friend who would have made the sacrifice of leaving you sooner had he suspected that he could ever stand between you and your happiness.

"And now the time has come. I will not wait to meet you again; you have had too many painful scenes through me already. I give myself until the candle burns out to be under the same roof with you, then I will look once more upon your face—that face which has grown so dear to me—as you sleep there next to me, and then take up my lonely life again. Good-by, dear Lewis. Burn this letter. I know you will respect my secret. Do not seek to find me. Do what your heart and judgment prompt you. I have confidence in both. I have confidence also in your future. God bless you!"

Lewis read these lines, incoherently, hurriedly dropped from a trembling pen. In the silence and cold of his solitude the misery of his dream returned upon him with an iron grip as he realized their import. His father, like his love, had left him—had faded out of his life forever.

Suddenly a flash of energy roused him. The words of the letter seemed to print themselves in fire upon his brain. "I give myself till the candle burns out." The candle had only just burned out. It was but a few moments ago since his father, that melancholy, aged figure, had towered over him, light in hand, and entered into his dreams—only a few moments ago that a door had really been opened, that the gate had closed, echoing in his half-conscious brain. Fargus was gone, indeed, but he could not be far off.

And at once, under the thought, the paralyzing horror of his nightmare gave way to a warm glow of reaction. With the fever of sudden resolution, he dashed into the hall and out of the house.

It was the opening of a sullen day. Drizzling rain slanted from heaven to earth, with fine, almost invisible, persistence.

He had reached that gently rising eminence which dominated so much of the country round; there, panting for breath, he paused and scanned the horizon with anxious, peering eye. Nothing but gray, gray sky and earth on every side—not a living being in sight.

And yet, "He cannot have gone far. The candle has only just burned out." In a sort of despairing anger at thus realizing in waking life the dread desertion of his dream, Lewis called out the words aloud, "He must be stopped—he must be stopped!"

Again he turned and slowly cast a straining glance around; at that moment a ray of yellow light darted between great banks of clouds in the east, and swept more warmly over part of the dull field of view; and then, across the gilded path of that blessed ray, was seen a dark point, slowly moving.

With a stifled cry of triumph, Lewis sprang in pursuit, with elbows pressed to his sides, bounding like a hound over the plain, conscious of but one thing, that he must cover the space between them before the figure disappeared.

It was not so far—half a mile at most, for Fargus had had but little start. And yet, in rage at his impotency, upborne by the intensity of his desire, he pressed on, on still, until it seemed as if he had been running for hours already.

He had gained on the figure markedly, yet now it seemed, as it swam and faded before his startling gaze, to be steadily increasing the distance between them once more. His feet were weighted down with iron weights, the cold and the numbness were reaching his knees; in another moment he knew that he would fall, and that his father would silently, fatally continue on his way and disappear forever. He stopped, and the whole of his life energy was thrown into a wild, appealing, angry cry:

"Halt! for Heaven's sake, halt!"

The call was, for all the effort it represented, but a feeble one, but it reached the lonely traveler in the silence of the moorland. He, too, came abruptly to a standstill, as if it had struck him like a shot, and then turned round, looking vaguely about him. Lewis waved his arm and beheld, as it were through a circling mist, how the figure began to retrace its steps and come toward him, first slowly, presently at a run.

For a moment he lost consciousness, all was dark before him; but the next minute his hands were grasped with a warm, living, strong pressure that seemed to send thrills of new life to his heart, to fill it with strange, unwonted comfort.

He looked up at the anxious, white face bending over him—the face of his father!

Tears welled into his eyes and flowed down his cheeks. He

did not know it. He only felt intense and keen relief and inexpressible comfort. Then he found himself speaking in hurried, passionate accents:

"You were going; I, too, must go; I cannot live here. We will go together. There can be no home for us here now; but the world lies wide before us. Will you not take me with you and remain my guide, friend, companion? Afterward we will return here—afterward, when we can come back together."

And then, receiving no reply, looking up in fear to meet no compliance in the loving eyes, which were so sad as they looked back at him, as sad as in his dream, there broke forth a cry from his very heart:

"Father, you will not leave me? *Father!*"

* * * * * * * *

The gathering sunlight had grown upon the dull day and driven the mists aside, and turned the drenching wet of leaf and grass-blade to a tangle of diamond and gold. Shoulder to shoulder, under the promise of a glorious noon, went father and son together across the moorland, on their way out into the world.

THE END.